C

The west must wait

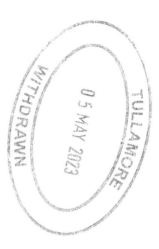

MANCHESTER
1824

Manchester University Press

The west must wait

County Galway and the Irish Free State 1922–32

ÚNA NEWELL

Manchester
University Press

The right of Úna Newell to be identified as the author of this work has been asserted by her in accordance with the Copyright, Designs and Patents Act 1988.

Published by Manchester University Press
Altrincham Street, Manchester M1 7JA, UK
www.manchesteruniversitypress.co.uk

British Library Cataloguing-in-Publication Data is available

Library of Congress Cataloging-in-Publication Data is available

ISBN 978 1 5261 0737 4 paperback

First published by Manchester University Press in hardback 2013

This edition first published 2017

The publisher has no responsibility for the persistence or accuracy of URLs for any external or third-party internet websites referred to in this book, and does not guarantee that any content on such websites is, or will remain, accurate or appropriate.

Printed by CPI Group (UK) Ltd, Croydon CR0 4YY

For my mother Sheila,
and for Caoimhe and Dara

Contents

Tables and figures

Acknowledgements

My first debt is to Manchester University Press for favouring this book.

At University College Dublin my doctoral thesis, on which parts of the book are based, was supervised by Michael Laffan. I acknowledge warmly his candour in comment and enviable erudition. For suggesting the subject and for his constant encouragement and support, I express my sincere gratitude. For introducing me to the writings of Kingsley Amis, David Lodge and many others, and impressing on me the great importance of the cadence of a sentence, I offer an additional word of thanks.

I owe a special debt of gratitude to the School of History and Archives and the Humanities Institute of Ireland, UCD; and particularly to the Irish Research Council for the Humanities and Social Sciences and the National University of Ireland, who provided invaluable financial assistance during the course of my research.

The staff of the National Library of Ireland, where much of this work was completed, went out of their way to help. I thank them all most sincerely. I also extend my gratitude to the staff of the National Archives of Ireland; the National Photographic Archive; UCD Archives Department; the James Joyce Library, UCD; the National Folklore Collection, UCD; Galway County Library; Galway City Council Archives; Galway Diocesan Archives; Tuam Archdiocesan Archives; and the James Hardiman Library and Special Collections Department, NUI, Galway, who offered me every assistance and courtesy in researching this book.

I am most grateful to John Newell and Alberto Alvarez, School of Mathematics, Statistics and Applied Mathematics, and HRB Clinical Research Facility, NUI, Galway, who generated the graphs that accompany the text. I also wish to thank William Nolan and William Jenkins for their permission to reproduce the reference map of County Galway, and Damian Duggan and James A. Farr for their meticulous attention to detail in providing the technical modifications that were required for its inclusion in the book.

I am fortunate to have many trusted friends at home and abroad. For your kindness, humour and generous hospitality, I offer my warmest thanks.

I am deeply obliged to Gearóid Ó Tuathaigh for his continued support. I also wish to acknowledge my late grandaunt Síle Ní Chinnéide. In addition, I am especially grateful to Mary E. Daly and Anne Dolan for their generosity with their time, for the welcome advice they offered and for drawing my attention to useful sources. I have also benefited immensely from conversations with Nicholas Canny, Marie Coleman, Catherine Cox, John Cunningham, Lindsey Earner-Byrne, Mark Empey, Diarmaid Ferriter, Sharon Leahy, Shane McCorristine, Ivar McGrath, William Murphy, the late Kevin B. Nowlan, Margaret Ó hÓgartaigh, Jonathan O'Malley, Paul Rouse and Karl Whitney. In sad times, Carole Holohan, Roisín Higgins, Adrian O'Connor and Aileen Broderick were towers of strength when it was needed most. You are true friends.

Jim Farr's inimitable personality has taken me to the other end of the world and back on more than one occasion. I thank him for his unfailing encouragement and for the endless summers we have shared.

What I owe to my mother Sheila, my father Martin, my four brothers, Kevin, Johnnie, Brendan and Micheál, and my extended family is different from all the rest. I thank them for their love and abiding friendship.

The book is dedicated to the memory of my mother, and to my eldest niece Caoimhe, and my eldest nephew Dara, whom she adored, as do I.

Abbreviations

ASU	Active Service Unit
BMH WS	Bureau of Military History witness statement
CÉ	Clann Éireann
CI	County inspector, Royal Irish Constabulary
CID	Criminal Investigation Department
CNG	Cumann na nGaedheal
CWT	Hundredweight
DE	Dáil Éireann
DF	Department of Finance
DJ	Department of Justice
DT	Department of the Taoiseach
FF	Fianna Fáil
GCCA	Galway County Council Archives
GDA	Galway Diocesan Archives
IG	Inspector general, Royal Irish Constabulary
IHS	*Irish Historical Studies*
INTO	Irish National Teachers' Organisation
IPP	Irish Parliamentary Party
IRA	Irish Republican Army
IRB	Irish Republican Brotherhood
ITGWU	Irish Transport and General Workers' Union
JGAHS	*Journal of the Galway Archaeological and Historical Society*
NAI	National Archives of Ireland
NL	National League
NLI	National Library of Ireland
NUI	National University of Ireland
PR-STV	Proportional representation by the single transferable vote
RA	Ratepayers' Association
RDC	Rural District Council

RIC	Royal Irish Constabulary
TAA	Tuam Archdiocesan Archives
TCD	Trinity College Dublin
TD	Teachta Dála (Dáil Éireann deputy)
UCC	University College Cork
UCD	University College Dublin
UCDA	University College Dublin, Archives Department
UCG	University College Galway
UDC	Urban District Council
UIL	United Irish League

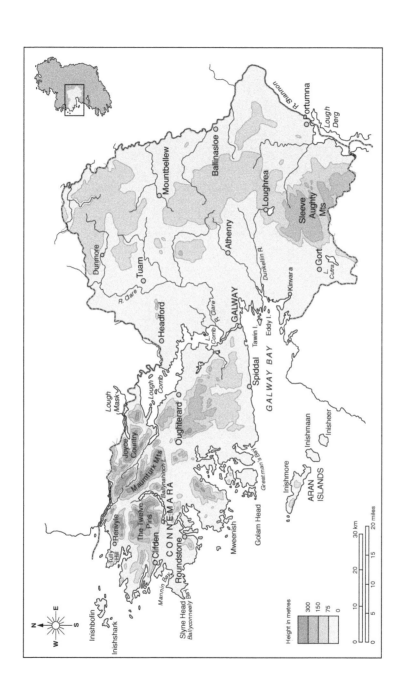

Height in metres

300
150
75
0

0   10   20   30 km
0   5   10   15   20 miles

N
W E
S

Inishbofin
Inishshark
Slyne Head
Ballyconneely Bay
Mannin Bay
Tully Hill
Renvyle
Clifden
Roundstone
CONNEMARA
The Twelve Pins
Maumturk Mts
Ballynahinch
Joyce Country
Lough Mask
L. Corrib
Lough Corrib
Oughterard
Mweenish
Golam Head
Inishmore
ARAN ISLANDS
Inishmaan
Inisheer
Greatman's Bay
Spiddal
GALWAY BAY
Tawin I.
Eddy I.
GALWAY
L. Corrib
R. Clare
Headford
R. Clare
Tuam
Dunmore
Mountbellew
Athenry
Ballinasloe
Dunkellin R.
Kinvara
L. Cutra
Gort
Loughrea
Sleeve Aughty Mts
Portumna
Lough Derg
R. Shannon

Prologue

While not wishing to 'give any one the impression that Galway is all dead', Robert Lynd put it thus in 1912:

> If you let the sexton take you up the bell-tower and show you Galway and its streets from that height, you will as likely as not get the impression that you are looking out upon a city where the very houses are death's-heads. Skulls of lofty mansions, the windowlessness of which gives an appearance as of empty eye sockets, line the streets in graveyard ruin. Other buildings lie in stony masses, like bones heaped and mixed together in an old tomb. No one who has not seen Galway from a height like this can realize to the full what an air the place has of a town awaiting a blessed resurrection. Little of the grand life has been left here. Emptiness sits in the places of abundance. Tall and smokeless chimneys rise everywhere, giving the town at noonday the appearance that other cities have at dawn. So hollow of joy and vigour does this grey town look from the tower of St Nicholas that it has been likened fitly enough to a scooped-out egg-shell. Flour-mills, factories – how many were there even thirty years ago that are now silent behind cobwebs and broken windows![1]

Galway's charm and economic success lay in days that had long since passed and in the 1920s the line of quays, empty warehouses and unused mills gave melancholy evidence of a former affluence. Yet while it displayed little of its ancient grandeur, Galway retained what Henry Inglis described as 'an air of a place of importance'.[2]

Galway was both an urban and a rural county, a congested district and a Gaeltacht region. It was a focal point of the Land War (1879–81) and the Ranch War (1904–8) and was one of the few areas outside Dublin that was 'out' in 1916. Yet it played only a minor role in the military struggle of the War of Independence (1919–21) in comparison with counties such as Tipperary and Cork. The pistol was widely used in Galway, but it was employed to force the surrender of land rather than the surrender of the British forces.

Prologue

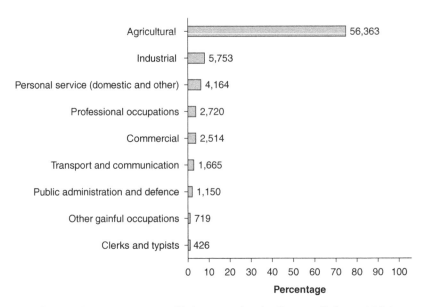

Figure P.1 Persons in specified occupation in County Galway, 1926

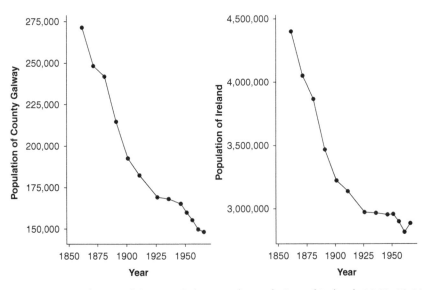

Figure P.2 Population of County Galway and population of Ireland, 1861–1966

Regional studies of the Irish revolution undertaken by David Fitzpatrick, Peter Hart, Marie Coleman, Michael Farry, Fergus Campbell, Joost Augusteijn and others have revealed the fact that Irish political experience is far more complex than the traditional one-dimensional

popular version. Fitzpatrick has spoken of how 'it is a regrettable historiographical accident that the political history of the Irish Revolution
has hitherto been focused on Dublin, as though Dublin were the spiritual capital of Ireland'.[3] This book builds on a significant emerging
genre. It extends the historical debate beyond the Irish revolution and
introduces a new study of post-revolutionary experience in Ireland at a
county level.

In 1922, Galway society was a mix of the haves and the have-nots,
of those challenging and those looking to consolidate the new state, of
loyal treatyites and avowed anti-treatyites, a professional middle class,
a conservative small-farmer community and a destitute rural poor. For
many people in Galway, poverty, not politics, was their primary concern.
For many others, the possession of land was an obsession more critical
than the attainment of an Irish Republic. Furthermore, the idealisation
of the west by cultural nationalists and literary revivalists, and the verit-
able chorus of comment in praise of the simple life it supposedly represented, contrasted with the reality of everyday life.

With a land valuation of £488,276, Galway was one of the poorest
counties in Ireland.[4] In some areas of the rural countryside the simple
fact was that in a community where 75 per cent of the workforce was
involved in agriculture, the rugged, undulating, exposed nature of the
land was incapable of sustaining many of the people except in a state of
near poverty (Figure P.1).[5] In 1926, the population of County Galway
stood at 169,366, but it was in a continual state of decline (Figure P.2).
The fundamental truth behind the image of rural Ireland as the reservoir
of native culture was that of an emigrating population.[6]

Emigration, of course, was not unique to the west of Ireland. Yet what
typified the *mentalité* of the rural emigrant was its penchant for moving
'from the known to the known', that is to say, 'from areas where the emigrant lived to places where their friends and relations awaited them'.[7] In
1904 Horace Plunkett wrote:

> Recently a daughter of a small farmer in County Galway with a family too
> 'long' for the means of subsistence available, was offered a comfortable
> home on a farm owned by some better-off relative, only thirty miles away,
> though probably twenty miles beyond the limits of her peregrinations. She
> elected in preference to go to New York, and being asked her reason by
> a friend of mine, replied in so many words, 'because it is nearer'. She felt
> she would be less of a stranger in a New York tenement house, among her
> relatives and friends who had already emigrated, than in another part of
> County Galway.[8]

Among a people who had 'for more than a century looked west across
the Atlantic to America as the nearest land, its nearest kin',[9] it was
Boston, Chicago or New York, and not Dublin or the Gaeltacht colonies

of County Meath that offered a sense of security and a sense of the familiar. As Máirtín Ó Cadhain wrote of his character Mairin in *The Year 1912*,

> she had been nurtured on American lore from infancy. South Boston, Norwood, Butte, Montana, Minnesota, California, plucked chords in her imagination more distinctly than did Dublin, Belfast, Wexford, or even places only a few miles out on the Plain beyond Brightcity.[10]

The lack of social mobility in rural Ireland produced a society where countless people had rarely, if ever, strayed outside a two- or three-mile radius from their own home. Such societal limitations fostered a solidarity and sense of place in the 'local' communities and 'local' village associations of the towns and cities of North America, Britain and elsewhere.

The continual high level of emigration was a clear adjustment to congestion, pressure on the land, and the lack of social and monetary mobility in rural Ireland. Economic want forced many people to emigrate. However, many others, beguiled by hopes of social betterment, chose to leave. Fitzpatrick has commented that

> as the impulse to emigrate altered from shove to tug to promotion, so the expression of farewell changed from casual to sorrowful to congratulatory. Emigration became a fact of life, a 'fashion', a 'fever'. As P. D. Murphy wrote in 1917 of 'the intending emigrant': 'You can tell him at a glance, for there is something in his appearance that betrays him. He is listless, restless, discontented … He has caught the fever that has depopulated the Irish countryside.'[11]

Unwilling to sacrifice herself to the drudgery of small holder west of Ireland rural life, many a young Irish girl, wrote George Russell, 'must have looked on the wrinkled face and bent back and rheumatic limbs of her mother, and grown maddened in a sudden passion that her own fresh young life might end just like this'.[12]

For some aspiring emigrants, the expression of farewell may well have changed from the sorrowful to the liberating, but for those compelled to emigrate, the newfound idealism of the Irish Free State stood in stark contrast to the reality of the continued rural depopulation of the west. In August 1927, a reporter for the *Galway Observer* captured the emotive pain of these departures.

> I saw heartbroken fathers and mothers with the snows of many winters on their heads and tear bedimmed eyes take their last farewell of strapping sons and splendid specimens of womanhood at the railway station on Wednesday. The young people were bound for America. It was a saddening, a never to be forgotten sight. One old man who I was told had come all

the way from a remote district of Connemara to say goodbye, embraced his daughter. He was assisted out of the station while the tears sparkling like summer sun stole down his wrinkled brow. A pearl of great price had passed out of his life forever.[13]

Here lay the emotional tragedy for those too poor in purse, Galway's silent exports, the sons and daughters of small farmers and landless men, the remnant of Irish history whose economy had passed them by and whose remittance cheques sent home from abroad would become of infinitely greater assistance to their local community than had they themselves stayed behind. In 1924–25 a government survey of fifteen west Galway districts found that only three areas had greater financial input from livestock than remittances.[14] Commenting on the number of eligible bachelors in the county in 1931 and the effect emigration was having on local society, Frank Fahy, Fianna Fáil deputy for Galway, stated:

> Of course, there were in every parish a few crusty old bachelors who keep a tight grip on the purse strings and refuse to get married for fear that they would have to spend a little in buying silk stockings for the ladies. But the average young man would get married if he could afford to do so. The large percentage of bachelors is one of the greatest indications that we are not as prosperous as members of the Government Party would lead us to believe.[15]

The book begins to build an image of regional political and social life in the immediate post-revolutionary period. With an unresolved land question, a tradition of radical agrarianism, pockets of extreme poverty and sectarian violence, a language question, a sense of distance from the capital, an east–west economic variance, and a divided political society, the Galway experience raises important questions concerning our understanding of the achievements and disappointments of the first decade of Irish independence. The establishment of the new state brought new expectations and new frustrations when these were not met.

The first part of the book discusses the turbulent years of 1922 and 1923, the local electorate's endorsement of the Anglo-Irish Treaty and the beginning of domestic Irish politics in what was a vastly altered post-treaty world. Part II examines four major themes in rural agrarian society – land, poverty, the Irish language, and law and order – and establishes the level of deprivation in local society that the Cumann na nGaedheal government had to confront. Part III is more political in tone and it attempts to relate the political record of the county to the existing socio-economic realities of local life. Particular emphasis is placed on the election campaigns, the issues involved, and the voting patterns and trends that emerged in Galway. Why did the people vote for pragmatism

over radicalism in 1922? Why did Cumann na nGaedheal fail to capitalise on this position over the next decade? How did the Cumann na
nGaedheal government address (or fail to address) Galway's social and
economic difficulties? Were the criticisms of local Cumann na nGaedheal party supporters justified? Was the party abandoning its republican
past? Was the government becoming too removed from the communities
it governed? Was it ignoring vital local issues? Did the political opposition offer any viable alternatives? Why did the west have to wait? These
are some of the fundamental questions addressed in the book. Selectivity
is inevitable. It is not a comparative text. The historiographical neglect
of other comprehensive socio-political regional studies of the Irish Free
State period makes such an extensive brief altogether impossible. Only
with further research will the complete range of regional experiences be
recovered and the fuller picture of the impact of the revolution and the
civil war on post-revolutionary Irish society become discernible.

On 6 December 1921, the Anglo-Irish Treaty was signed in London
and confirmed dominion status on a twenty-six-county Irish Free State.
The settlement represented a significant advancement on earlier offers
of Home Rule, but it failed to secure an Irish Republic. On 7 January
1922, the Dáil approved the treaty by a narrow margin of 64 votes
to 57. Among the citizenry there endured a blithe belief that an Irish
government with its own autonomous legislature would help solve the
pressing social and economic problems of the west. The pro-treaty government now had an opportunity to test the strength of this assumption
on the creative potential of political independence. Galway, along with
the rest of the country, waited with much anticipation and, in certain
cases, apprehension. What follows is a study of a people and its government in one of the key problematic areas in the nascent Irish Free State.

Notes

1 Robert Lynd, 'Galway of the Races', in Seán McMahon (ed.), _Robert Lynd:
   Galway of the Races: Selected Essays_ (Dublin, 1990), pp. 64–5.
2 _Thom's Directory 1923_ (Dublin, 1923), p. 1163; a phrase Henry Inglis attributed to Galway on his visit to the city in 1834. Cited in M. A. G. Ó Tuathaigh,
   '"… the air of a place of importance": aspects of nineteenth-century Galway',
   in Diarmuid Ó Cearbhaill (ed.), _Galway: Town and Gown 1484–1984_
   (Dublin, 1984), p. 136.
3 David Fitzpatrick, _Politics and Irish Life 1913–1921: Provincial Experience
   of War and Revolution_ (2nd edn, Cork, 1998), p. xiii.
4 _Census of Ireland 1926_ (Dublin, 1927), Population, Area and Valuation, vol.
   I, pp. 19–29. According to the census County Galway measured 1,467,639
   acres and, as noted, had a land valuation of £448,276. County Mayo (also in

Connacht), a similarly poor region, measured 1,333,941 acres and recorded a land valuation of £338,321 and County Clare (in Munster) measured 787,768 acres and had a land valuation of £325,243. By way of comparison, County Meath (in Leinster), which measured 577,816 acres, had a land valuation of £555,904 and County Cork (in Munster), an area of 1,843,590 acres, recorded a land valuation of £1,316,117.

5 *Ibid.*, Occupations, vol. II, pp. 20, 21.

6 *Ibid.*, Population, Area and Valuation, vol. I, p. 5; R. F. Foster, *Modern Ireland 1600–1972* (London, 1988), p. 538.

7 *Commission on Emigration and Other Population Problems, 1948–1954, Reports* (1955), p. 137. Cited in Terence Dooley, *'The Land for the People': The Land Question in Independent Ireland* (Dublin, 2004), p. 135.

8 Horace Plunkett, *Ireland in the New Century* (London, 1904), p. 49. Cited in Dooley, *'The Land for the People'*, p. 135.

9 Máirtín Ó Cadhain, 'The year 1912', in *The Road to Brightcity and Other Stories*, translated by Eoghan Ó Tuairisc (Dublin, 1981), p. 7.

10 *Ibid.*, p. 33.

11 David Fitzpatrick, *Irish Emigration 1801–1921* (Dublin, 1984), p. 42.

12 AE (G. W. Russell), *Cooperation and Nationality* (Dublin, 1912), p. 66. Cited in J. J. Lee, *Ireland 1912–1985: Politics and Society* (Cambridge, 1989), p. 376.

13 *Galway Observer*, 13 Aug. 1927.

14 Micheál Ó Fathartaigh, 'Cumann na nGaedheal, the land issue and west Galway 1923–1932', *Journal of the Galway Archaeological and Historical Society*, vol. 60 (2008), p. 158. For many uneconomic holders who had survived on credit all year, the remittances sent at Christmas enabled them to settle their debt with the shopkeeper for another year. In 1927 the *Connacht Tribune* reported that a sum estimated at £20,000 was sent to County Galway from emigrants in North America during the Christmas season.

15 Speech by Frank Fahy at a Fianna Fáil meeting in Glinsk (Connemara). *Connacht Tribune*, 7 Mar. 1931.

Part I

Conflict

1

The Anglo-Irish Treaty and the June pact election

The treaty

In January 1922, a visiting correspondent for the London *Times* wrote:

> I have talked with many inhabitants of Galway, and they all look to a revival of the industries of the city – jute mills, flour mills and other industries – which aforetime promised a reign of prosperity for the West of Ireland. The vision is bright with promise, and it is not surprising that most of the people of the county desire to see the establishment of peace and the opportunity for development.[1]

Yet the approval of the Anglo-Irish Treaty was received with little of the boisterous enthusiasm which used to mark local political events. The Republic seemed lost in the small print and among the people a pressing mood of relief rather than triumph greeted the endorsement of the treaty by the Dáil. An editorial in the *Connacht Tribune* on 4 February 1922 asked 'where are the rejoicings and the jubilations of a liberty-loving and impulsive race which has regained its freedom after seven-and-a-half centuries of bondage? As far as can be judged, they are entirely absent.'[2] The *East Galway Democrat* noted 'an entire absence of anything like jubilation', but acknowledged that 'nobody would doubt that all were relieved that the great strain was over at last, and the issue decided formally'.[3]

It is of course, as J. J. Lee and more recently John M. Regan have argued, too simplistic to paint all pro-treaty supporters as instinctive democrats and all anti-treaty supporters as instinctive autocrats.[4] To cast the treaty debate as a battle between the pragmatists and the idealists is equally unfair. We can certainly argue that Michael Collins was pragmatic in signing the treaty, but it is difficult to argue that he was not also an idealist. There was a mix of moderates and radicals on both sides, and it was precisely because the split was not so clear-cut that it became so divisive. The treaty debate hinged on several issues. Broadly speaking, and even this may be an over-simplification, the debate was fought over the oath of allegiance to the Crown (more correctly an oath of fidelity), the Republic and essentially over power. It was not fought over class or partition. Cyclically, the same questions were rehearsed over and over on the floor of the Dáil. Was the treaty an abandonment of the Republic, or did it contain the seeds of further development? Was there ever to be a 'living Irish nation', was Ireland always going to be 'the dead past or the prophetic future', to use Arthur Griffith's phrase, or indeed, had the treatyites, as Eamon de Valera later maintained, abandoned their journey across the desert on catching their first glimpse of an oasis, when paradise may have been just over the horizon?[5] This notion that, if they stopped, the people might get comfortable and they might never regain their momentum was repeated over and over in the speeches on both sides of the House. For Galway's Patrick Hogan,[6] the treaty was not a final settlement – the words 'forever' and 'permanent', he maintained, should not be used in connection with the treaty.[7] But Frank Fahy[8] (Galway), while accepting that the stepping-stone theory was comprehensible, feared that 'this road under other guides may also lead rapidly to the sacrifice of principles to the Imperial idea, to smug prosperity, and obese content'.[9] Writing in *An Saorstát* a few months later, Griffith attempted to counter such criticisms.

> Certain well-fed people have expressed a fear that if the body of Ireland be well nourished the soul of Ireland may get gross. Let them be reassured, the children of the Irish farmer, the children of the Irish artisan, the children of the Irish labourer will not love Ireland the less if they get butter and jam on their bread … The Irish poor will not cease to be true to their love of Ireland when the Irish Free State has abolished pauperism and provided them with [the] means of [a] decent livelihood.[10]

The difficulty was that up until this point 'the Republic' had never really been specifically clarified. The time-honoured demand was for independence but it was clear that the Republic meant different things to different people.[11] Was it to be a Gaelic Republic, a Workers' Republic, an all-Ireland Republic, an externally associated Republic? The definition was clouded in ambiguity. In 1918, the general election was fought on the basis of self-determination; in 1921 it was fought for the continuance of a republican government, but Irish statesmen had at no time shown an inclination to be meticulous about defining what the words the 'Irish Republic' actually meant. The form in which independence should clothe itself was secondary to its actual attainment. The Republic was as much a rallying-cry as it was something tangible. The treaty forced a debate on what form Irish independence would now take and the cracks began to show openly. As Brian Cusack[12] (Galway) made clear to the Dáil, 'we have visualised this Republic far more clearly than we ever visualised this Free State'.[13]

In the Dáil, the seven Galway deputies voted four to three in favour of the treaty settlement. Patrick Hogan, Padraig Ó Máille, George Nicholls and Joseph Whelehan voted in favour of its ratification. Liam Mellows, Frank Fahy and Brian Cusack voted against it. However, this division is somewhat deceptive. When the treaty was first published Joseph Whelehan[14] acknowledged that he was more or less against it, but knowing that his actions would misrepresent his local (north Galway) Sinn Féin executive, he felt bound to stand for the agreement.[15] Had he not done so, Galway would have returned a verdict of four to three against the treaty.

Of the three anti-treaty deputies, Mellows[16] dismissed the treaty out of hand; Cusack, like many of his republican colleagues, stressed the inviolability of his oath to the Republic; and Fahy put it to his colleagues, 'Is not the declaration of the Republic ... *a fait accompli*, or have we been playing at Republicanism?'[17] For the Galway anti-treatyites, the war-weary western people had to be saved from themselves. By rejecting the treaty, they argued, they were preserving the virtue of their constituents who were unwittingly abandoning the Republic. Material might must not vanquish moral right. Virtue must not be subjugated by fear. As Fahy explained:

> Had a vote been possible prior to the Rising of 1916, does any Deputy imagine that we would have received the sanction of 10 per cent of our people? Yet the people now admit that our action was justified ... should a demand inspired by terror be hearkened to as the real voice of the people?[18]

Endorsing Fahy's belief that 'the great majority of the people are in favour of acceptance, lest worse befall',[19] Mellows claimed that

> the people are being stampeded; in the people's mind there is only one alternative to this Treaty and that is terrible, immediate war ... the people who are in favour of the Treaty are not in favour of the Treaty on its merits, but are in favour of the Treaty because they fear what is to happen if it be rejected. That is not the will of the people, that is the fear of the people.[20]

In their view, and in the minds of some of their anti-treaty colleagues, the majority of the Irish people were supporting the treaty on tactical grounds, and not on principle.[21] But even Mellows, in his emotional appeal that 'we would rather have this country poor and indigent, we would rather have the people of Ireland eking out a poor existence on the soil; as long as they possessed their souls, their minds, and their honour',[22] seemed to have lost sight of the fact that many people in the west of Ireland were already poor and indigent, and looked upon the treaty as a means of economic and social salvation.

Protesting against a hostile press, Cusack complained that the daily papers in Ireland were full of 'ratify the Treaty' resolutions.[23] Arguing on the same lines, Fahy declared that 'a venal Press that never stood for freedom and now with one voice advocates ratification has, by *suppressio veri* and *suggestio falsi*, prejudiced the issue and biased public opinion'.[24] Their protests were not unfounded. Terms such as 'disorder', 'chaos', 'ruin', 'war' abounded in the local press as its editors tried to impress on their readers what would ensue if the treaty was rejected. The effusive *Tuam Herald* was particularly forthright in its attacks on the anti-treatyites. Commenting on the necessity for people to accept the treaty settlement, it declared that 'they cannot possibly do otherwise unless they are bereft of intelligence and that they have been drugged and thereby their common sense is abandoned'.[25]

The difference between the oath agreed to by the plenipotentiaries and that proposed by de Valera in his alternative to the treaty – Document No. 2 – sparked little debate in the local pro-treaty press. The *Tuam Herald*, rather flippantly, deemed it a matter more verbal than vital and reiterated John Devoy's claim that de Valera's amendment would establish little more than a 'Royal Irish Republic'.[26] In similar fashion the *East Galway Democrat* cast it as a choice between Tweedledum and Tweedledee.[27] Described somewhat disparagingly in the Dáil as 'a quibble of words' by Arthur Griffith and 'a red herring' by Eoin MacNeill, de Valera's bold concept of external association – of an Ireland associated with but not part of the British Empire – was a formula undoubtedly ahead of its time.[28] Yet the differences between the proposals in Document No. 2 and those of the Articles of Agreement were portrayed as nothing but a 'shadow'. Deploring the manner in which his alternative was handled by the pressmen, de Valera accused them of being guilty of 'a violation of the canons of all reputable journalism'.[29]

The treaty did not grant unfettered freedom for Ireland, and if one recalls the famed remark of Seán Lemass in 1928 that Fianna Fáil was 'a slightly constitutional party', then perhaps it could be argued that, for the pro-treaty Galway deputies, the peace settlement presented 'a slightly independent treaty'. In the Dáil, Galway's pro-treaty deputies, and Patrick Hogan in particular, challenged the attitude adopted by their anti-treaty colleagues over divine right and majority right. Public opinion could not be flouted. Reiterating Michael Collins's call for government by the consent of the governed, Hogan reminded those assembled that any deputy who voted in favour of the treaty, knowing that his or her constituents were against it, was doing wrong. 'That may be a bitter thing', he conceded, 'but it is democracy'.[30] While acknowledging that the treaty did not provide complete independence, local solicitor George Nicholls[31] (pro-treaty) argued that it brought them very near to what they wanted. Responding to those who were expounding constitutional law in connection with the treaty, he stated:

> One of my constituents was speaking to me, and he used these words to me: 'We are bewildered and moidered with high faluting talk about constitutional law ... But we do feel certain of one thing; that is, if we once get the British forces out of Ireland, it will require more than constitutional law to get them back.'[32]

Adhering to public opinion, and echoing Collins's reluctance to commit the people to a renewed war without their consent, Padraig Ó Máille[33] (pro-treaty), a celebrated member of the West Connemara IRA flying column, stated that he supported the treaty because he believed it was what the people of Galway wanted.[34] Defending the treaty in a later speech, he argued that 'when a man got nine-tenths of a road, that man was a fool if he went back to the starting point, and began the journey again'.[35] Ó Máille's speeches in favour of the settlement gained him the congratulations of the *Connacht Tribune*, which applauded his 'shrewd intuition, common-sense, and moral courage', acknowledging that this was a tribute that they were pleased to pay him inasmuch as they actively opposed his return at the 1918 election.[36] For Joseph Whelehan (pro-treaty), like Collins, and like Ó Máille, the situation and the decision which must follow was 'not a Republic *versus* Association with Great Britain', but whether 'this Treaty be approved or, shall we commit the country to war'.[37]

While the Articles of Agreement fell short of the people's expectations, public opinion in Galway, as in much of the country, expressed a desire for peace. Support for the treaty was stronger among the citizenry than the small margin of victory (64 votes to 57) in the Dáil suggested. But it was difficult to gauge accurately. As one local reporter noted, 'into one ear is whispered an assurance that public opinion is solid for the Treaty, and into the other an assertion that it is Republican to the core'.[38] On 30 December 1921, Galway County Council passed a resolution stating that

> although the terms of the Peace treaty between England and Ireland do not satisfy the aspirations of the Irish people we are of the opinion that it is the best that our plenipotentiaries could have got under the circumstances. On that account, and on that account only, we, on behalf of the people of Galway, approve of it, and we call upon our representatives in the Dáil to vote for its ratification.[39]

This was hardly a resounding endorsement of the treaty, particularly coming from what was a rather conservative body. Other political groups were more outspoken. In a letter to Brian Cusack, the Tuam Town Commissioners wrote that 'the people of Tuam, who were among your most ardent supporters in the 1918 election, are almost unanimously in favour of ratification. By opposing the Treaty you are acting in direct opposition to their wishes and the wishes of the men who worked so hard for your return.'[40]

Across the county the local Sinn Féin organisation was also divided. At a meeting of the South Galway Comhairle Ceanntair at Loughrea on 2 February, members narrowly voted by 15 votes to 14 to support the republican policy at the Árd Fheis. In Galway city, the standing committee of the Thomas Ashe Sinn Féin Club carried a similar amendment by 36 votes to 22. The North Galway Comhairle Ceanntair, on the other hand, was unanimous in its support of the treaty and the East Galway Comhairle Ceanntair also voted in favour of the agreement by 18 votes to 8. While many Sinn Féin clubs instructed their delegates to support the treaty at the February Árd Fheis, not an insignificant number declared in favour of de Valera.[41]

In addition, two of the three Western Divisions of the IRA, contained within the county boundary, declared against the treaty.[42] Yet the recurrent procurement and relinquishing of local barracks across the county by both factions of the army did little to clarify the situation. In one episode, Portumna barracks (south Galway), recently vacated by the RIC, changed hands three times in one week.[43] In Galway city, Renmore barracks, previously the depot of the Connaught Rangers, was taken over by Commandant Thomas Duggan on behalf of the Republican (anti-treaty) forces of the IRA, while the Regular (pro-treaty) forces, under Commanding Officer Austin Brennan, commandeered the Railway Hotel in Eyre Square. Commenting on her new 'tenants', Miss Clancy, the manager of the hotel, remarked:

> The lounge of the building has been turned into a guardroom. It is worth noting that the British who were recently in occupation took over the best rooms in the hotel, whilst the I.R.A. have left the best rooms for the visitors, whom they have endeavoured to inconvenience as little as possible.[44]

The anti-treaty IRA, as has been well documented in other accounts of the civil war, held the dominant position in the country during the first months of 1922. In Galway, the influx of new recruits to the republican cause ever since the ratification of the treaty – 'trucileers' or the new playboys of the western world (as the treatyites perceived them to be) – was a source of bitter resentment among local pro-treaty supporters.

There was, however, to be no military standoff between the IRA rival units in Galway. Unlike the initial crisis that developed in Limerick city, a degree of civilised cooperation existed between the pro- and anti-treaty troops in Galway city. The wounding of Captain Seán Hurley (pro-treaty IRA) outside the Railway Hotel on 3 April was an isolated incident. At a public meeting held in Eyre Square to condemn the shooting, Austin Brennan declared

> we are not here for intimidation … we are not here for war, but I wish to warn the other side that we are not here to be made cock-shots of either. We will afford protection to the people of Galway … I will control my men and I will let the other side do the same, and I hope we will come together again.[45]

While reconciliation seemed increasingly unlikely, both sections wished to avoid military confrontation. Similarly in Limerick, despite Ernie O'Malley's plan to take over the provisional government positions in the city, and his warnings that the pro-treaty forces would gain an advantage if the republicans did not act decisively, the majority of the anti-treaty leadership showed no desire for a military showdown.[46] The tension between rival forces in Limerick, however, was more pronounced than in Galway. Locally, despite the wounding of Hurley, the *Connacht Tribune* reported that good feeling appeared to prevail between the two sides and they moved about the city freely without arms.[47] Speaking at Clifden in Connemara on 8 April, Padraig Ó Máille (pro-treaty) conveyed a similar sentiment: 'I knew that even though some of my friends of the flying column may differ from me they would not stand for anything in the nature of tyranny. Thank God that in this county, at least, we are able to keep our heads.'[48]

However, in an isolated but significant local incident, the ugly underside of the struggle surfaced in the town of Ballinasloe in east Galway in May and June 1922 when a campaign of violence and intimidation was directed against ex-soldiers, ex-policemen and local Protestant traders. Their homes were attacked and raided by gunmen and their commercial properties deliberately targeted and damaged. On 30 May 1922 the residence of John Wood, draper and outfitter on Main Street, Ballinasloe, was destroyed by fire. The previous week a bomb was thrown into his shop, but it failed to explode.[49] Two ex-policemen were shot and seriously wounded and a number of others were badly beaten. William Crawford, the local stationmaster, and several other residents and their families were ordered to leave the town.[50] A threatening letter delivered to John Davidson, an employee of the Post Office, read: 'The North east corner for you Jack – This within four days … No Damn North men here – Clear [out] … death after that … Bring your family if you're wise.'[51] On 1 June, the head of a monument erected at Cleaghmore to commemorate William Thomas Le Poer Trench, third Earl of Clancarty, was removed and thrown through the window of the premises of Edward Rothwell, local auctioneer. While the incident was fuelled by agrarian tension over the sale of Garbally Court, in which Rothwell, in his capacity as auctioneer, had been employed, inscriptions on the decapitated monument read: 'Western Orangemen clear out' and 'Revenge for Belfast'.[52] In Ahascragh, a few miles north of Ballinasloe, the local Protestant church was burned down. Responding to the situation, Thomas Sterling Berry, Church of Ireland, Killaloe, wrote:

> If the campaign against Protestants which has been carried on there [Ballinasloe] since the end of last month is continued in similar intensity for a few weeks more, there will not be a Protestant left in the place. Presbyterians and members of the Church of Ireland, poor and well-to-do, old and young, widows and children, all alike have suffered in intimidation, persecution and expulsion … In one case, an old man who had not left when ordered to do so was visited by a gang, who smashed everything in his cottage … Under such coercion as this a large number of Protestants have left … The list of those proscribed is added to constantly, and every Protestant is simply waiting for his turn to come.[53]

At a joint pro- and anti-treaty Sinn Féin rally, held to protest against the attacks in Ballinasloe, Fr J. P. Heenan condemned the outrages as 'uncharitable, un-Christian and un-Irish'.[54]

Between 1911 and 1926, the total Protestant community in County Galway (including 3,544 Episcopalians, 495 Presbyterians and 152 Methodists) had dropped from 2.3 per cent of the population to 1.1 per cent. While the percentage figure is slight, it represented a substantial decrease of over half of the Protestant population from 4,191 persons in 1911 to 1,938 persons in 1926.[55] However, census reports do not indicate the internal turnover of membership within the religious communities and the possible enlistment of new members and the outward movement of other members. Nor do they list the year-by-year rate of regression. Some obvious explanations for the rapid decline in numbers during this period would include the casualties suffered by Protestants during the Great War, the withdrawal of the British armed services stationed in Galway, the disbandment of the Royal Irish Constabulary and the departure of some of its members and their dependents from the county (although it must also be noted that membership of these forces was certainly not an exclusively Protestant phenomenon). A lack of social amenities, mixed marriages, family formation and cessation, and emigration also account for the precipitate decline. The Protestant community did not sink in the face of revolution. But Fergus Campbell's research demonstrates that Protestants were a target of revolutionary terror, particularly in an agrarian guise, and in Galway this ranged from cattle drives and arson attacks to shootings and murder. Some people were forced to leave the county. Disillusioned, many others chose to leave. Nevertheless, convincing evidence of a systematic sectarian campaign in the west of Ireland has yet to emerge.

In 1922 the violence and intimidation inflicted on Protestants in east Galway – whether inspired by ancestral agrarian grievances, covetousness, the settling of local scores, deliberate sectarian motivations or revenge for anti-Catholic atrocities in Belfast – drove Protestant families out of their shops, farms and homes. This is an indubitable fact. Yet, it is a relatively rare trend that affected a minor fraction of the community. From a wider perspective, the Ballinasloe case cast doubt on the provisional government's ability to impose civic order and safeguard Protestant political and economic interests in the newly independent state. Comparisons with Hart's tentative but provocative ethnic cleansing speculations on West Cork, however, are injudicious.

The pact election

With the party and the army deeply divided, the Collins–de Valera electoral pact of May 1922 was designed to salvage the fragile unity of Sinn Féin by denying a popular verdict on the treaty. Under the provisions of the pact, a joint panel of Sinn Féin candidates, proportionate to their existing strength in the Dáil, would be offered to the voting public in the hope that electoral contests would be reduced to a minimum. After the election, a national coalition government representing the rival pro- and anti-treaty factions of Sinn Féin would be formed. A crucial aspect of the agreement, however, was the clause that allowed other 'third parties' to run candidates against the Sinn Féin panel and, despite republican intimidation, many of them did so.

In Galway, in an election contest with eight candidates for seven seats, the question was not who would win but who would be eliminated. The pact election result saw the ousting of the most prominent republican candidate, Liam Mellows, by the Labour nominee and general secretary of the Irish National Teachers' Organisation (INTO), T. J. O'Connell. The republicans were the only ones to suffer a defeat in Galway, and had other pro-treaty candidates entered the contest their position might have been more vulnerable.

According to the published figures, Galway registered the lowest percentage turnout in all the contested constituencies, recording a figure of

44.81 per cent compared to the national average of 60.27 per cent.[56] With an estimated population of a little over 170,000 people in 1922, 48 per cent of the population of Galway (81,455) was eligible to vote in the election, yet less than half of the electorate (36,497) recorded their vote on 16 June. If only half of the population was eligible to vote and if only half of this half actually voted, could the government really claim such a decisive victory? A general election, however, was the only way, even in an admittedly imperfect manner, in which public opinion could be measured. The clause enabling other parties to contest the election was the ultimate contradiction, but the pact did affirm 'the primacy of the ballot box, at a time when this seemed very much in the balance'.[57] And this is precisely what Collins needed – a popular mandate for the treaty and for peace. The pact enabled an election to take place. Without it, it seems likely that the anti-treaty IRA would have attempted to forcibly prevent any election contest from being held. Yet not even Collins could have expected it to have worked so well – every minor party vote cast in the election was translated as a vote in favour of the treaty, and these successes came at the expense of the anti-treaty candidates, not candidates who supported the treaty.

If, for the anti-treatyites, the pact was designed to silence or at least 'muzzle' the electorate, it failed.[58] In Galway, the treaty dominated the local election campaign. The central message, stressed by both sides, was that responsibility for acceptance or rejection of the settlement rested with the people. George Nicholls (pro-treaty), at a public meeting in Clifden, advised those gathered that if 'you do not want the Treaty and are prepared to face the consequences, and if you think that we did wrong, your absolute duty is to kick us out'.[59] On the same day, the *Galway Observer* reported a speech made by Frank Fahy (anti-treaty) at a republican meeting in Athenry.

> It was to secure a Republic he trained his men there in 1915. He and those with him in the rising of 1916 took seriously the declaration of the Republic. If the people wished by acceptance of the treaty to turn down the Republic he was willing to give [his] place to somebody who would better express their changed opinions. It was a question entirely to be decided by the people.[60]

But 'if you turn me down', he later proclaimed at Loughrea, 'be honest and admit that it is not because you accept the Articles of Agreement, but because of the fear of war or of injuring your business'.[61]

Much to the frustration of the press, local issues almost entirely failed to impinge on the debate. On 8 April, the editor of the *Connacht Tribune* stated 'unemployment is rife, everywhere, although the stern fact has been lost sight of in the political ferment. It is doubtful if any of those who talk politics so glibly realise the menacing groundswell of discontent that is heaving in their very midst.'[62] The pact was widely criticised by the local pro-treaty press. Claiming that it was a negation of the first principle of democracy, the *Tuam Herald* insisted that 'it is not a real election for its effects will be practically a mere stereotyping of the present situation'.[63] William O'Malley declared the election to be 'a farce'.[64] Yet however inflated and frenzied the pronouncements of this former Irish Party MP for Connemara were, the election campaign in one of the largest constituencies in the country produced little enthusiasm among the voting public. After months of debate on the merits of the treaty, the people, as the *East Galway Democrat* noted, were 'tired of talking'.[65]

Apart from Labour's T. J. O'Connell, no other non-panel candidate came forward. However, unlike in Sligo, Clare, Mayo and elsewhere, there were few reports of disruptions at public meetings and intimidation preventing other candidates from contesting the election. The tempestuous meetings which characterised the election campaign in Sligo-East Mayo, the only other Connacht constituency where an election was held, were for the most part absent in Galway, where cordial fellowship seemed to abound between the two factions of the army and the local body politic. In Sligo-East Mayo the campaign was particularly bitter. Two pro-treaty Sinn Féin candidates – John Hennigan and Seamus McGowan – refused to withdraw from the contest, as the pact required them to do, and the republicans were especially hostile and aggressive in consequence.[66]

Until O'Connell's entry into the contest it seemed as though County Galway would fall into the habit of its nearest neighbours and not hold an election at all. The Galway branch of the Irish Farmers' Union, recognising that Patrick Hogan and Padraig Ó Máille (both pro-treaty) were themselves farmers and members of the organisation, decided not to nominate candidates for the election and agreed instead to give first and second preference votes to them.[67] It was hardly surprising then that, in a county where such a large majority of the work force was engaged in agriculture, Hogan from east Galway and Ó Máille from west Galway topped the poll on the first count (Figure 1.1). Overall in Galway, pro-treaty Sinn Féin won 54.5 per cent of the vote compared with anti-treaty Sinn Féin's 32.3 per cent and Labour's 13.2 per cent.[68]

The Labour Party's decision to offer a challenge to the Galway panel candidates was significant. Labour, on the whole, was not very well organised in the county, although the Town Tenants' League and local trade associations were occasionally visibly active. In May 1922, for instance, one month before the election, in a protest against the conditions of the tenants on the Clanricarde estate (east Galway) and the Urban District

Council's inability to provide adequate housing in the city, the Galway branch of the Town Tenants' League, led by Stephen Cremen, pulled down the bronze statue of Lord Dunkellin which stood in Eyre Square, paraded it through the town, and unceremoniously hurled it into the sea at Nimo's Pier.[69]

In selecting T. J. O'Connell the Labour Party chose a prominent figure to contest the June election and with the help of local trades councils and supporters of the INTO, a strong political union, it ran a short yet effective campaign. Perhaps the size of the constituency influenced its decision. As O'Connell pointed out at the opening of his campaign in Ballinasloe, there were seven seats and Labour was looking for only one. O'Connell also recognised a growing spirit that was 'antagonistic to the ordinary people having a say in the affairs of the country'.[70] While some support for the party could be perceived as a reactionary vote against Sinn Féin, Labour also clearly identified a frustration among a populace tired of hearing about the nation and eagerly seeking an end to economic stagnation.

The local Urban and Rural District Councils' minute books are filled with entries relating to the severe distress prevalent in parts of Connemara and the housing, unemployment and agricultural crisis affecting the whole county. Labour's ability to sidestep the treaty debate and identify with these immediate social and economic concerns was certainly advantageous. The alleviation of the destitution in Connemara may well have been an overriding factor among a voting community that was merely striving to exist on patches of bog and rocks. O'Connell ascribed a certain level of political naivety to the Galway populace when he asked: 'what did the starving fisherman in the West of Ireland, the houseless workers, the men living in unsanitary slums care whether there was a governor-general here, or whether they signed Document No. 1 or Document No. 2?'[71] Yet he expressed a clear understanding of the com-promising mindset of a war-weary western people desperate to follow any course that might improve their social conditions. O'Connell did not crawl in in last place but was elected on the first count, receiving the third-largest number of votes in the county (Figures 1.1 and 1.2). The majority of the electorate, by recording the highest number of first preference votes for the two farming pro-treaty Sinn Féin representa-tives and the Labour candidate, and by rejecting a principal member of the republican garrison in the Four Courts, made a clear statement in favour of peace, the treaty and economic regeneration. The local elector-ate decisively voted for pragmatism over radicalism.

In theory, the coalition panel presented a united front to the elector-ate, but the cracks and fissures within Sinn Féin were perceptible and

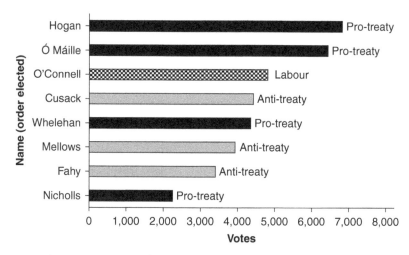

Figure 1.1 First preference vote in County Galway, June 1922

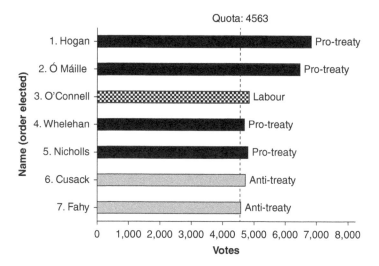

Figure 1.2 Result in County Galway, June 1922

palpable. The vibrant and resourceful campaign fought in 1918, in an election characterised by the swift organisation of the party, was on this occasion altogether absent. In June 1922, Sinn Féin, as a unit, won 86.8 per cent of the votes cast in Galway. This figure is often quoted to indicate its strength, but in an election contest in which seven of the eight candidates were guaranteed to be returned, the result, relative to the provisions of the pact, was a disappointment (although the treatyites were no doubt pleased to oust one of their most fervent opponents).

The government candidates retained each of their four seats. The successful election of the Galway city representative George Nicholls, who polled the lowest number of first preference votes, illustrated a clear loyalty in transfer votes on the part of the pro-treaty supporters (Figures 1.3 and 1.4). Nicholls was elevated to fifth place, overtaking the anti-treatyite Brian Cusack whom he trailed by four places and 2,167 votes after the first count. With the republicans already losing one seat to Labour, the final seat was fought out by two of the republican camp's most divergent supporters – Frank Fahy, the moderate republican, and Liam Mellows, the uncompromising radical.

Fahy urged restraint throughout the campaign. At an anti-treaty meeting at Athenry, he declared that he 'would rather let the Free State win, without a contest, than to see a divided army and Irishmen who had fought side by side, turn their arms against one another in fratricidal strife'.[72] No doubt, as the *Connacht Tribune* suggested, his speeches in favour of the restoration of order and goodwill brought him an accession of supporters from all classes.[73] Mellows, on the other hand, rarely left his position in the Four Courts to address the Galway electorate during the contest. Failure to address one's electorate in person, however, did not make inevitable a failure to secure election in Galway. In 1918, both Fahy and his other republican colleague Brian Cusack were elected for Sinn Féin while interned in Birmingham as a result of the German Plot allegations.[74] On this occasion, however, the electorate may well have felt there was less excuse for a candidate's absence, especially one who was not a 'native' of Galway. Mellows had been returned unchallenged in 1918 and 1921. Perhaps he took the electorate somewhat for granted.

The closely run fight between these two republican figures reveals some interesting voting patterns. Fahy received the second-highest number of transfers from Hogan's surplus, coming second to Nicholls and gaining 103 more votes than Joseph Whelehan, the other pro-treaty candidate (Figure 1.3). Hogan's large surplus was clearly a factor in Fahy's high tally, but he was also the beneficiary of a certain degree of localism with both Fahy and Hogan hailing from Loughrea in south Galway. Mellows secured the highest number of surplus votes among the anti-treaty candidates on the third count (Figure 1.4). However, it was the distribution of O'Connell's surplus which was most revealing (Figure 1.5). Electors who gave their first preference to Labour clearly paid little heed to the social policy of Mellows and showed no desire to pass on their lower preferences to the man who in 1916 had brought about a short-lived merger of

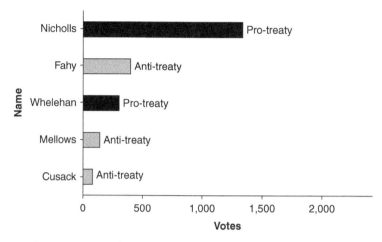

Figure 1.3 Distribution of Patrick Hogan's surplus, June 1922

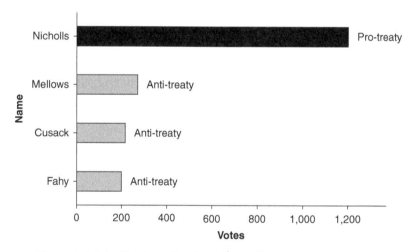

Figure 1.4 Distribution of Padraig Ó Máille's surplus, June 1922

land and revolution in east Galway. Lower transfers, of course, contain a more random element, but they still produced a high margin of 70, 71 and 88 per cent in favour of Fahy over Mellows. Fahy had trailed his fellow anti-treatyite after each successive count, yet secured sufficient pro-treaty and Labour transfers to beat Mellows to the final seat by a slim margin of 39 votes on the seventh count.

The defeat of Mellows was unexpected. To lose such a commanding figure of the republican army and one of their most outspoken leaders

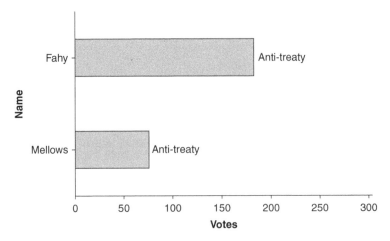

Figure 1.5 Distribution of T. J. O'Connell's surplus, June 1922

was a disappointment to the anti-treatyites. Of the three anti-treaty candidates, Cusack seemed to be in the weakest position but he polled the highest number of first preference republican votes, narrowly failing to be elected on the first count. Cusack's high tally may well have been the result of anti-treaty supporters giving their first preferences to their weaker candidate, expecting both Mellows and Fahy to be elected on merit, thus securing each of their three seats.[75]

The national result was conclusive: 58 pro-treaty Sinn Féin, 17 Labour Party, 7 Farmers' Party, 6 Independents and 4 Unionists, amounting to 92 candidates that could be expected to support the treaty in the new Dáil, against 36 anti-treaty Sinn Féin candidates.[76] However, as long as the Collins–de Valera pact could be regarded as still in existence, the result could be interpreted (and was interpreted by the republicans) as a vote which returned a total of 94 pro- and anti-treaty Sinn Féin candidates to form a coalition government as originally negotiated in the electoral agreement. The deterioration of the military situation, the attack on the Four Courts republican garrison on 28 June and the outbreak of heavy fighting in Dublin shelved any lingering likelihood of the continuation of Sinn Féin's dualist approach. In truth, any such possibility had been extinguished with Collins's alleged repudiation of the spirit of the pact days before the poll, the decision of non-panel candidates to contest the election, and the publication of the new Free State constitution on the morning of the poll in a form, insisted upon by the British government, that was wholly unworkable for the republicans.

Notes

1 Cited in *Tuam Herald*, 7 Jan. 1922.
2 *Connacht Tribune*, 4 Feb. 1922.
3 *East Galway Democrat*, 14 Jan. 1922.
4 Lee, *Ireland 1912–1985*, p. 67; John M. Regan, *Myth and the Irish State: Historical Problems and Other Essays* (Kildare, 2013), pp. 1–38, 43, 89.
5 *Dáil Éireann treaty deb.*, 7 Jan. 1922, p. 338. De Valera used the oasis metaphor in a letter to John Hagan, Rector of the Irish College in Rome, on 13 January 1922. See Dermot Keogh, *The Vatican, the Bishops and Irish Politics, 1919–1939* (Cambridge, 1986), p. 82.
6 Patrick Hogan: solicitor, farmer, vice-president of the Irish Farmers' Union and member of Sinn Féin. He became TD for Galway (uncontested) in May 1921. He served as Minister for Agriculture from 1922 to 1932. For more details on Hogan, see Chapter 3.
7 *Dáil Éireann treaty deb.*, 20 Dec. 1921, p. 63.
8 Frank Fahy: teacher, general secretary of the Gaelic League, Sinn Féin and Irish Volunteer veteran, and a student at King's Inns, Dublin. He served as second in command to Edward Daly in the Four Courts area during the Easter Rising. He spent terms in several British jails and was released in June 1917. He was elected as a Sinn Féin deputy for South Galway in December 1918. Active during the War of Independence, he was returned (uncontested) for Galway in May 1921. He later became a Fianna Fáil TD and was Ceann Comhairle of the Dáil from 1932 to 1951.
9 *Dáil Éireann treaty deb.*, 3 Jan. 1922, p. 196. Some pro-treaty supporters, Collins in particular, argued that the treaty be accepted as a stepping stone toward the ultimate attainment of complete independence in the fullness of time.
10 Cited in *Tuam Herald*, 4 Mar. 1922.
11 F. S. L. Lyons, 'The meaning of independence', in Brian Farrell (ed.), *The Irish Parliamentary Tradition* (Dublin, 1973), p. 229.
12 Brian Cusack: medical doctor. Founding member of the Irish Volunteers in Galway and member of the IRB, he was elected as a Sinn Féin deputy for North Galway in December 1918 and was returned (uncontested) for Galway in May 1921. A War of Independence veteran, he spent most of the civil war period in the Curragh internment camp.
13 *Dáil Éireann treaty deb.*, 4 Jan. 1922, p. 253.
14 Professor Joseph Whelehan: teacher. He was elected (uncontested) for Galway in May 1921 when the county became a single electoral constituency.
15 *Tuam Herald*, 18 Mar. 1922; *Dáil Éireann treaty deb.*, 21 Dec. 1921, p. 93.
16 Liam Mellows: clerk in Dublin in 1905. Son of a British army sergeant, he joined Fianna Éireann in 1909 and the IRB in 1912, and was full-time organiser for the Irish Volunteers in County Galway in 1914–15. The radicalisation of the Galway Volunteers, particularly in east Galway, is synonymous with the name of Mellows, who led the local insurrection in Easter 1916. However, the tradition of agrarian crime and unrest in the west and

the incessant hunger for land division and land redistribution all helped dictate the pattern of the Galway rebellion. Mellows was elected (uncontested)
for Sinn Féin in East Galway in December 1918. In America (where he
escaped to after the Rising) he worked on the *Gaelic American* and assisted
de Valera's tour in 1919–20. After his arrival back in Dublin, he acted as
IRA director of arms purchases in 1921 and was returned (uncontested) for
the Galway constituency. Despite losing his seat at the pact election, 1922,
he was appointed minister for defence in the republican government. After
the surrender of the Four Courts anti-treaty garrison, he was imprisoned
in Mountjoy jail. He was executed on 8 December 1922 by the provisional
government in reprisal for the killing of Seán Hales TD.

17 *Dáil Éireann treaty deb.*, 3 Jan. 1922, p. 195.
18 *Ibid.*, p. 197.
19 *Ibid.*
20 *Ibid.*, 4 Jan. 1922, p. 229.
21 See Lee, *Ireland 1912–1985*, p. 67, for his interpretation of this argument.
22 *Dáil Éireann treaty deb.*, 4 Jan. 1922, p. 231.
23 *Ibid.*, p. 252.
24 *Ibid.*, 3 Jan. 1922, p. 196.
25 *Tuam Herald*, 25 Feb. 1922.
26 *Ibid.*, 18 Feb. 1922.
27 *East Galway Democrat*, 14 Jan. 1922.
28 *Dáil Éireann treaty deb.*, 19 Dec. 1921, p. 21; *Dáil Éireann private ses-
    sions*, 15 Dec. 1921, p. 161. For further details on de Valera's comprom-
    ise proposal see, for example, 'The Anglo-Irish Treaty and Mr de Valera's
    Alternative' (Dublin, 1924), NAI, Department of the Taoiseach (hereafter
    DT), S9302/A; Lee, *Ireland 1912–1985*, p. 51; Jeffrey Prager, *Building
    Democracy in Ireland: Political Order and Cultural Integration in a Newly
    Independent Nation* (Cambridge, 1986), p. 63; Lyons, 'The great debate', in
    Farrell (ed.), *The Irish Parliamentary Tradition*, pp. 249–52. For another dis-
    cussion on de Valera's policy of external association and Griffith's belief in
    a dual monarchy see Michael Laffan, *The Resurrection of Ireland: The Sinn
    Féin Party, 1916–1923* (Cambridge, 1999), p. 425.
29 Eamon de Valera, 'The alternative to the treaty', 1923, NAI, DT, S9302/A.
30 *Dáil Éireann treaty deb.*, 20 Dec. 1921, p. 61.
31 George Nicholls: solicitor, founding member of the Galway branch of the
    Irish Volunteers in December 1913, first president of the Thomas Ashe
    Sinn Féin Club in Galway city and chairman of Galway County Council
    (1920–25). He was arrested on the morning of the local rebellion in 1916
    along with other Volunteer organisers including Padraig Ó Máille. Interned
    in Britain, he was released in December 1916 and was elected (uncontested)
    for Sinn Féin in Galway in May 1921.
32 *Dáil Éireann treaty deb.*, 3 Jan. 1922, p. 198.
33 Padraig Ó Máille: farmer, Gaelic League organiser and Sinn Féin activist. A
    prominent member of the Irish Volunteers, he was arrested on the morning
    of the Galway rebellion in 1916. He was interned in Wandsworth prison,

Frongoch and Reading jail and released in December 1916. He was elected as a Sinn Féin deputy for Connemara in December 1918 and was returned (uncontested) for Galway in May 1921. A charismatic War of Independence veteran, he was shot and wounded on 7 December 1922 outside the Ormond hotel in Dublin by republican forces during the civil war. His travelling companion and fellow pro-treaty deputy Seán Hales was killed in the attack.

34 *Dáil Éireann treaty deb.*, 22 Dec. 1921, p. 140.
35 *Galway Observer*, 15 Apr. 1922.
36 *Connacht Tribune*, 21 Jan. 1922.
37 *Dáil Éireann treaty deb.*, 21 Dec. 1921, pp. 92–3.
38 *East Galway Democrat*, 25 Feb. 1922.
39 Minutes of Galway County Council, 30 Dec. 1921, Galway County Council Archives (hereafter GCCA), Galway County Council minute books, GC1/3.
40 Cited in *Tuam Herald*, 31 Dec. 1921.
41 *Connacht Tribune*, 4 Feb. 1922.
42 The 2nd and 4th Western Divisions of the IRA declared against the treaty. The 1st Western Division supported it.
43 *Connacht Tribune*, 15 Apr. 1922.
44 *Ibid.*, 8 Apr. 1922.
45 *Galway Observer*, 8 Apr. 1922.
46 Michael Hopkinson, *Green against Green: The Irish Civil War* (2nd edn, Dublin, 2004), p. 63.
47 *Connacht Tribune*, 8 Apr. 1922.
48 *Galway Observer*, 15 Apr. 1922.
49 Letter from Sec. Home Affairs to Peter Ennis, Chief of Police, 3 June 1922, NAI, Department of Justice (hereafter DJ), H5/330; *Connacht Tribune*, 3 June 1922.
50 *Connacht Tribune*, 17 June 1922.
51 NAI, DJ, H5/412.
52 *Connacht Tribune*, 3 June 1922.
53 *Church of Ireland Gazette*, 16 June 1922; Peter Hart, 'The Protestant experience of revolution in Southern Ireland', in Richard English and Graham Walker (eds), *Unionism in Modern Ireland: New Perspectives on Politics and Culture* (London, 1996), pp. 91–2.
54 *Irish Times*, 16 June 1922.
55 *Census of Ireland 1926*, Religion and birthplaces, vol. III, p. 16.
56 Michael Gallagher (ed.), *Irish Elections 1922–44: Results and Analysis* (Limerick, 2003), p. 14.
57 Michael Gallagher, 'The pact general election of 1922', *Irish Historical Studies*, vol. 21, no. 84 (Sept., 1979), p. 421.
58 Here the use of the word 'muzzle', in a political context, imitates that employed by Arthur Griffith during the treaty debate when he criticised his detractors' attempts to try to silence or suppress the voice of the people: 'The Irish people will not be deceived ... Some of you will try to muzzle it; but that voice will be heard, and it will pierce through ... Distrust the people, muzzle the people, where then is gone self-determination for the people?' *Dáil Éireann treaty deb.*, 7 Jan. 1922, p. 341.

59 *Connacht Tribune*, 15 Apr. 1922.
60 *Galway Observer*, 15 Apr. 1922.
61 *East Galway Democrat*, 6 May 1922.
62 *Connacht Tribune*, 8 Apr. 1922.
63 *Tuam Herald*, 27 May 1922.
64 *Galway Observer*, 17 June 1922.
65 *East Galway Democrat*, 17 June 1922.
66 For additional information on the Sligo-East Mayo contest, reports of intimidation, the alleged kidnapping of personation officers acting for the two independent candidates and the two sides' different degrees of commitment to the pact, see Michael Farry, *The Aftermath of Revolution: Sligo 1921–23* (Dublin, 2000), pp. 64–74.
67 Letter to the editor by Martin Egan, Galway Executive member of the Irish Farmers' Union, explaining its decision not to nominate candidates for the election. See *Connacht Tribune*, 10 June 1922.
68 Gallagher (ed.), *Irish Elections 1922–44*, p. 7.
69 For further details on this incident, see *Connacht Tribune* 27 May, 3 June 1922; NAI, DJ, H5/313.
70 *Connacht Tribune*, 10 June 1922.
71 *Galway Observer*, 17 June 1922.
72 *Connacht Tribune*, 15 Apr. 1922.
73 *Ibid.*, 24 June 1922.
74 In an attempt to stifle the separatist movement, and, in part, in response to the stand-off over conscription, a large proportion of the Sinn Féin leadership was arrested on the night of 17–18 May 1918 under allegations of treasonable contact with Germany.
75 For an expansion of this theory see 'The count at Galway', *Connacht Tribune*, 24 June 1922.
76 Gallagher (ed.), *Irish Elections 1922–44*, p. 15.

2

Civil war society and the August 1923 election

Civil war society

The war in the west, as has often been suggested, was an isolated campaign. On 2 July 1922, republican forces in Galway, following the national pattern, abandoned attempts to hold fixed positions, destroyed their posts and evacuated the city. Four buildings – Renmore barracks, the Naval base at the Docks, Eglinton Street police barracks, and the Freemasons' Hall on Presentation Road – were set on fire. A fifth republican base at Dominick Street police station was spared. A notice posted by Thomas Fahy, O/C at Dominick Street, explained that the house was left intact because it was felt that a fire started in the building would endanger the entire street and the lives of non-combatants.[1]

At once, abandoned republican posts in the city were targeted by looters. The *Connacht Tribune* reported that at Renmore barracks 'every portable piece of property that remained after the evacuation was looted. Doors, tables, kitchen furniture, window-sashes, even permanent woodwork were torn down ... and removed.' At the Naval base, military tables were carted off on donkeys and all sorts of other vehicles and at the Freemasons' Hall, which had not been badly damaged by the fire, looters carried away doors, window-frames, furniture and floors. One man was in the process of removing the kitchen range when the National troops arrived and put a stop to it.[2]

The withdrawal of the republican forces and the re-employment of guerrilla war tactics in the countryside, however, meant that Galway city did not become a focal point of the military struggle. Unlike in Dublin and in Limerick, there was no military showdown in Galway. Limerick city had considerable strategic importance. If controlled by the anti-treaty IRA a link between Munster and the west could have been established, leaving Michael Brennan's command in Clare and Seán MacEoin's command in Athlone dangerously isolated. Conversely, if the city was held by the pro-treaty IRA, republican units in Clare and the midlands would

have been cut off from their colleagues in Munster.[3] Galway city, in a
military sense, was not such a strategic pivot.

The civil war, particularly the disintegrated guerrilla phase of the war,
did not spread across the whole county. Republican resistance in Galway
was strongest in Connemara and in north Galway, but it appeared to
lack precise direction. In east Galway agrarian agitation shaped the
nature of civil war violence (this aspect of the campaign is discussed in
the next chapter).

Seventeen big houses were destroyed in Galway during the war. Of the
more prominent residences, Castlegrove House, the property of Thomas
Lewin in north Galway, was burned by republicans on 26 July 1922.
In south Galway, Roxborough House, the home of Major W. A. Persse
and birthplace of Isabella Augusta Persse (later Lady Gregory of Coole),
was destroyed on 9 August 1922. Castlehackett House, a three-storey
mansion built by the Kirwan family in the early eighteenth century, was
burned down on 4 January 1923. Describing the destruction of this his-
toric north Galway mansion the *Connacht Tribune* wrote that

> the splendid library, magnificent ballroom, drawing room with polished
> oak floor and beautiful plastered panel ceiling, billiard room, and all the
> antique furniture of priceless value, family relics centuries old and historic
> articles, all were consumed to dust.[4]

In February 1923, Renvyle House, Connemara, the country home of
Senator Oliver St John Gogarty, was burned. In April 1923, Spiddal
House, Connemara, home of Lord Killanin, was totally destroyed.
Significantly, at Coole, in east Galway, Lady Gregory's enquiries in May
1922 as to what might happen to her were met with the response: 'Oh,
nothing to your ladyship – but terrible things will happen.'[5]

Within the local community, raids on banks and post offices, the
destruction of roads, bridges and railway lines, the interruptions to the
postal service and telegraphic communications, the prevention of market fairs, theft, the postponement of the Galway Races festival, and the
damage to public and private property inflicted widespread disruption
on economic life. Reporting on the effect the cancelling of local markets
was having in the county, the *Irish Independent* noted: 'The amount
lost through injury to fairs and markets and the slump in cattle prices is
incalculable. There is a tendency to hoard money. Thus the circulation
of currency has been checked.' A Dublin trader who came to the county
with accounts amounting to £600 had, after three weeks of difficult
travel, only collected £25.[6] In Tuam, in north Galway, the destruction
of the Crumlin bridge near Ballyglunin, prevented a rail service running from Athenry to Tuam for three months. As the main road from

Galway to Tuam was also impassable in places, people wishing to get to Tuam from Galway had to travel a circuitous route by train to Athenry and then continue by road to Tuam. In July 1922 a journey of 22 miles became a journey of 46 miles.[7] In Galway city, in an effort to conserve food supply and prevent profiteering, the Urban District Council ordered that no trader was to charge more for any goods than the market price of 1 July and that all citizens were to be as sparing as possible in the use of foodstuffs and report any waste to the council.[8] In Oughterard (west Galway) old age pensions, which had not been received since July, were finally delivered when the first train to travel on the Clifden line since the outbreak of the war ran from Galway to Oughterard and Maam Cross on 17 October. In a letter to the Department of Home Affairs on 1 August, J. B. Hill, resident magistrate, Oughterard, described how

> The shops [here] are small and hold a very small stock. All is now used up ... fever has broken out at Recess, and [because] of the road to Galway being blocked ... the patients cannot be got to the fever hospital in Galway ... Those who have and keep cattle can sell neither as fairs cannot be held or animals got away ... This large and remote area with a population without any reserve in food are always only a little ahead.[9]

From Roundstone, Connemara, Dr T. T. Collins, dispensary medical officer for the area, wrote: 'we are absolutely cut off here, no post or telegraph communication, no railway, and ... no petrol ... I have appealed to the IRA (the Irregulars) in Clifden (who have seized the available supplies) but with no result.'[10]

The civil war was an intimate war, it was a bitter war and it was a public war. Trade was disrupted, food supplies were at times limited and some areas became increasingly isolated, but everyday life also went on.

The Catholic hierarchy

The declaration of the majority of the electorate in favour of the treaty in June 1922 strengthened the Galway bishops' initial uncompromising stance in support of the provisional government. Preaching in Loughrea on 2 April 1922, the Bishop of Clonfert, Thomas O'Doherty, had offered a scathing criticism on the formation of the republican military executive in Dublin. Emphasising the need to obey lawful authority, he deplored the refusal of this 'military junta' to accept majority rule and declared that 'its proclamations and orders have no moral force whatever'. 'Should these men order you to destroy property', he added, 'the men who give the order and the men who execute it are jointly and severally bound to restitution according to the ordinary laws of justice.'

Death inflicted under their orders 'is nothing but murder'.[11] O'Doherty's anti-republican pronouncement gained him the congratulations of his episcopal colleagues. In Tuam, Archbishop Thomas Gilmartin judged his sermon to be a 'splendid opportune and clear statement'. Writing to O'Doherty, Bishop Michael Fogarty (Killaloe) declared that 'it is perfect in phrase and teaching. It is timely as well as excellent … I believe the de Valera crowd are bent on wrecking everything.'[12] On 26 April, a joint statement issued by the Catholic Church reaffirmed much of O'Doherty's earlier pronouncement. In it, the hierarchy urged 'the young men connected with this military revolt' not to 'make shameful war upon their own country'; warned that if they did so they would be 'parricides and not patriots' and forcefully denounced military despotism as 'scandalous and incalculable criminality'.[13]

Six months later, arranged to coincide with the government's offer of amnesty to the republicans and the implementation of the Public Safety Act, they issued a pastoral letter collectively condemning the republican cause. The bishops declared that the provisional government was 'the legitimate authority in Ireland'; that the republican campaign of guerrilla warfare was 'without moral sanction'; and that the killing of National soldiers was 'murder before God'. Those who disregarded the bishops' teachings would 'not be absolved in Confession, nor admitted to Holy Communion'.[14] While the partisan tone of the October pastoral bolstered the provisional government, it brought the hierarchy into conflict with those who rejected the legitimacy of the new state. The allegation cast against the bishops was that, in signing the pastoral, they acted from party bias rather than spiritual zeal and that, out-stepping the proper sphere of their activity, they played the part of political partisans rather than pastors of their people.[15] Republican supporters contended that priests, in essence, had become policemen, ordering and directing rather than counselling and advising the Catholic laity. 'One needs to have a mind like the hide of a rhinoceros',[16] wrote James O'Dea, Galway diocesan secretary, in reference to the bundles of republican literature, received by the bishops in the wake of the October pastoral, deploring the 'traitorous' bishops of the Irish 'Freak State'. An excerpt from one such pamphlet read:

> Our condemnation of the Freak State and the English Government is but a gentle reprimand compared to the intensity of feeling and anguish of soul with which we irrevocably condemn and forcefully denounce the Roman Cabal and the Bishops of Ireland who planned and plotted with England to bring forth that unspeakable and monstrous abortion called the Freak State of Ireland … The signing of the drunken treaty, drunkenly arrived at, on the 6th Day of December 1921, by the traitors of Ireland, was the supreme

spiritual treason committed by the Invincible Government of the Roman Church and the Bishops of Ireland against the Irish Nation.[17]

James O'Dea, however, did not favour the treaty, and his opposition to the provisional government intensified as the war progressed. Protesting against the execution of Liam Mellows, Rory O'Connor, Joseph McKelvey and Richard Barrett in Mountjoy jail on 8 December 1922, he declared that a 'Government that murders its prisoners deserves no support'.[18] His bishop, Thomas O'Dea of Galway, while supporting the treaty, adopted a more measured tone than his two Galway colleagues, O'Doherty and Gilmartin. Rather than denouncing the republicans from the pulpit, he appealed for reconciliation.[19] His conciliatory stance was welcomed by republican clerical supporters, particularly John Hagan, the Rector of the Irish College in Rome. In a prophetic letter, written on a visit to Ireland in August 1922, Hagan wrote

> I am particularly depressed by the tone of some recent Episcopal utterances which seem to me to be calculated to do much harm in the years that lie ahead. I wish they would all imitate the tone of the Bishops of Galway and Dromore ... I have little hesitation in forming a forecast that in half a dozen years the Republican Party will command the majority of the country. In that event it will not be pleasant or profitable to remember that more than one Bishop today was responsible for the denying of absolution to those, who rightly or wrongly, have made up their minds as to the lawfulness of resorting to certain methods for the realisation of the republican ideal.[20]

Hagan, however, demonstrated no inclination to return to Ireland on a permanent basis and continued to offer pronouncements from the sanctuary of the Irish College. On the death of O'Dea in April 1923, Hagan immediately dissociated himself from the vacant diocese of Galway. Writing to Gilmartin, he stated:

> My knowledge of the history of Ireland during the past three hundred years has made me as certain as I am of my own existence that the experiment of introducing outsiders into another province as Bishops is doomed to failure and will lead to mischief; and I could not think of making myself a party to such an experiment.

'As regards Galway in particular', he added, 'I assume that some practical knowledge of Irish is essential; whereas I have no knowledge whatever of that ancient tongue.' Insisting that the position held no attraction for him whatsoever, he strongly appealed on the grounds of his ill health not to be made 'stand a winter in Ireland after all these years in a sunnier land'.[21]

By December 1922, the numerically superior National army, equipped with far greater resources, had successfully subdued most of the county.

As the war dragged on republican activity became increasingly isolated. One of the last significant engagements of the civil war was an assault on the barracks occupied by the Free State forces in Headford in north Galway on 8 April 1923.[22] On 11 April six IRA prisoners were brought from Galway jail and executed in Tuam as a reprisal for the Headford attack. The timing of the executions, coming at a point when republican armed resistance to the state was practically at an end, and the government's decision to bring the prisoners to Tuam rather than execute them in Galway provoked a strong local reaction. Coinciding with a period of mourning in the city on account of the death of the Bishop of Galway, the executions could not have been carried out in the city. However, Thomas Costello's remarks to the Tuam District Council that the executions were carried out in Tuam 'to make the volleys ring in the ears of the Archbishop' implied that the selection of that location was deliberate. By the end of 1922, Gilmartin, while supporting the institutions of the new state, had adopted a more conciliatory position towards the war.[23] His calls for clemency were at variance with the Cosgrave government's repressive measures in defence of the state. Nevertheless, it was far more likely that the decision to execute the prisoners in Tuam was a demonstration of the government's political strength and its adamant refusal to yield to republican resistance in the region. Gilmartin was not in Tuam on the day of the executions. He was attending the funeral of a friend in Maynooth. Writing to John Hagan in Rome, he explained: 'I knew nothing of the executions in Tuam until they were all over and I doubt if I could have stopped them. They inspired horror all round. They were of course a sequel to the Headford attack which was insane.'[24] Others were less sympathetic. Padraig Ó Máille TD defended the action of the government, stating that 'these young men had themselves entirely to blame. They got ample opportunities recently of ceasing the struggle against their countrymen, but unfortunately they persisted in their mistaken course.'[25] Patrick Hogan TD deplored what he termed the 'benevolent neutrality' of the local commissioners and questioned how far such an attitude of public men towards those in armed rebellion against the state was responsible for the condition of the country.[26]

The passivity of the people in promoting the new state is significant. While they offered their political support to the Free State, the people seemed less forthcoming in offering an out-and-out defence of it and there seemed to have been a degree of sympathy for the republicans. Addressing a Cumann na nGaedheal meeting in Tuam, Monsignor Macken stated

> I was out on the hills … and met some of the boys, and you would not be
> too hard upon them if you saw their mental and physical suffering, and

realised their mental needs. He would be a cold Irishman who would not try to stop that thing and do all in his power to bring them all together again.[27]

The ceasefire was called on 30 April and the republicans, demoralised, dumped their arms on 24 May 1923.

The condition and morale of the IRA

It has been argued, particularly in regard to republican activity and sup-port in the west of Ireland, that the people were more active in this region because they were poor, their situation was more desperate and therefore they had less to lose – in short, that revolutions were more easily made when people were starving. Revolutions, however, require energy and many would-be Volunteers were too poor or too weak to fight. Some Volunteers could not afford to leave their land untended and take to the hills or go on the run. The economic cost to those they would leave behind would be, and often was, far too high (the consequences of such activities had already been seen in other parts of the county after the widespread arrests and imprisonments of local Galway 'sympathis-ers' in the aftermath of the Easter Rising in 1916).[28] For those people who did fight, the localised nature of Volunteer enlistment, activity and loyalty were important factors, as were the aspirations towards an Irish Republic and the anticipation of a radically altered way of life. For many others the desire for land and land redistribution was as fundamental as any patriotic objective.

Nonetheless, the poverty in many of the western areas, coupled with a lack of food supplies and a shortage of arms, was an important element in reducing the prospect of effective republican activity. Reporting on the conditions in East Connemara, Colm Ó Gaora of the 4th Western Division wrote to his divisional O/C in December 1922 stating that

> since the commencement of hostilities last June our A.S.U.s [Active Service Units], numbering about 80 men, are in a pitiable and most desperate con-dition [and] in need of proper clothing and feeding, especially since the Winter months ... the shops in our area which are small did not stock the stuff required by our men, and therefore the necessaries needed could not be commandeered.

The people 'who have stood with us are of the poorest type in Ireland', he continued, 'and I consider it a crime to trespass much longer on their hospitality'. Ó Gaora ended by stating that if a sum of at least £800 was not immediately provided the fighting spirit of his men would be broken.[29] The O/C of the West Connemara Brigade offered a similarly depressing account, writing that his men could not stand it always being out in the cold and rain without overcoats and with wet feet.[30]

A report on the general state of the Western Command compiled on 14 March 1923 stated that the 2nd Western Division was weak in officers, arms, and ammunitions. The 4th Western Division was in a stronger position, but the round-up before Christmas had a demoralising effect. Communications were 'very bad all round' and it was considered a very good result if a reply to a dispatch from the 4th Western Division HQ to Connemara reached the Division in less than seven days.[31] Maurice Twomey, reflecting on the position in the west after the civil war, noted that

> Before hostilities began a great proportion of the Brigade Officers deserted to the enemy. Even worse still others ... remained only to desert a short while after hostilities began. The result is that these areas never properly recovered from the effects of these desertions and consequent disorganisation.[32]

Notwithstanding the earlier advent of new volunteers to the republican side, the local organisation was in a particularly poor condition. Participation in the Sinn Féin clubs was also unsatisfactory. A report submitted in December 1923 recorded that the clubs simply existed nominally, that meetings were poorly attended and that no business was transacted. The 'right type of man', it noted, 'does not control the Clubs' and 'several volunteers have walked out ... in disgust'. The report also criticised members of the committee who arrived at meetings with their accounts in a bundle of raggy papers, with no balance sheets, no appearance of satisfactory business, and concluded: 'no wonder people ask are we really serious'.[33]

In June 1922, the majority of people supported the treaty and voted for peace and stability. Yet Galway was not playing at republicanism. Although a defeated, depleted and dejected force by the spring of 1923, the anti-treaty IRA retained a reservoir of support in the west.[34] However ineffective they might have been in the immediate aftermath of a demoralising military defeat, republicanism was a still a potentially potent force,[35] and the continued presence of this rumbling if not particularly radical republican bloc posed a challenge to the process of legitimising the new state.

August 1923

In the aftermath of the civil war, the August 1923 general election was fought on the Free State government's terms. Many prominent republicans and their supporters were interned, on the run, dislocated or dead.

Their political activities were subject to harassment by the police, and the national press and the Catholic hierarchy were unsympathetic and unforgiving.[36] Under such inequitable circumstances, Frank Fahy TD questioned the merits of Sinn Féin contesting the election. In a letter to de Valera in June he wrote: 'As there will be no freedom of the press, as the register is not at all satisfactory, as lying and corruption will be rampant, I think it is not wise to run Republican Candidates at all at [the] next elections.' The main question under consideration, he contended, was whether or not the treaty should be accepted and the Republic disestablished.

> The breaking of the Pact, the attack on the soldiers of the Republic – the war, and the unconstitutional action of the Free State in general – whilst for some of us they were determining factors in our attitude since June last, are for most Republicans secondary matters only.[37]

Fahy had opposed the civil war. He defended those who fought for the Republic, but he did not follow de Valera's precipitate enlistment into the republican army. Like de Valera he remained ardently against the treaty, but he consistently called for peace and restraint among the IRA rather than aggravating the drift towards civil war. The pro-treaty press and the *Connacht Tribune*, in particular, had commended his appeals to end the war.

> If every Republican were like Mr Frank Fahy, there would be no fresh-made graves throughout Ireland to-day, no terrible legacy of bitterness, no wasted island ... The forum would be the battleground, and the ballot box would replace the bullet ... He recognised and honoured the truism that preventable war was a crime and ... steadfastly refused to take up arms against his brother Irishmen. Yet he would have preserved faith even unto death against the alien enemy. Even those who oppose him politically can be proud of such Irishmen as he.[38]

At a later republican meeting in Dublin, Fahy reiterated that under no circumstances 'would he agree to a renewal of the Civil War with half of Ireland and all of England against us'.[39] Fahy declared himself to be a constitutional republican and drifted towards a position of constitutional opposition to the treaty and the Free State. But this was a rather disingenuous position as he refused to take the oath and recognised neither the 1922 constitution nor the third Dáil. Constructive republicanism is perhaps a better representation of his moderate political principles and instinctive democratic tendencies in 1923. He was certainly not bereft of democratic culture.

In June 1923, he was approached by the Farmers' Party to run in the election on its behalf, but he declined. On 2 July, a month before the election, and worn down, he wrote again to de Valera declaring that he was 'sick of politics' and that he believed he could do better work for Ireland in the Gaelic League.[40] By August, however, he was less morose and threw his weight behind the republican campaign.

Cumann na nGaedheal, the newly constituted pro-treaty Sinn Féin party, painted the August election as a contest between the constitutionalists and the militarists; a choice between peace and security or anarchy and commercial ruin. In his election address 'To the People of Ireland', W. T. Cosgrave, as President of the Executive Council, outlined the record of the government's achievements during the past year. It had framed a constitution, introduced universal adult suffrage, organised the departments of the state, established the Civic Guard and the District Courts of Justices, built up a national army and defeated the armed resistance against the new state.[41] The republicans, on the other hand (who retained the name Sinn Féin), campaigned against what they viewed to have been a year of 'Raids, Imprisonment, Flogging, Torture and Death' inflicted upon them by the government.[42] One republican handbill carried the heading: 'There is no use you saying you were against the executions if you again return the men who carried them out.'[43]

Locally, Cumann na nGaedheal selected a complete panel of nine candidates and expected to poll strongly. A correspondent for the *Manchester Guardian* predicted that had the contest been fought on the old electoral system of a single non-transferable vote the result, for the Free State supporters, would have meant 'a sweep even cleaner than that which disabled the English Conservatives in 1906 or the English Liberals in 1918'.[44] The Galway electorate reacted quite differently. In the contest for nine seats, four Cumann na nGaedheal, three Sinn Féin, one Labour and one Independent candidate polled the highest number of first preference votes in the county (Figure 2.1). An exhaustive count of nineteen rounds effected only one change in the result, substituting one Sinn Féin candidate, Colm Ó Gaora, for another, Louis O'Dea (Figure 2.2). While Cumann na nGaedheal retained the four seats it won in June 1922 (as pro-treaty Sinn Féin), it made no new ground in the county.

The party's cautious approach had brought about peace, stability and a desire for progress. Cumann na nGaedheal's election manifesto, however, contained little of the language or socio-economic aspirations of the revolution and Galway society was impatient for economic development. The government's attitude to fiscal spending would be slow and steady and conservative. During a visit to the city in July, Cosgrave, standing at the proposed site of a new transatlantic port for Galway at Furbo, had told those gathered:

> There is a very warm corner in every Irishman's heart for Connacht ... The
> Gael was driven here in times gone by and he has extracted a livelihood

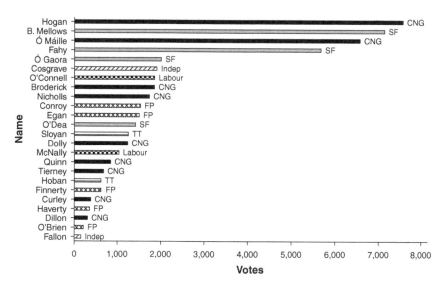

Figure 2.1 First preference vote in County Galway, August 1923

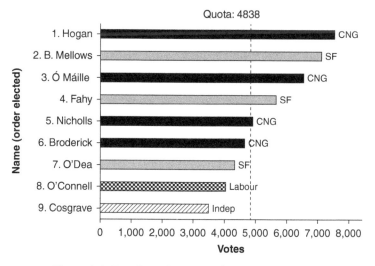

Figure 2.2 Result in County Galway, August 1923

from an unwilling soil ... We must, however, postpone immediate consideration for an important scheme of development such as this ... After all public life, as well as private life, must be based on honest dealing, and it is a man's first duty to discharge his debts before he undergoes any other expenditure.[45]

Reporting on his stay in Galway, the *Connacht Tribune* declared that the President 'had won the heart of the west'.[46] However, the party's rigorous conservatism failed to excite the local electorate. It also failed to excite some of its more prominent supporters. Speaking at an election rally in Mountbellew (north-east Galway), Professor Michael Tierney explained that

> He was far from believing this Government was the best on earth, or did everything possible that could be done, but ... he had come to the conclusion that if Ireland is to go on the road to peace and prosperity and be an honour amongst nations, there was no other Government possible but the Government presently in power.[47]

It was hardly a ringing endorsement.

Local issues, such as the provision of housing, the distribution of land, the relief of unemployment, the construction of better roads, the support for a transatlantic port scheme, and the development of the Gaeltacht and the Irish language, were referred to on the election platforms. However, politics, not economics, dominated the election campaign. In 1923, given the fragility of the new state, the issue was not that of the town tenant, farmer or worker; it was between the Free State and the Republic. Sectional interests were waived and candidates were defined by the treaty split.

Galway again registered the lowest percentage turnout in the country, recording a figure of 45.47 per cent compared to the national average of 59.05 per cent. Of the 106,378 people listed as eligible to vote, only 48,375 valid votes were returned.[48] In a contest where twenty-four candidates stood for election, three times the 1922 number, a less than 1 per cent increase in the voting turnout was recorded. Yet the abstention from the polls was not necessarily a vote against the establishment of the new state, but more an expression of dissatisfaction with the government's performance.

Additionally, there were fundamental problems with the electoral register. In 1923, Galway had 7,977 more people listed on the register than existed in the adult population. As a result the turnout figure for the county was artificially low (the matter of the local register is referred to again in the course of the discussion in Chapter 7).[49] Nonetheless, the *Connacht Tribune* noted that 'never before did candidates take the elections with such apparent indifference'.[50] Basil Chubb has attributed the low turnout in the west to the fact that the mountainous landscape and scattered nature of the communities made communications difficult.[51] Undoubtedly, the poor infrastructure and economic hardship of much of the rural countryside did inhibit many voters from travelling to the polling stations. In addition, the selection of a Monday as Election Day and declaring it a public holiday was intended to allow the electors ample opportunity to exercise the franchise. Instead, it induced many people to make the most of this unexpected time off. The wisdom of the government's decision was questioned in the national press, which carried reports of hundreds of Dublin professionals flocking to the seaside resorts instead of casting their votes.[52] The contrasting torrential rain that fell on the morning of the election in the west, however, had a less joyous effect on the local electorate. Furthermore, the large size of the constituency prevented an intense election campaign from developing. Candidates particularly well known in one region of the county were often strangers in another and as a result tended to concentrate their efforts in their own local areas of support. The length of the ballot paper, listing all twenty-four candidates, also caused confusion among some voters (the party affiliation of candidates was not listed on the ballot papers until 1965).[53] Reports from the polling booths stated that the name Hoban (Town Tenants' Association) was occasionally mistaken for Hogan (Cumann na nGaedheal) and the independent candidate James Cosgrave (formerly of the IPP) for the president, W. T. Cosgrave.[54] The electorate, more familiar with a two-horse race, was unaccustomed to having such an array of candidates representing both national and sectional interests. In 1923 the people were electing candidates to form a new government in their own Irish Parliament as distinct from deciding 'which particular hundred mendicants would be sent to Westminster'.[55] Dáil Éireann was now an official body recognised by law, and the flood of new candidates who stood for election in 1923 clearly saw it as a more appealing and advantageous career choice than it had appeared to be in 1918. Yet, on the morning of the poll, Galway was described as being 'more like a graveyard' than the scene of a general election.[56]

The August contest was the first to be fought on a universal adult suffrage. Modifications made to the electoral law extended franchise rights to women between the ages of twenty-one and thirty. A woman voter, the *Connacht Tribune* noted, 'need no longer be married, need no longer give information that she has reached the sensible age of thirty … She need only be twenty-one, and she can, provided she gets her name on the register, vote for the man of her choice.'[57] Local press reports commented on the number of young women who took the opportunity to cast their votes, but it remained the case that 'she' could only vote for the 'man' of her choice. While some women did sit on Galway's local political bodies, the county had not escaped the male-dominated system. No female candidate stood for election in any of the general election contests held in Galway between 1922 and 1932.

In 1923, the local electorate, as noted, recorded a split vote. Two Cumann na nGaedheal candidates, Patrick Hogan and Padraig Ó Máille, and two Sinn Féin candidates, Herbert 'Barney' Mellows (younger brother of Liam) and Frank Fahy, were elected on the first count (Figures 2.1 and 2.2). A certain degree of localism was evident in the voting trend. In Connemara, for instance, ballot papers were returned recording only three votes, one for each of the three local candidates – Padraig Ó Máille (CNG), Colm Ó Gaora (SF) and Patrick Conroy (FP).[58] Broadly speaking, transfer loyalty was notably strong among the two main parties. For example, Patrick Hogan (CNG) was the first candidate to be elected and 64 per cent of his surplus went to the seven remaining Cumann na nGaedheal candidates. George Nicholls received the largest share of the surplus, gaining 35 per cent or 956 of the 2,725 available transfers. However, Cumann na nGaedheal also lost a number of lower transfers to other pro-treaty groups – the Farmers' Party, Independents and Labour (Figure 2.3). The Sinn Féin candidates, in contrast, were not exposed to such a division. Barney Mellows (SF), who was in prison in Mountjoy, was the second candidate to be declared elected and 86 per cent of his surplus went to the two remaining Sinn Féin candidates. Louis O'Dea received 62 per cent, securing 1,425 out of the 2,293 available transfers, and Colm Ó Gaora received 24 per cent, gaining 556 transfers. Labour's T. J. O'Connell, who obtained the third-largest share, received just 3 per cent, gaining 69 transfers (Figure 2.4).[59]

The large number of candidates, representing different interest groups, resulted in a protracted count. The tallying of votes which began on 29 August, two days after polling day, did not lead to a final result being declared until the evening of 31 August. After the first four candidates were elected on the first count, it took another fourteen counts before the fifth candidate, George Nicholls, was declared elected and a further four counts before all nine seats were filled. Ten candidates, including Professor Thomas Dillon, President of the Galway branch of Cumann na nGaedheal, failed to obtain a third of the quota and lost their deposits. The election of James Cosgrave (Independent), although somewhat of a surprise, was as much in appreciation of the work he had done for the tenant farmers on the Lisduff, Ballyhannery, Killadulisk and Clanricarde estates as it was a testament to the loyalties of his old Irish Parliamentary Party supporters in east Galway.

In June 1922, Labour had benefited from the votes of those who refused to support the Collins–de Valera pact. In August 1923, it failed to capitalise on this protest vote, now divided across a plethora of interest groups. T. J. O'Connell retained his seat, but the party (despite fielding two candidates) failed to increase its vote in Galway. Its support dropped from 13.21 per cent of the total vote in 1922 to 5.97 per cent in 1923. Local political commentators also forecast that the Farmers'

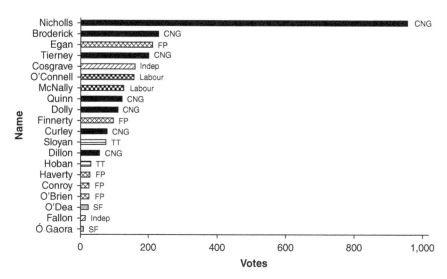

Figure 2.3 Distribution of Patrick Hogan's surplus, August 1923

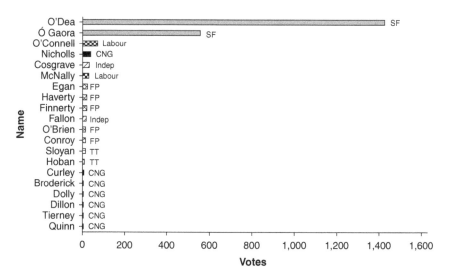

Figure 2.4 Distribution of Barney Mellows's surplus, August 1923

Party, which had ambitiously nominated five candidates, would gain at least three seats.[60] It failed to win a single one. The setback to Labour and the Farmers' Party rebuff indicated the extent to which political loyalties overshadowed both sectional interests and local personalities.

The government had invited the people to scrutinise the work they had done and to endorse it with their approval at the polls.[61] Nationally, all but two sitting ministers were triumphantly returned at the head of the poll and all twelve were re-elected. Yet Cumann na nGaedheal failed to increase its percentage of the national vote by a significant margin, only narrowly advancing from 38.48 per cent in June 1922 to 38.97 per cent in August 1923. Furthermore, in 1923 the number of Dáil seats expanded from 128 to 153. The party gained only five new seats, increasing from 58 seats in 1922 to 63 seats in 1923. The outcome was a blow to the government. Locally, Hogan again topped the poll, but Cumann na nGaedheal failed to secure either of the two new seats on offer in the county and as already mentioned it lost a number of votes to the array of smaller parties that stood for election. Its first preference vote in Galway fell from 54.51 per cent to 43.67 per cent. In Connacht, Cumann na nGaedheal recorded its highest percentage vote in the two Mayo constituencies, recording a figure of 53.90 per cent in Mayo South and 53.76 per cent in Mayo North (Appendix A.3).

In Galway, the practical patriotism espoused by Cosgrave's government was given a grudging if not an unbridled citizenry endorsement. One Cumann na nGaedheal supporter, in a letter titled 'The Galway election fiasco', berated the local result and the lack of support for the government party; a result which nearly secured for the county 'the unenviable reputation of being like a few other counties [–] fully Republican now that the Anglo-Irish war is over'.[62] Yet, while apathetic at the polls, the greater part of local society did favour the treaty, the constitution and the new state. Although it did not return Cumann na nGaedheal with an overwhelming majority, six of the nine candidates elected in Galway belonged to pro-treaty groups. After the election the *Connacht Tribune* wrote that 'so far as the results have been declared, anyone who seeks to read into them any weakening of the determination to reap the utmost benefit from the Treaty that has been won is hugging to himself a huge delusion'.[63] There was no delusion. The result demonstrated majority support for peace, democratic government and economic regeneration.

However, it must also be pointed out that the strong performance of Sinn Féin was regarded as a considerable achievement by the republicans. While they did not win the election, republicanism, as a political force, had not been wiped out. On a national level, the party received its highest percentage vote (47.38 per cent) in County Clare. The Mayo North constituency recorded the highest percentage vote (39.80 per cent) for the party in Connacht (Appendix A.4). In Galway, Sinn Féin increased its vote from 32.28 per cent in 1922 to 33.54 per cent in 1923. While the increase is marginal, the result was significant. Of the three parties that contested the June pact election in the county, Sinn Féin was the only one to improve its percentage vote in Galway in August 1923. Despite its abstentionist policy and its refusal to acknowledge the legitimacy of the Dáil, Sinn Féin won three of the four seats it contested. Its reservoir of political support remained intact. The electorate's instinct to lend such strong support to the republican candidates was unsurprising in a county long accustomed to voting for a party that would not gain power. The republicans also benefited from the low turnout and indifference of the government supporters. Sinn Féin gained one new seat in Galway and only narrowly lost a fourth seat by 155 votes on the final count to the independent candidate, James Cosgrave. The election of Barney Mellows was, in part at least, a direct emotional response to the execution of his older brother. More importantly, the result indicated a consolidation of electoral support for non-violent political republicanism in Galway. This in turn denied Cumann na nGaedheal a decisive victory.

Nationally, Sinn Féin increased its vote from 21.26 per cent in June 1922 to 27.40 per cent in August 1923. Considerable opposition to the state persisted. The republicans were jubilant. Reminiscing many years later, Peadar O'Donnell remarked:

> We had done miserably in the 1922 election and no wonder. A year later we bettered our position by eight seats … It was really fantastic that, after a military defeat and with our best people in jail, the country responded so strongly. We went half wild with delight.[64]

Cumann na nGaedheal, on the other hand, was determined to demonstrate that the new state was legitimate. Ultimately, the treaty had been accepted in two successive elections by the electorate. As the practical reality of the Free State's independence strengthened, the point at issue was whether local republican support would expand or subside? Would the people, as O'Halpin has questioned, continue to vote for a party that had vouched to boycott the existing political system, when that system displayed every sign of operating effectively?[65] Would de Valera and his slightly constitutional colleagues be content to remain on the margins of Irish politics?

Speaking to a representative of the *Irish Independent*, W. T. Cosgrave admitted that the policy Cumann na nGaedheal put forward at the August election was a cautious one. It may be a complaint 'that we adopted a too conservative policy', he conceded, 'but the people have declared themselves to be very well satisfied that we had not undertaken or promised anything which we have not been able to carry out'.[66] With such a conformist mentality, would Cumann na nGaedheal confront the critical problems in local Galway society – land, distress and the depopulation of the Gaeltacht areas?

Notes

1 *Connacht Tribune*, 8 July 1922.
2 *Ibid.*
3 Hopkinson, *Green against Green*, pp. 63, 150.
4 *Connacht Tribune*, 13 Jan. 1923; *Irish Times*, 9 Jan. 1923.
5 Daniel J. Murphy (ed.), *Lady Gregory's Journals*, vol. 1, Books 1–29 (Gerrards Cross, 1978), p. 355.
6 *Irish Independent*, 22 Aug. 1922.
7 *Connacht Tribune*, 29 July 1922. The bridge was repaired in October 1922, but other bridges around Tuam were also destroyed.
8 Minutes of Galway Urban District Council, 6 July 1922, Galway City Council Archives, Galway UDC minute books, GA3/8/116.
9 J. B. Hill to Dept. Home Affairs, 1 Aug. 1922, NAI, DJ, H65/65.
10 Cited in *Connacht Tribune*, 29 July 1922. The letter was sent from Roundstone by boat.
11 *Irish Independent*, 5 Apr. 1922.
12 Thomas Gilmartin to Thomas O'Doherty, 5 Apr. 1922; Michael Fogarty to Thomas O'Doherty, 6 Apr. 1922, Galway Diocesan Archives (hereafter GDA), O'Doherty papers, Box 45/38–9.
13 Statement issued by the Cardinal Primate and the Archbishops and Bishops of Ireland, 26 Apr. 1922, GDA, O'Dea papers, Box 39/197; *Irish Catholic Directory* (Dublin, 1923), pp. 598–602.
14 For the full text of the October pastoral, see Patrick Murray, *Oracles of God: The Roman Catholic Church and Irish Politics 1922–37* (Dublin, 2000), pp. 425–30.
15 Murray, *Oracles of God*, p. 13.
16 James O'Dea to Michael Browne, 15 Dec. 1922. Cited *ibid.*, p. 233.
17 Pamphlet issued by the Chicago Padraig Pearse Council, America Association for the Recognition of the Irish Republic, 9 Dec. 1922, GDA, O'Dea papers, Box 40/228.
18 James O'Dea to Michael Browne, 15 Dec. 1922. Cited in Murray, *Oracles of God*, p. 141. The four men were captured in July during the attack on the Four Courts.
19 Pastorals, Lent 1922, GDA, O'Dea papers, Box 31/1; *Connacht Tribune*, 12 Aug. 1922. For brevity's sake, the diocese of Galway, Kilmacduagh and Kilfenora is at times referred to in the text simply as the 'diocese of Galway' or the 'Galway diocese'.
20 Letter from John Hagan, 22 Aug. 1922, GDA, O'Dea papers, Box 39/204.
21 Hagan to Gilmartin, 26 May 1923, Tuam Archdiocesan Archives (hereafter TAA), Gilmartin papers, Box 96, B4/05-vii/1.
22 For further details on the military aspect of the civil war in County Galway see Hopkinson, *Green against Green*; Cormac K. H. O'Malley and Cormac Ó Comhraí (eds), *The Men Will Talk to Me: Galway Interviews by Ernie O'Malley* (Cork, 2013); Cormac Ó Comhraí, *Revolution in Connacht: A Photographic History 1913–23* (Cork, 2013); Nollaig Ó Gadhra, *Civil War*

in Connacht 1922–1923 (Dublin, 1999). For details of the republican attack on Costello Coast Guard station, Connemara, and Mountbellew barracks, north Galway, and other assaults on isolated Free State positions in July 1922, see *Connacht Tribune*, 8 July 1922. For the republican attack on Clifden, see *Connacht Tribune*, 4 Nov. 1922. For details of an attack on Free State forces in Gort in July 1922 and the subsequent funeral ambush at Coshla, see *Connacht Tribune*, 22 July 1922. For details of the Headford ambush, see *Connacht Tribune*, 14 Apr. 1923.

23 *Tuam Herald*, 28 Apr. 1923. For details of Gilmartin's New Year's message of peace, see *ibid.*, 6 Jan. 1923.

24 Gilmartin to Hagan, 23 Apr. 1923. Cited in Dominic Price, *The Flame and the Candle: War in Mayo 1919–1924* (Cork, 2012), pp. 252–3.

25 *Connacht Tribune*, 5 May 1923.

26 *Ibid.*

27 *Tuam Herald*, 21 Apr. 1923.

28 See, for instance, Erhard Rumpf and A. C. Hepburn, *Nationalism and Socialism in Twentieth Century Ireland* (Liverpool, 1977), pp. 61–2; Peter Pyne, 'The third Sinn Féin party: 1923–1926', *Economic and Social Review*, vol. 1, no. 2 (1969–70), pp. 229–42. For a further discussion on the effect these imprisonments had, particularly on the families of those belonging to the small farming classes, see Gilbert Morrissey's witness statement to the Bureau of Military History. NAI, BMH, WS 1138, Gilbert Morrissey, O/C Athenry Battalion Irish Volunteers, recorded on 25 June 1953.

29 Hopkinson, *Green against Green*, p. 219.

30 *Ibid.*

31 Report on condition of the Western Command, 14 Mar. 1923, University College Dublin, Archives Department (hereafter UCDA), Twomey papers, P69/30 (222–3).

32 General report on the 2nd Western Division, 30 Sept. 1924, *ibid.*, P69/104 (7).

33 Report on the Council Meeting, 2nd Western Division, 21 Dec. 1923, *ibid.*, P69/104 (108).

34 Hopkinson, *Green against Green*, p. 212.

35 Eunan O'Halpin, *Defending Ireland: The Irish State and its Enemies since 1922* (Oxford, 1999), p. 39.

36 Eunan O'Halpin, 'Politics and the state, 1922–32', in J. R. Hill (ed.), *A New History of Ireland, vol. VII. Ireland 1921–84* (Oxford, 2003), pp. 91–2.

37 Fahy to de Valera, 12 June, 8 Apr. 1923, UCDA, de Valera papers, Communications between Ministers, P150/1710.

38 *Connacht Tribune,* 12 May 1923.

39 Report of meeting of Republican TDs, 19 Sept. 1923, UCDA, de Valera papers, P150/1944.

40 Fahy to de Valera, 12 June, 2 July 1923, *ibid.*, P150/1710.

41 W. T. Cosgrave, 'To the people of Ireland', 1923, NLI, Pamphlet collection, LO P117/55.

42 Republican pamphlet, *ibid.*, ILB 300 P3/83.

43 *Ibid.*, LO P117/11.
44 Cited in *Tuam Herald*, 8 Sept. 1923.
45 *Connacht Tribune*, 21 July 1923.
46 *Ibid.*
47 *Ibid.*, 11 Aug. 1923.
48 Gallagher (ed.), *Irish Elections 1922–44*, pp. 34, 45.
49 Richard Sinnott, *Irish Voters Decide: Voting Behaviour in Elections and Referendums since 1918* (Manchester, 1995), pp. 82–7.
50 *Connacht Tribune*, 1 Sept. 1923.
51 Basil Chubb, *The Government and Politics of Ireland* (London, 1970), p. 334. Cited in Sinnott, *Irish Voters Decide*, p. 85.
52 See *Tuam Herald*, 8 Sept. 1923.
53 Richard Sinnott, 'The electoral system', in John Coakley and Michael Gallagher (eds), *Politics in the Republic of Ireland* (3rd edn, London, 1999), p. 100.
54 *Irish Independent*, 28 Aug. 1923; *Connacht Tribune*, 1 Sept. 1923.
55 Tom Garvin, 'Democratic politics in independent Ireland', in Coakley and Gallagher (eds), *Politics in the Republic of Ireland*, p. 353.
56 *Connacht Tribune*, 1 Sept. 1923.
57 *Ibid.*, 21 Apr. 1923.
58 *Irish Independent*, 30 Aug. 1923.
59 *Connacht Tribune*, 1 Sept. 1923; Gallagher (ed.), *Irish Elections 1922–44*, p. 34.
60 *Connacht Tribune*, 23 June 1923. The Irish Farmers' Union was a highly organised body. It had successfully established new branches throughout County Galway and as such it should have been in touch with local rural opinion. Yet while it claimed to represent the ordinary man, the small farmers did not look upon the Union or its political offshoot, the Farmers' Party, as the guardians of their interests. Although the party fought an active campaign, it hopelessly miscalculated its chances. In the 1940s, the success of Clann na Talmhan proved that it was viable to stand on behalf of a particular interest group in Galway, but in Clann na Talmhan the small farmers saw a party that was representing their best interests. In the 1920s the Farmers' Party was more closely identified with the large farmers and on the two occasions when the party contested the general elections in Galway (August 1923 and June 1927) it failed to win a seat.
61 Cosgrave, 'To the people of Ireland', 1923.
62 *Connacht Tribune*, 8 Sept. 1923.
63 *Ibid.*, 1 Sept. 1923.
64 Cited in Uinseann Mac Eoin (ed.), *Survivors* (Dublin, 1980), p. 30.
65 O'Halpin, 'Politics and the state, 1922–32', pp. 91–2, 96.
66 *Irish Independent*, 31 Aug. 1923.

Part II
Society

3

Land and reform

Land and the Irish revolution

Would the people migrate to richer lands? 'They might and they might not', one visitor to Connemara wrote in February 1924, 'the truth being that it would require an infantry brigade to move them from the barren rocks.'[1] Why in places of such poverty was there such a reluctance to leave the land? Why was land, and more specifically the possession and ownership of land, so prized and venerated in the west? Here the number of written assumptions that Ireland's land question was resolved before the Irish revolutionary period of 1916–21 deserves careful consideration. The key judgement is that not only was the Irish War of Independence the social revolution that never was, but there was never any potential that it might have been so. According to two commentators, 'there is little evidence of a social component within the Irish revolution and less again in its settlement'[2] and 'any chance of real social revolution had been substantially undermined by land reform and the creation of an increasingly conservative peasant proprietorship in Ireland'.[3] That may well be true in some cases. Between 1870 and 1916 the number of occupiers of Irish agricultural holdings who became owners of their land rose from 3 per cent to 64 per cent.[4] However, in the west of Ireland, the series of Land Acts from 1881 to 1909 brought little fundamental change in the pattern of land *structure*. Tenant purchase had been very effective in raising the living standards in some parts of the country, but the Land Acts had not solved the problems of the small holders and landless men whose grievance, as Ó Tuathaigh has argued, had not been their status as tenants 'but rather the size of their holding or its poor quality, or both … land redistribution lay outside the scope of the Land Purchase Acts'.[5]

In the 1920s the landscape of County Galway still contained large landlord properties and untenanted grazing lands, and alongside these a mass of smallholdings survived. Vast tracts of land that could support men and animals continued to support only livestock. According to the

1926 census, 19 per cent of male farmers in County Galway lived on farms of under 10 acres in size; 33 per cent held less than 15 acres; 66 per cent had less than 30 acres; and 87.4 per cent occupied less than 50 acres. In addition, of the 33 per cent living on 1 to 15 acre farms the highest numbers were located in the Oughterard and Clifden rural districts of west Galway. Only 12.6 per cent of male farmers in County Galway lived on farms averaging more than 50 acres in size. This compares with a figure of 43 per cent of farmers in County Tipperary (Figures 3.1–3.3).[6] In the west of Ireland, where congestion greatly intensified the strain on the land, farm size, land valuation and economic viability were critical matters. For many the traditionally emotive slogan 'the Land for the People' was taken to mean 'a redistribution of land as well as a transfer of land ownership'.[7]

In January 1917 the Royal Irish Constabulary (RIC) county inspector for west Galway wrote, 'when a man gets his land he settles down and there is no one more conservative than an Irish small farmer'.[8] The key word worth emphasising here is 'when' a man gets his land. And, as Rumpf suggested, 'to make the tenant farmer the owner of his land did little or nothing to moderate the craving for land on the part of men without land, or with an insufficient amount of it; on the contrary, it tended to stimulate demand'.[9] In such an agriculturally dominated society, the possession of land, particularly for the small holders and landless men, was synonymous with liberation and social status. As one of George Bernard Shaw's characters remarked after Matthew Haffigan bought his farm in the Land purchase: 'Oh ... sure ... Hes [sic] independent now.'[10] That farm ownership provided social standing in rural communities helps rationalise the emotive, obsessive attachment to these small fields often won from bog and rocky soil with back-breaking toil and great endeavour. In the early 1900s, a Congested Districts Board inspector analysed the amount of labour involved in fertilising one acre of land in west Galway:

> some stable manure mixed with heather, sedges, and weeds was used, and in addition seaweed was brought from the shore, where it had previously been collected and dried. For 1 acre, 36 horse or donkey loads, or 200 'women's basket loads' were needed; the donkey with its baskets, would make the journey six times a day and six days of good weather, rarely consecutive, would be needed. Under such circumstances it is not remarkable that the arable acreage on a farm rarely exceeds 2–3 acres divided between oats and potatoes: equally significant is the concentration on the seaboard.[11]

Nonetheless, land ownership without the benefit of land redistribution did little to affect the economic standing of the rural farmer. It did little to reverse atavistic tendencies. Despite the claim by Patrick Hogan,

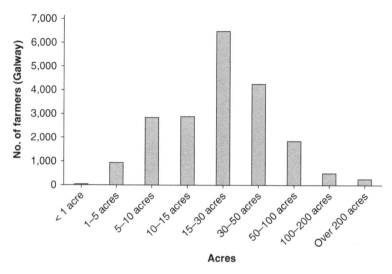

Figure 3.1 Number of male farmers in County Galway classified by size of farm, 1926

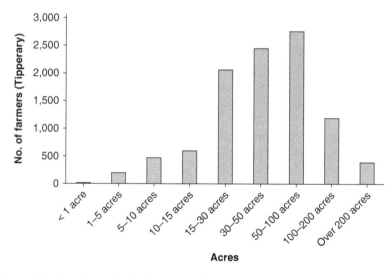

Figure 3.2 Number of male farmers in County Tipperary classified by size of farm, 1926

Minister for Agriculture, in the Dáil in July 1923 that land ownership made a 'tremendous difference' to farming practices, innovation on such small uneconomic holdings was almost impossible.[12] As Eugen Weber observed in his study of late nineteenth- and early twentieth-century

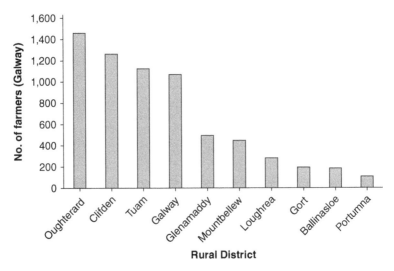

Figure 3.3 Number of male farmers on 1–15 acre size farms in each Rural District, 1926

French peasants, 'routine connoted not mindless labour but precious experience, what had worked and hence would work again, the accumulated wisdom without which life could not be maintained'.[13] On the small west of Ireland holdings, the risk of failure was too great. Persisting with traditional techniques, these farmers were, as Padraig Ó Máille TD recognised, 'the last by whom the new was tried and the last to lay the old aside'.[14]

The periodic recurrence of land agitation, in 1898–1902, 1907–8, 1917–18, 1920 and later, indicated that significant elements in Irish rural society felt that the agenda of agrarian reform had by no means been resolved.[15] In 1917 and the spring of 1918 the Sinn Féin party, at a local level, supported the agitation for the acquisition and redistribution of grazing land.[16] The RIC county inspectors' reports contain several accounts of local Sinn Féin clubs organising forcible land seizures, branding impropriated cattle with the letters 'SF' or 'IR' and flying tricolours above occupied farms. In a county in which one fifth of farmers occupied holdings that were too small to provide a reasonable standard of living, the association of Sinn Féin with the land campaign was a profitable one in terms of mobilising political support for the separatist cause in preparation for the anticipated general election to be held at the conclusion of the First World War.[17] According to Campbell's figures, 69 per cent of farmers and farmers' sons who were members of local Sinn Féin clubs between 1916 and 1918 lived on small holdings

valued at less than £20 and 38 per cent lived on farms which were classified by the Congested Districts Board as being too small to provide an
acceptable standard of living for the occupier.[18] In February 1918 the
county inspector for east Galway reported that 'Sinn Féin is now being
worked in this Riding as an agrarian movement for the forcible possession of lands ... This new phase ... will bring many young men into the
movement which had no attraction for them here-to-fore.'[19]

However, in the summer of 1920, as more violent agitation intensified, the Sinn Féin leadership, at a national level, refused to sanction
land seizures in the name of the Republic. In the west, the appetite for
land was sharpened by the trebling of Irish agricultural prices between
1913 and 1920 in response to the dislocation of world trade during
the First World War.[20] At the same time, the British government wartime restrictions on emigration, the curtailing of the powers of the
Congested Districts Board to purchase and redistribute land, and
the letting of untenanted land, acquired by the Board, to graziers on
the eleven-month system greatly increased the demand for more land.
In Galway, the deliberate targeting of the RIC by the IRA, the demoralisation of the police force and their withdrawal from outlying barracks
was seized upon chiefly by small farmers, tenants and the landless to
initiate a campaign of agrarian violence in order to force the redistribution of grazing land. With the retreat of the RIC and the removal
of the protection previously afforded to the landed gentry, lawlessness
flourished in the rural countryside. Cattle drives, land grabbing, extensive destruction of property and vicious attacks on landlords and land-
owners became more widespread. For instance, in March 1920, Frank
Shawe-Taylor was murdered as he motored to the Galway fair from his
house at Moorpark, Coshla, Athenry. A considerable landed proprietor,
his response to an earlier deputation of locals who wanted him to sell his
estate was 'You'll never see a perch of my land.'[21] In his Lenten pastoral,
1920, Bishop Thomas O'Dea of Galway condemned what he described
as this 'wicked desire for land', warning local agitators, 'what use is land,
if it brings God's curse on them and their acres, as it surely does, if they
get possession of it by foul means?'[22] In June 1920, J. D. Blake, who had
also refused to give up his grazing lands to some of his tenants, was shot
and wounded as he walked to Mass in Kilconly. In July 1920, a north
Galway grazier was shot dead and three herdsmen employed by other
graziers were also killed. In another incident, a Franciscan brother of
the Agricultural College, Kilkerrin, Ballinasloe, whose lands had been
cleared of stock and seized, was severely beaten on the roadside as he
attempted to round up the scattered cattle. Furthermore, as judicial commissioner Kevin O'Shiel recalled, anonymous letters signed 'IRA' and 'SF'

were often distributed at will, commanding the recipient to surrender all or part of his land to a local land committee or to clear out on pain of getting 'Shawe-Taylor's medicine'.[23] In March 1920, the RIC Inspector General reported that agrarianism in east Galway had been 'fostered by Sinn Féin to popularize the party in the Riding, but its strength is due to the land hunger always so prevalent in County Galway'.[24] At a time when pressure on the land greatly increased, the desire, need and, in some cases, greed for land intensified.

Why, at the height of the War of Independence, did Sinn Féin not manipulate the land campaign to mobilise support for the national struggle? The destabilising effect of this western challenge to British rule could have advanced the IRA's military campaign, but for the Sinn Féin leadership social anarchy in the countryside and the threat of a class war pitting desperate small holders and landless men against the more substantial farmers was an alarming prospect. The battle lines of the agrarian conflict were not simply landlords versus tenants, but also small farmers versus graziers, small farmers versus large farmers and labourers versus farmers.[25] Understandably, its leaders feared a new land war that 'would deflect energies from military and political campaigns, and which might even result in large-scale desertion from the cause by followers more concerned with land than with politics'.[26] The party's refusal to endorse the land campaign was also a direct appeal to the moderate, wealthier elements of Irish society including larger farmers, graziers and businessmen whose support, and particularly whose financial support, Sinn Féin relied upon if it was to be successful in running and maintaining the government of the underground republic. Equally, in order to gain international recognition for Dáil Éireann, the cabinet had to demonstrate its ability to provide responsible and respectable government that represented all elements in Irish society. To their opponents and proponents alike, the widespread land seizures in the west could be viewed not only as a defiance of British law and order but also as a potential threat to the authority of the Dáil. For the Sinn Féin leadership, encouraging agrarian social radicalism was simply not good politics.

Yet in the past the land question had repeatedly been used as a metaphor for freedom. Land and rebellion, independence and social betterment, were powerful motivating factors, factors that Liam Mellows successfully employed in east Galway in Easter 1916. The nation, as Fitzpatrick has written, was 'a vessel into which each man could pour his own dream'.[27] And for the small holders and landless men of the west, their vision of freedom had a very practical economic dimension.[28] Some senior IRA officers drew on this conviction. Michael Brennan, O/C East Clare Brigade, IRA, later recounted that he had not the slightest interest in the land agitation, but had every interest in using it as a means to get these men into the Volunteers.[29] There is little doubt that IRA engagements in the west were in many cases 'thinly disguised land seizures'.[30] This is not surprising, given that the majority of the rank and file of the local IRA came from a farming background. However, other IRA leaders were more suspicious of attempts to mix social aims with the pure cause of the national struggle, perhaps recognising that for some local agitators 'the Sinn Féin tricolour was no more than a flag of convenience' and any movement would have served the same purpose.[31] The cautious agrarian policy of Sinn Féin and the Dáil did not necessarily dissuade local farmers from joining the Volunteers. However, the geography of the War of Independence and the low level of IRA engagements in County Galway, before the reorganisation of the local force in the spring of 1921, indicate that the areas where the most violent agrarian agitation occurred were not the centre points of the national struggle.[32] The party's unwillingness to combine the land movement with the national campaign limited its military appeal in the west. Yet its support for a non-violent redistributionist land reform policy, through the establishment of national arbitration courts and a special land commission to adjudicate claims, directly appealed to the more moderate elements of local society. Although the Dáil courts, as O'Shiel recollected, 'hardly touched the fringe of the great agrarian problem',[33] they did provide Sinn Féin with an opportunity 'to assert the legitimacy of its own embryo state institutions'[34] and thereby tempered the appeal of violent forceful agrarianism.

It is true that the Irish revolution did not seriously attempt a change in the social balance of power.[35] Indeed, one struggles to hear the voice of Connolly or see the educational vision of Pearse and his desire for a Gaelic Ireland in the rhetoric and campaigns of a socially conservative movement that regarded agrarian militancy as something to be curbed and contained rather than channelled and harnessed. The Irish revolution was a struggle for national independence. However, that does not imply that the potential for social upheaval or what O'Shiel identified as a budding 'revolution within a revolution',[36] particularly in the west of Ireland, did not exist.

Land agitation and the civil war

The civil war fanned a recrudescence in acute agrarian agitation in the west. Once more the absence of civil authority in many parts of the county provided the conditions for tenants, particularly in east Galway, to seize and clear the grazing ranches. James Glynn, for instance, who rented land on the eleven-month system on the Ashtown estate, Woodlawn, outlined in a series of letters to the provisional government the type of intimidation and sabotage that was being carried out on the estate. The walls were knocked down, several iron gates were removed, the plough was broken and his stock was driven off the land. On 4 May he wrote, 'the damage is still going on. My meadow [was] trespassed on. I am looking for five cattle since Tuesday morning and if I get them I expect they will be greatly reduced after being driven all over the country. My sheep have been driven and left unmarketable being daubed with colour.'[37]

Agitation during the civil war varied from the usual unauthorised knocking down of walls and non-payment of rents, to cattle driving, forcible occupation of land, illegal ploughing, threats of violence and shootings. In May 1922 Hutchinson Davidson, solicitor and agent for the Arres-Maher estate, Ballinasloe, complained to the Department of Defence that cattle had been driven off the farm and seven or eight shots were fired at the house. 'This sort of thing', Davidson wrote, 'is so common now, it is looked on as a trifling matter.'[38] On the Hearnesbrook estate, Killimore, several trees were cut down; the windows and doors of the Gate Lodge were broken; grates and chimney pieces were removed; graves were dug on portions of the estate; and the lands were overrun by cattle belonging to small farmers in the neighbouring districts.[39] In June 1923, the solicitor of George MacPhail (owner of Hearnesbrook) wrote to the Minister for Agriculture complaining that 'trespass on the lands was greater than before and still continues'. Every field, he explained, 'is overrun … the matter is really urgent'.[40] On the Dunsandle estate, located between Athenry and Loughrea, William Callan, steward of the estate, who had already been the victim of gross intimidation, was fired at and wounded in the head on 21 November 1922.[41] In January 1923 Walter Joyce, landlord of Corgary estate, Mountbellew, was killed while on his way to Mass.[42] In addition, a number of threatening letters were sent to Pat Gormally, herdsman of Corgary, stock was driven off his land and unauthorised tillage took place. On 17 March Gormally wrote: 'I … found two sheep dead like as if they would be killed and torn by dogs. I am [sic] nineteen sheep missing and nine lambs whether they are stole[n] or not yet I cannot say.'[43] In April, John Creavan, a tenant on the Corgary estate, was shot dead and six other tenants were severely beaten, and in September, in a separate incident, the house of Patrick Cahill, herdsman, Caltra, was burned down.[44]

In December 1922, Hogan warned Richard Mulcahy, Minister for Defence, that 'the land war is coming'.[45] This was undoubtedly a grave exaggeration. Yet civil war created the lawless conditions for agrarian radicals to act freely.[46] In the Dáil, the Minister for Home Affairs, Kevin O'Higgins, accused local agitators, many of whom had played no part in the national struggle, of seizing land 'under [the] cover of an Irregular campaign',[47] or as Seán Moylan, a senior IRA officer (and later Fianna Fáil Minister for Agriculture), put it, 'to cash in on the work of the IRA'.[48]

Reiterating his previous declarations on land seizures, Thomas O'Dea, Bishop of Galway, warned

> that three conditions are required for the lawful taking and division of other people's land: first, that the public good really require the division; second, that the land be taken and divided by public authority, and not by private individuals, who may be interested, or untrained to such work, and who, besides, have no mandate to act; third, that due compensation be paid to the owner. To allow those wanting land to take it on their own authority, is Lynch Law, or mob law, and therefore no better than anarchy.[49]

In January 1923, Hogan wrote disparagingly that the people behind this unrest were from

> the worst elements in the country districts with a pretty liberal sprinkling of wasters from the towns. They are practically all landless. The great majority have no genuine claim to land and would not make a success of farming.[50]

However, the land seizures were often more than simply the *vive moi* actions of rural malcontents. During the civil war, some prominent republicans such as Liam Mellows, Peadar O'Donnell and P. J. Ruttledge favoured utilising the agrarian agitation to generate anti-government support. On 1 May 1922, the Army Council of the IRA ordered local commandants to seize and hold certain lands in the name of the Irish people.[51] On 9 May 1922, Colonel Maurice Moore wrote to Mulcahy stating that

> The anti-treaty politicians and IRA, finding themselves in a hopeless minority, have adopted a policy very dangerous to the country and to the present ministry ... they are now making a bid for support through an agrarian movement.[52]

In December 1922, Hogan admitted that such a bid 'would have the advantage of being much more popular, in fact quite in the best traditions. The "land for the people" is almost as respectable an objective as the "republic" and would make a much wider appeal.'[53] Allying the land seizures of the civil war to anti-government resistance could have undermined the fledgling state and, in particular, undermined the confidence of the people in the capacity of the provisional government to preserve law and order in rural Ireland. Although republicans supported the agrarian campaign, no coherent, organised strategy emerged. Many of the leading anti-treaty political figures, including the redundant de Valera, distanced themselves from the social radicalism propounded by Mellows, O'Donnell *et al.* The war, Hogan argued, became 'a war by different sections, different interests, and different individuals, with no common bond except ... that all have a vested interest in chaos, and bringing about a state of affairs where force is substituted for law'.[54] This lack of collective organisation among the IRA leadership, coupled with the absence of a well-defined policy, inhibited the channelling of the revival of subversive land agitation into active support for republican armed resistance against the state. It reflected the general fracturing of the republican campaign, the lowering of morale, and definitive military defeat in April 1923. From the outbreak of hostilities, opposition to the state, particularly in east Galway, increasingly took the form of settling local disputes and personal scores rather than strict military engagements with the Free State army. Fuelled by the civil war, the agrarian agitation in the west in 1922–23, although cutting across the national struggle, once again remained largely independent of it.

Hogan and O'Higgins, as O'Halpin has argued, greatly exaggerated the extent and depth of social disorder in the countryside, as well as its links with republicanism.[55] Nonetheless, the renewed land agitation and violent attacks on landed property put the provisional government in a difficult position. Numerous letters, testimonies and deputations from large property owners and local graziers called on the government to prevent further trespass on their lands, seizures of their property and injury to their stock. Major Denis Daly, landlord of Dunsandle estate, wrote:

> a strong government would show that blackguardism is not going to be allowed to override law and order, and it would have a very good effect in the district round here if shown that the Government were willing and able to protect those who were simply carrying out the duties that earn them a living, and that they would not allow a few blackguards (and I am sure it is the work of a very few) to terrorise honest men.[56]

Additionally, as Dooley has suggested, if landlords resorted to the courts to have their rents paid and 'were granted the opportunity to press for arrears or alternatively evict their tenants, the new government was likely to be accused of being no different from British governments in the past' favouring 'the old landed class over the new order'.[57] Furthermore, persistent attacks on substantial farmers, the mainstay of the agricultural industry, posed a threat to the fiscal economy of the country. Strong government, the restoration of law and order in the disturbed rural areas, and the prompt introduction of land legislation were fundamental aspects for the survival of the new state. Harsh repression would be combined with land reform.[58]

Both Hogan and O'Higgins advocated the use of military detachments to subdue agrarian outbreaks. Consequently in February 1923 a Special Infantry Corps, made up of contingents of Free State soldiers who would be deployed to districts outside their local areas, was established. These new-styled small flying columns would occupy seized farms in disturbed areas, clear trespassed land, impound stock found illegally grazing on the land and enforce court orders. A fine would be imposed on the perpetrators for the release of their stock. Failing payment, the seized stock would be auctioned and the sum obtained in the sale awarded to the owner of the land. A summary list of unit operations for No. 1 Company Special Infantry Corps, stationed at Renmore barracks, for March–April 1923 is a typical catalogue of activities:

13 March: Served court writs, decrees in Athenry. Collected £50 11s 0d.
20 March: Searched for stolen timber at Kilconly. Ordered that it be handed back and warned against further theft. Issued warnings against trespass by stock on land near Tuam.
21 March: Supervised an eviction at Corrandulla.
23 March: Writs served at Moylough and Mountbellew. Collected £7 due to the Land Settlement Commission. Made arrests in connection with land trouble in Gort.
26 March: Executed a decree for eviction at Killimore.
28 March: Served writs in the Ballinasloe area and collected £150.
2 April: Served a writ at Oughterard and collected £16 5s 10d. Executed a decree at Roscahill and seized 1 cow and 2 calves.
14 April: Arrested two men who were involved in illegal tillage on an estate near Raheen.[59]

Reporting on conditions in Galway, Captain M. Higgins, O/C No. 1 Company, wrote 'It is perpetually raining down here, but there is a fine crowd of officers.'[60] In April, Hogan was able to inform the President that the forces operating in the county were particularly successful in clearing seized lands and re-establishing effective police control.

Galway was in the past the worst County in Ireland from the point of view of agrarian outrage. It is probably the best at the present moment as a result

of the operations of the Columns, and if every other County was in the
same state as Galway they would be almost ready for the Land Bill.[61]

The seizing of stock and the enforcement of tangible fiscal pun-
ishment on the guilty parties had a strong effect. In August 1923,
Superintendent Burke reported to Eoin O'Duffy, Garda Commissioner,
that compensation by the County Court was granted for the cattle
drives that had taken place on the Arres-Maher estate, Ballinasloe,
adding: 'It is believed that this will have a good effect as the offenders
are beginning to realise that they are only placing a financial burden
on themselves.'[62]

However, despite Hogan's assertions, the actions of the Special
Infantry Corps were also the cause of some local resentment and their
methods, particularly the auction of seized goods, were at times an
evocative reminder of the practices of the Land War. In March 1923, an
article in the *Western News* questioned: 'Is the Army a tool of indecent
and extortionate investors in landlordism, or is it the servant of the
people's honour?'[63] The dispute that arose in connection with a grass
farm owned by James Mongan in Mynish, Connemara, exemplified the
disparate attitudes of the local community towards the actions of the
army columns. In April 1922 tenants took possession of land belonging
to Mongan. In May, he obtained an injunction against the tenants to
restrain them from using the land. The tenants, however, ignored the
court order and continued to till the land and graze their stock into
the following year. Writing to Padraig Ó Máille TD on 20 April 1923,
Mongan explained:

> These parties took forcible possession of our holding in April 1922
> and have possession of it ever since ... We got an injunction against
> them ... but owing to misfortune [civil war] it has not been executed ...
> they don't seem to think any authority can put them out of it ... believe
> me if the holding was cleared nothing more popular could be done for the
> sake of law and order ... I am trying to keep my lads quiet as I could get
> it cleared by a crowd but this would mean murder and I don't want any
> such thing.[64]

On 1 July 1923 the land was cleared by the military, stock seized and
the tenants fined £54 for the release of their animals. In addition to
seizing the livestock, the military arrested five of the tenants including
Coleman Ridge and his son John Ridge. From Mongan's point of view,
the actions of the Special Infantry Corps were necessary and justified.
However, within the local community there was considerable sympathy
for the tenants. Canon McHugh, parish priest Carna, received a letter of
complaint concerning the manner in which the columns had carried out

their duties at Mynish. Ó Máille, after meeting with McHugh, wrote to O'Higgins on 13 July.

> It is stated ... in the letter which Canon McHugh received this morning, that 'James and Joseph Mongan and some of the Military went to Mynish late last night and kicked up a terrible racket about Ridge's house, smashed chairs and said they would shoot the Ridge boys' ... The Government should not allow all this bully work to go on ... the Mongans have put eight or ten cattle upon the farm in dispute with the view of destroying the potato crop which the poor Mynish people planted on a small portion of that land. This action of the Mongans should not be permitted ... The law should be as strong in checking illegalities performed by them as it is in dealing with the poor people of the place.[65]

In response to Ó Máille's letter, Henry O'Friel, secretary to the Department of Home Affairs, stated that the government did not seek to set up a system of terrorism, but insisted that 'the illegal interference with the rights and properties of others is so widespread that gentle methods could not succeed at the present time'.[66] The five Mynish tenants were brought to the Curragh internment camp and later transferred to Dundalk prison. Writing on 5 August (three weeks before the general election), McHugh warned Ó Máille that the continued detention of the men would not help the government candidates at the election.[67] The following week the Carna Branch of the Irish Farmers' Union passed a resolution stating that unless the men were liberated from jail they would refuse to vote for any parliamentary candidate who was a supporter of the government.[68] After much petitioning, the prisoners were released in February 1924.

On the whole, the introduction of the Special Infantry Corps was successful in restoring a semblance of civil authority to the disturbed areas. Ultimately, legislative reform and the completion of land purchase would, in the fullness of time, successfully subdue the underlying agrarian tension and unrest in the west.

Agricultural policy

By 1922, Irish agriculture was in the middle of a severe slump as wages and prices fell after wartime inflation.[69] As Kevin O'Higgins recognised in 1924, 'the Free State was unfortunate in being born when prices were at a peak and the main producers had been working since on a falling market. It was hard luck that a period of unprecedented depression had set in with the evacuation of the British.'[70] But in Patrick Hogan, Galway had a knowledgeable local Minister for Agriculture. Born in Cloonmain, Kilreekill, Loughrea, in May 1891, Hogan was of strong farmer stock. His father Michael Hogan was an extensive agriculturalist and stock raiser and for many years had served as chief inspector of the Estates Commission. His sister was married to the secretary of the Irish Agricultural Organisation Society and he was elected vice-president of the Irish Farmers' Union in 1921. At University College Dublin he was a distinguished scholar. He qualified as a solicitor in 1915 and built up an extensive practice in County Galway. During the War of Independence he was identified with the administration of the Republican Courts and the settlement of land disputes in the west. In 1920 he was arrested and interned in Ballykinlar, County Down, where he remained until the Truce. During his internment he occupied himself by reading material published by the Department of Agriculture and Technical Instruction. He was elected uncontested for Galway in May 1921 and appointed, at thirty years of age, Minister for Agriculture in the provisional government in February 1922, a post he held for ten years until Fianna Fáil came to power in March 1932. In the Dáil, his sharp wit, sarcasm, candid language and abhorrence of fatuity gained him the reputation of a skilful and merciless debater. A master of the incisive phrase, his parliamentary speeches and election addresses were models of clarity. The successful enactment of the 1923 Land Act during a period of political and social conflict was testament to his ability as a minister. He died in a car accident in Aughrim in July 1936. In the Dáil, de Valera paid tribute to his implacable rival – 'Many of us differed profoundly from Deputy Hogan on matters of public policy, but I am sure that there is no member of the Dáil who did not admire his courage and frankness in stating his views, his energy as an administrator and his rare effectiveness in debate.' Reacting to the news of his death, W. T. Cosgrave announced: 'Our best man is gone.'[71] Hogan was a nationalist and a realist. He was 'conservative but not cautious'.[72] Crucially, in matters agricultural, he was 'well-connected and well-informed'.[73]

Hogan was guided and influenced by his friend George O'Brien, Professor of Economics at University College Dublin, and later by James Meenan (O'Brien's pupil and successor in UCD).[74] The Minister's policy, as O'Brien explained, began from the assumption that agriculture would remain the most important industry in the Free State, and the touchstone by which other economic measures would be judged was its effect on the wealth of the farmers. The keynote of Hogan's policy for the recovery of the export market was better quality of produce, improved efficiency, stronger marketing and increased output of the goods for which Ireland had the greatest comparative advantage: that is, cattle, bacon and dairy produce.[75] The government, through the Agricultural Credit

Corporation and the Board of Works,[76] would be willing to offer credit to make this happen. In short, Hogan, much like his predecessor Horace Plunkett, 'wished to help the farmer to help himself'.[77] He believed that the farmers knew what was best for the farmers and he looked to maximise their profit by minimising their costs of production. If the individual did well then collectively everyone would do well, and therefore the country would do well. There were, of course, many flaws in such an approach. As Lee has argued, a prosperous farmer did not automatically equate to a healthy agricultural community.[78] Personal interest and personal circumstance would naturally guide the farmer's state of mind. A more coherent state-guided principle might have had a better impact (although Fianna Fáil's record demonstrates the effects of taking such a policy too far). Moreover, the interests of the large farmer did not reflect those of the small marginal farmer. And in Galway, as noted, two thirds of the male farmers in the county lived on farms of less than 30 acres. The ordinary farmer in the west was the 20-acre man, not the 200-acre man. For Irish agriculture to reach its productive potential, the status of the numerous uneconomic smallholders in the west would have to be improved.[79]

Although Hogan's performance as Minister for Agriculture won him particular respect in political circles abroad, his policy enjoyed limited success. The total value of Irish exports peaked in 1924 at £51.6 million, fell to £42 million in 1926, and recovered to £47 million in 1929.[80] Farming, by its nature, will always be exposed to outside factors such as weather (particularly poor in County Galway in 1923 and 1924), trends in agricultural prices and market conditions.[81] Even Hogan could not have forecast the economic crash in 1929, the great slump in world trade, and Britain's decision to abandon free trade in the early 1930s. Nonetheless, his programme of modernisation (including the Dairy Produce Act 1924; Agricultural Produce (Eggs) Act 1924; Livestock Breeding Act 1925; Agricultural Produce (Fresh Meats) Act 1930; and Agricultural Produce (Potato) Act 1931) made great advances in improving the breeds of sheep, cattle and other livestock and the quality, cleanliness and reliability of Irish dairy products. However, in a county dominated by small holdings, were the local farmers to be satisfied only with 'a few pedigree bulls and boars'?[82] At a national level, large-scale cattle farming and export industries proved to be a powerful lobbying group. Bank balances accumulated during the Great War reflected the satisfaction of the bigger farmers, and their support for law and order and the status quo.[83] The government's civil service advisors offered little encouragement towards changing social categories that, according to Lynch, 'now owed more to the conventional wisdom of Whitehall than to Pearse or Connolly'.[84] Hogan's export-led agricultural policy, a 'beer, biscuits, cars and cattle coalition', as Daly put it, emphasised cost cutting, education, and quality control but 'it offered little to those facing emigration or inadequate living standards'.[85] Addressing a crowd in Gort (south Galway) in 1928, Hogan declared that 'every phase of Government policy was designed to build up a self-reliant farming community'.[86] But where he wanted to see more stock-rearing, the small holders of the west wanted more tillage and more land division.

The promised land

The question of land redistribution was one of the most difficult and complex questions which Hogan and the state had to manage. Despite the fact that his policies were not directly serving the needs of the small farmers of the west, there seemed to be a sense of trust in the local minister. Hogan retained a strong personal vote in Galway and was successfully returned at the top of the poll at each general election in the county until 1932 (see Chapter 7). The small landholders bordering the larger grazier farms and untenanted estates clearly anticipated that the forthcoming Land Act would work to their advantage.[87]

Under the terms of the 1923 Land Act, the Cosgrave government took over all existing schemes of land purchase. The newly constituted Land Commission absorbed the functions of its predecessor (the Land Settlement Commission) as well as those of the Congested Districts Board and came under the administrative control of the Department of Agriculture in its early years and the newly created Department of Lands and Fisheries after 1927. All land to be transferred, whether tenanted or untenanted, was to be vested in the Commission, the scale of the policy of acquiring and dividing land to relieve congestion was expanded to include the formerly non-congested counties, and compulsory purchase powers (with certain exemption clauses) were introduced.[88] The act was devised with the dual purpose of putting all Irish farmers on an equal footing as land owners and of relieving the congestion caused by the overcrowding of small and uneconomic holdings.[89] In January 1923 Hogan, rather ambitiously, told the Dáil:

> It is our policy to complete land purchase; it is our policy to make every tenant in the Saorstát the owner of his holding. It is our policy to make every holding in the Saorstát economic. It is our policy to buy up the congested areas and to buy up the ranch lands outside the congested areas.[90]

However, Hogan also supported the safeguarding of large commercial farms and the substantial contribution they made to the financial revenue of the nascent state. There would be no radical redistribution of land. There would be no fundamental restructuring of the agrarian economy. Land settlements would be channelled through 'the safer conduits of the Land Commission'.[91] In May 1923 Hogan estimated that the completion of land purchase was going to cost the state £30 million.[92] The money was raised via a loan from the British government. In March 1925 he declared

> It is an enormous loan, when compared ... with the development of the Shannon, a gigantic scheme, but at the onset which is only going to cost about five million pounds. Thirty million pounds for land purchase is a very expensive matter.[93]

It was also a matter which would greatly restrict government spending in wider areas of social and economic reform.

Hogan's distribution policy, as Dooley has argued, stemmed from a belief 'that the maximum number of uneconomic holders, particularly in the designated congested areas of the west, had to be catered for at the expense of the minimum number of landless men'.[94] In the creation and expansion of economic small holdings, the relief of congestion would take priority over confronting the needs of the landless. In May 1923 Hogan wrote that 'the Irish countryman believes that nature intended him to be a farmer, and there is an idea that there is enough land for all'.[95] The utopian dream, the rural panacea of the land for the people, fuelled by years of nationalist propaganda, would not and could not be realised and was ultimately quashed. Promptly recognising the limitations of land purchase, Hogan candidly told the Dáil that 'unless you drain the sea' there simply was not enough land available to cater for all the landless men and the tenants living on congested land.[96] It was an impossible task.

Hogan favoured migrating the larger western landholder (if he could be persuaded to move) 'so as to create a pool of redistributable land for the relief of local congestion'.[97] The breaking up of the ranch land would then facilitate the creation of small economic holdings for 'deserving' applicants. Hogan's 'hierarchy of allottees', as Dooley has outlined, in order of priority, consisted of local congests, migrants, ex-employees, evicted tenants or their representatives and the landless (once they could satisfy the Land Commission of their ability to work the land).[98] Such a policy, however, pitted small holders, labourers and the landless against one another as prospective allottees vied for their share of the spoils. In February 1926 Kevin O'Higgins stressed that land distribution was

going to be a most difficult and thorny matter and a highly invidious
one for the Department that had the responsibility of selecting from the
enormous numbers of applicants the comparatively few who could be
dealt with.[99] And despite Hogan's system of allocation, several disputes
arose at a local level over who was deemed the most deserving of the first
claim when it came to the division of land. For instance, in July 1926 the
tenants, labourers and landless men on the Pollock estate (east Galway)
passed a resolution stating

> That in the proposed distribution of the Pollock and Laurencetown estates
> in this locality we insist on first consideration being given to the uneco-
> nomic holders, deserving landless men and labourers of the district before
> the needs of outsiders are considered. While recognising that people who
> surrender land in other places, in order to increase holdings there, are
> entitled to receive land elsewhere, we insist that such should be done only
> after local needs are met. Under our own native government we confi-
> dently looked, after weary years of waiting, for a peaceful and just settle-
> ment of the land question in this district. We are entirely dissatisfied with
> the arrangements that we learn are about to be made, and we earnestly
> warn the Government and all concerned that if they persist in forcing
> outsiders on us while our own have no prospects but the emigrant ship,
> the peace of the district will be seriously endangered. We are determined,
> if the injustice is persisted in, to resist it by every legitimate means in our
> power.[100]

Additionally, in many other cases, the area of untenanted land made
available to the Land Commission for distribution was too small or too
unevenly arranged to bring the size of uneconomic holdings up to the
standard required. Therefore, instead of dividing small parcels of land
among the tenants surviving on 5 acres or less, the land was distributed
to augment existing viable (although still small) farms of 10 or 20 acres.
In theory, this was a logical step which brought at least some holdings
up to an economic level and produced some tangible evidence of the
successful workings of the Land Commission. However, the allocation
of additional land to such persons ahead of the men with no property or
those occupying the smallest holdings, coupled with what was perceived
as the dilatory methods of the Commission in acquiring and distribut-
ing other, more suitable, larger properties, was the source of much local
criticism. The Ballinasloe Rural District Council declared that

> this Council views with extreme concern the hopelessness and bankrupt
> condition into which the interests of the small farming community of the
> Twenty Six Counties is drifting daily ... The high hopes built on the Land
> Bill which was introduced with such rosy promises are crumbling day by
> day and the poor farmers are fast recognising that these promises were only

paper promises and the Land Bill only a paper Bill, meant only to catch votes.[101]

The Land Commission did not publish annual statistics until the 1930s. In addition, as Dooley noted, the figures for the number of applications made to the Land Commission from people in individual counties requesting transfers to other holdings or seeking new holdings in their own localities are unavailable and possibly may never have been collected.[102] The precise data for the period 1923–32 therefore may require revision in the future, but according to Dooley and Varley's figures between 1923 and 1932 the newly constituted Land Commission spent £4,324,582 and acquired and divided 330,825 acres among 16,587 families in the Free State. In Connacht 133,499 acres of untenanted land was distributed.[103] By 1929, in County Galway a total area of 163,201 acres of untenanted land and 153,855 acres of tenanted land had been declared suitable for processing, but only 68,757 acres of untenanted land and 14,169 acres of tenanted land had been vested by the Land Commission.[104] Despite the Commission's criticism of what it termed the 'peculiarly stubborn character' of the western congests and their anxiety to stay within their own area, the slow, uneven tempo of land distribution was not producing sufficient numbers of socially desirable small holdings in the west.[105] For example, the Land Commission held the Daly estate in Furbo (west Galway) for twenty years without vesting ownership in the tenants.[106] At Mynish (Connemara), the unfortunate congests were still looking over the ditch and asking when the Land Commission was going to divide the land. In a letter to Kevin O'Higgins in January 1925, Seamus Mac an Iomaire, a local Mynish teacher, wrote:

> There is a farm on this island … about 70 acres. There are poor people around this farm living from hand to mouth, who have only from one to five acres of poor, rough, stony land, the soil on which is not more than a foot deep … This farm is used for the rearing and fattening of bullocks and sheep. Would it not be more appropriate that the need of the human beings should get first consideration?[107]

Hogan's enemies labelled him the 'Minister for Grass', a term particularly favoured by D. P. Moran in the *Leader*.[108] James Cosgrave, Independent TD for Galway, accused him of having 'congests on the brain' and the IRA newspaper *An Phoblacht* decried a government that 'preferred bullocks to people'.[109] Martin Corry TD, one of Fianna Fáil's most outspoken rural campaigners, denounced Hogan's policy as being a scheme for 'the land for the bullock and the men for the road'.[110] Such cries were clever electioneering ploys. By the same token, however, the timing of the passing of the Land Act on 9 August,

less than three weeks before the 1923 general election, had also been
sharp electioneering practice by the Cumann na nGaedheal government. Undoubtedly the 1923 Land Act did much to quell local agrarianism and temper support for the republican campaign during and
after the civil war. In January 1923 Hogan had asked the government
'to consider whether people who in future seize lands should not be
debarred in any future scheme of land purchase from getting land'.[111]
In May 1923 O'Higgins urged the Minister for Agriculture to ensure
that people who had pressed their claims by violence and illegalities
be placed outside the benefits of the Land Bill.[112] Furthermore, while
the restoration of law and order in the countryside and the settling of
the land issue was the mainspring behind the passing of the legislation,
the Act also provided an opportunity for the government to promote
the positive aspects of the Anglo-Irish Treaty and an Irish government
governing Irish affairs. To secure the passing of the bill so swiftly after
the civil war, procure British acceptance of its terms, acquire British
credit to fund land purchase and placate resident landlords and large
graziers was a notable political achievement. Moreover, the promise of
land redistribution could have strengthened the party's popular appeal.
However, in County Galway, Cumann na nGaedheal's first preference
vote fell from 54.51 per cent in June 1922 (as pro-treaty Sinn Féin) to
43.67 per cent in August 1923. The root of the problem, as a pragmatic
Hogan was at pains to point out, was the scarcity of land.

In south Connemara, experiments were undertaken to reclaim areas
of blanket bog land in an effort to provide new holdings. In the mid
1920s the Land Commission acquired an area of 23,000 acres in the
Cloosh Valley district for the construction of houses and the 'planting'
of local tenants from the Gaeltacht areas. A sum of £8,000 was allocated
for the construction of roads, reclamation works, drainage and fencing.
Initially six families were installed on the land and each family was supplied with farming implements, seeds and instruction on how to reclaim
additional acres.[113] Summarising the favourable features of the scheme,
the Land Commission reported:

> The migrants will be removed but a small distance from their native place;
> they will be given a class of land which they are used to labouring, and their
> average annuity for these better holdings will not be so very much in excess
> of what they have been accustomed to pay. Their holdings will be used in
> ameliorating the conditions in the neighbourhood from which the migrants
> have been taken ... In the opinion of the Commissioners this plan is the
> most practical way of relieving congestion by the process of migration in
> the maritime Gaeltacht areas.[114]

The scheme, however, was eventually abandoned when the Commission adjudged it to be too costly to warrant further colonies. Only six of the promised fifty holdings materialised.[115]

The recommendations of the Gaeltacht Commission, 1926, to implement a scheme of large-scale migration from the Gaeltacht to areas in east Galway, east Mayo and Roscommon or, if sufficient land was unavailable in the west of Ireland, to the inland counties of Leinster were also rejected by the government on the grounds of being too expensive for the limited amount of land available for distribution. Outlining Cumann na nGaedheal's party policy in 1927, W. T. Cosgrave declared that

> The extensive migration schemes proposed by the [Gaeltacht] Commission do not recommend themselves to us ... Migration, even where there is no opposition or hostility on the part of the migrants themselves or on the part of the owners of the land to which they are being migrated, is costly. Any scheme of wholesale migration to lands which could only be rendered available by a second migration of the present occupiers is, to our minds, unthinkable.[116]

Yet the government's efforts to relieve the chronic congestion of the Gaeltacht, in the Gaeltacht, proved unsuccessful. The recommendations of the Gaeltacht Commission for the migration of small holders beyond the western counties would eventually be adopted in the 1930s by the Fianna Fáil government.

According to William Nolan, this new scheme of assisted internal migration did not originate in Fianna Fáil circles but with Muintir na Gaeltachta, a group of Irish-language activists based in Connemara, who tried to pressure the government into implementing the migration policies recommended by the commission.[117] Gaeltacht migrants would not be installed on reclaimed local bog land but on more fertile holdings in counties Meath, Westmeath and Kildare. Between 1935 and 1940 sixty-three families moved from Galway to the townlands of Rathcairn, Kilbride and Allenstown in County Meath. This figure accounted for over half of the total number of 122 families – Galway (63), Mayo (18), Kerry (21), Donegal (18) and Cork (2) – who migrated to various Irish-speaking colonies in Meath during this period.[118] Patrick Sammon, in his memoirs of life in the Land Commission, recalled how

> The Gaeltacht colony scheme involved a great deal of detailed planning and preparation – the acquisition of large tracts of land, the laying-out and equipping of compact holdings, the siting and marking of over four miles of road, the provision of water supplies, the negotiations to persuade the most suitable tenants to migrate, the mass transfer of entire families with their

stock and other personal belongings and finally, the tactful encouragement
and help afforded them in their new surroundings.[119]

The scheme, however, provoked much criticism from local uneconomic
holders and members of the Old IRA Association who, unsurprisingly,
argued that their claims to any divided land should be met ahead of
those of prospective migrants from the west.[120] These receiving counties, they reminded the government, had local congests of their own.
In County Meath, for instance, slogans such as 'This land is not for
Connemara people. It is for Meath men' were written on the walls. In
June 1927, Hugh Colohan TD (Kildare, Labour) told T. J. O'Connell,
Labour TD for Galway, to 'keep his migrants in his own county'.[121] As
the scheme developed through the 1940s and early 1950s, it became
standard policy to deal with local uneconomic holders before the western migrants were brought in.[122] And while such efforts placated some
local claimants, it did not allay an inherent animus from manifesting
itself against the arriving occupants who were frequently received as
'foreigners' – who had come to occupy the vacant land eyed by the land-
hungry in the localities. Opposition also arose against the resettlement of
Irish speakers from the Gaeltacht areas on the grounds that it threatened
the survival of the Irish language. In the new inland colonies, the settlers
would be removed from the taproot of their Gaelic traditions and customs and the Gaeltacht districts would be weakened by the migration of
its native speakers. In addition, local Cumann na nGaedheal representatives, rather foolishly, claimed that the creation of the Gaeltacht colonies
was simply part of a 'Fianna Fáil strategy to transfer supporters from
areas where they had large majorities to constituencies which were more
equal in terms of the respective voting strength of the major parties'.[123]
Such a fortuitous outcome would not have displeased de Valera, and
despite the on-going difficulties, these Gaeltacht colonies in the midlands
of Ireland no doubt warmed his heart. De Valera is remembered 'in his
distinctive long coat, on a visit to Gibbstown in 1937 walking down a
Land Commission road conversing in fluent Irish with a migrant from
Corca Dhuibhne in Co. Kerry. For him perhaps, the resurgent sounds
and cadences of a language silent for centuries on the demesne lands of
the Gerrard estate was the supreme achievement.'[124]

The removal of migrants out of the congested areas had varied effects.
For the old, many were lost on the day they arrived. They 'lost the life
of the boats, the life of the sea and the strand, going and coming to the
Aran Islands with turf and many other things'.[125] Hanging in the brand
new landlocked cowshed of one Kerry migrant were the fishing nets he
had brought with him from his home.[126] Many of the younger adults
were glad of the opportunity. For the children, it was an adventure. One

'colonist', who had come to Rathcairn as a boy in 1935, recalled: 'It was a terrible great change for us. We thought we were in heaven, that there was no need for us to do anything, that we were on the pig's back. We were searching for stones and not a stone to be found.'[127]

Cullen reflects that in the long term Hogan's formula of assisting the most efficient and hardworking may have been the correct policy.[128] But the flaws of such a strategy were greatly exposed by Cumann na nGaedheal's inability to retain the local electoral support of the small farmer when a valid, constructive and challenging political alternative was eventually provided by Fianna Fáil from May 1926. At the party's first Árd Fheis, de Valera proclaimed that Fianna Fáil's first economic objective would be to 'complete land purchase, break up the large grazing ranches, and distribute them as economic farms among young farmers and agricultural labourers, such as those compelled at present to emigrate'.[129] The party's anti-rancher rhetoric, its desire to settle as many families as possible on the land and its promise of a more expedited approach to land acquisition and division, resonated with many frustrated small uneconomic farmers. The introduction of the 1923 Land Act heightened local expectations of what a native government could achieve. It was an ambitious attempt to resolve what, in the west of Ireland, was considered unfinished business. However, the lengthy legislative process of land redistribution was slow, arduous and costly and the performance of the Land Commission was inconsistent. Questions of inspection, title, price and in many cases improvements to the land (all of which had to be settled before the plots could be allotted) led to many delays. Criticising the methods of the Commission, the Cumann na nGaedheal standing committee wrote:

> There is widespread lack of confidence in the Land Commission which a western member of ours described the other day as 'The Chamber of Horrors' and of which a Cumann na nGaedheal T.D. wrote recently 'It is impossible to make the people believe that there is not some "old gang" running the Land Commission and in league with the old gang left in the country.'[130]

Despite some successes and the government's insistence that land division was 'proceeding as rapidly as possible',[131] demand for land both locally and in the colonies far exceeded the supply made available. Commenting on the situation in the Gaeltacht, the Commission informed the government that

> All the Land Commission (with its present powers, resources and material) can hope to do … is to increase considerably the share of land of a percentage of these people, and perhaps with the aid of improvement grants to

give them better housing facilities, and, in certain cases, improve old roads and open up new ones. Were congestion confined purely to these regions, or even to the maritime counties of the West, the matter would be much simpler; but, unfortunately it is widespread throughout the country. Small uneconomic holders of land requiring attention and having under the law a right to that attention are to be found in large numbers in the province of Leinster and North Munster, as well as in Connacht, Ulster and West Munster.[132]

The fundamental outcome was that a large number of small holdings in County Galway would remain as they were for the reason that there was no land available to meet their claims. In February 1932 Hogan was not rejected by the Galway electorate, but in the first preference poll he was relegated to third place behind two of the Fianna Fáil deputies endorsing that party's more radical call for more land, more tillage and more rural employment. Cumann na nGaedheal's defeat left Hogan dejected but he remained wilful. 'Cant has beaten us', he conceded, 'but the people are sound. They will come back when they have learned their lesson.'[133]

Notes

1 'An Atlantic slum-land', *Freeman's Journal*, 15 Feb. 1924. 'W. K.', the *Freeman's* correspondent who wrote the article, was brought on a visit to Connemara by two of the Galway Cumann na nGaedheal deputies, Padraig Ó Máille (Deputy Speaker of the Dáil) and Seán Broderick, to witness the poverty of the region first hand.
2 Mike Cronin and John M. Regan, 'Introduction: Ireland and the politics of independence 1922–49, new perspectives and re-considerations', in Mike Cronin and John M. Regan (eds), *Ireland: The Politics of Independence, 1922–49* (Basingstoke, 2000), pp. 1–2.
3 John M. Regan, *The Irish Counter-Revolution 1921–1936: Treatyite Politics and Settlement in Independent Ireland* (Dublin, 1999), p. 377.
4 M. A. G. Ó Tuathaigh, 'The land question, politics and Irish society, 1922–1960', in P. J. Drudy (ed.), *Ireland: Land, Politics and People* (Cambridge, 1982), p. 167.
5 *Ibid.*
6 *Census of Ireland 1926*, Occupations, vol. II, pp. 204–5, 223–4. The figures for County Tipperary represent the North and South Ridings combined.
7 Tony Varley, 'Irish land reform and the west between the wars', *Journal of the Galway Archaeological and Historical Society*, vol. 56 (2004), p. 213.
8 Monthly report of the county inspector for Galway (West Riding), Jan. 1917, NLI, Colonial Office records, CO 904/102.
9 Rumpf and Hepburn, *Nationalism and Socialism in Twentieth Century Ireland*, pp. 52–3.

10 George Bernard Shaw, *The Plays of Bernard Shaw: John Bull's Other Island* (London, 1927), p. 54. For a further discussion on why the possession of land was so venerated in Irish society see, for instance, J. J. Lee's comments on the 'possession ethos' in *Ireland 1912–1985*, pp. 390–2 and Dooley '*The Land for the People*', pp. 4–5. Lee criticises it as a retarding force against Irish social and economic progress.

11 T. W. Freeman, *Ireland: A General and Regional Geography* (4th edn, London, 1969), p. 416.

12 DE, vol. 4, 6 July 1923.

13 Eugen Weber, *Peasants into Frenchmen: The Modernization of Rural France 1870–1914* (Stanford, 1976), p. 480.

14 Lecture by Padraig Ó Máille TD to the Gaelic Society's meeting at Trinity College Dublin. Cited in *Connacht Tribune*, 8 Mar. 1924.

15 Ó Tuathaigh, 'The land question, politics and Irish society, 1922–1960', p. 168.

16 Úna Newell, 'Awakening the West? Galway 1916–1918', MA thesis, University College Dublin, 2004.

17 Fergus Campbell, *Land and Revolution: Nationalist Politics in the West of Ireland 1892–1921* (Oxford, 2005), p. 247. The Representation of the People Act 1918 extended the voting franchise in Ireland to all adult males of twenty-one years and granted it for the first time to women aged over thirty who were themselves householders or else married to a householder. Nationally, the Act generated a threefold increase in the number of people eligible to vote. In County Galway, the electorate increased from 29,625 in 1911 to 82,276 in 1918.

18 Campbell, *Land and Revolution*, p. 229.

19 Monthly report of the county inspector for Galway (East Riding), Feb. 1918, NLI, Colonial Office records, CO 904/105.

20 Fitzpatrick, *Politics and Irish Life 1913–1921*, p. 58. Irish agricultural prices slumped after 1920. The agricultural price index, which had risen from 100 in 1911–13 to 288 in 1920, fell to 160 in 1924. James Meenan, *The Irish Economy since 1922* (Liverpool, 1970), p. 91.

21 Dooley, '*The Land for the People*', p. 41; Campbell, *Land and Revolution*, pp. 252, 266, 267. A perch was a system of measurement used especially for land. A perch is equal to 5½ yards (approximately 5.029 metres). A square perch is equal to 160th of an acre or 30¼ square yards (approximately 25.29 square metres).

22 Pastorals, Lent 1920, GDA, O'Dea papers, Box 31/1.

23 Dooley, '*The Land for the People*', p. 40; Campbell, *Land and Revolution*, pp. 252–3; Kevin O'Shiel, 'Memories of my lifetime: the last land war', *Irish Times*, 22 Nov. 1966.

24 RIC Inspector General's monthly report for March 1920. Cited in Tony Varley, 'Agrarian crime and social control: Sinn Féin and the land question in the west of Ireland in 1920', in Ciaran McCullagh, Mike Tomlinson and Tony Varley (eds), *Whose Law and Order? Aspects of Crime and Social Control in Irish Society* (Belfast, 1988), p. 59.

25 Dooley, '*The Land for the People*', p. 40.

26 Michael Laffan, "'Labour must wait": Ireland's conservative revolution', in Patrick Corish (ed.), *Radicals, Rebels and Establishments, Historical Studies XV* (Belfast, 1985), p. 205.

27 Fitzpatrick, *Politics and Irish Life 1913–1921*, p. 122.

28 Ó Tuathaigh, 'The land question, politics and Irish society, 1922–1960', p. 169.

29 Cited in Hopkinson, *Green against Green*, p. 45.

30 David Fitzpatrick, 'The geography of Irish nationalism 1910–1921', *Past and Present*, no. 78 (Feb., 1978), p. 119. For instance, in March 1918 a note was posted on a farm in Gort stating that the land had been taken over by 'the Irish Republic'. The farm belonged to Patrick Deviney. It was being taken over by his brother. See Dooley, *'The Land for the People'*, p. 36.

31 Laffan, *The Resurrection of Ireland*, p. 317.

32 Rumpf and Hepburn, *Nationalism and Socialism in Twentieth Century Ireland*, p. 55.

33 O'Shiel, 'Memories of my lifetime: fellow travellers', *Irish Times*, 17 Nov. 1966.

34 Varley, 'Agrarian crime and social control: Sinn Féin and the land question in the west of Ireland in 1920', p. 69.

35 Laffan, *The Resurrection of Ireland*, p. 315.

36 NAI, BMH, WS 1770 (part VIII), Kevin O'Shiel, Judicial Commission, Dáil Land Courts 1920–22, recorded on 25 Mar. 1959.

37 Series of letters from James Glynn to Sec. Provisional Government, 30 Jan., 9 Mar., 1, 2, 4 May 1922, NAI, DJ, H5/28.

38 Hutchinson Davidson to Sec. Dept. of Defence, 26 May 1922, *ibid.*, H5/907.

39 Report by Civic Guards to Sec. Home Affairs, 6 Nov. 1922, *ibid.*, H5/532.

40 Longfield, Kelly & Armstrong, Solicitors, to Patrick Hogan, 22, 28 June 1923, *ibid.*

41 Henry O'Friel, Sec. Home Affairs, to Eoin O'Duffy, Commissioner, Civic Guard, 20 Dec. 1922, *ibid.*, H5/578.

42 *Connacht Tribune*, 13 Jan. 1923; NAI, DJ, H5/704. Corgary House, the residential holding on the estate, was later burned by republican forces operating in the area. Report on malicious burning of houses submitted by Supt. H. J. Keegan, Garda Síochána, Galway, to Eoin O'Duffy, 7 May 1923, NAI, DJ, H5/1308.

43 Patrick Gormally to Raoul Joyce (Agent for Corgary estate), 17 Mar. 1923, NAI, DJ, H5/704.

44 Raoul Joyce to William Roach (solicitor for Walter Joyce), 13 Apr. 1923, *ibid.*; telegraph from Inspector E. Tobin, Garda Síochána, Athenry, to Dept. of Justice, 24 Sept. 1923, *ibid.*, H5/976.

45 Patrick Hogan, 'Memorandum: seizures of land', 22 Dec. 1922, Military Archives (hereafter MA), A/7869. Cited in Campbell, *Land and Revolution*, p. 282.

46 Dooley, *'The Land for the People'*, p. 42.

47 DE, vol. 2, 1 Mar. 1923.
48 Cited in Campbell, *Land and Revolution*, pp. 283–4.
49 Pastorals, Lent 1923, GDA, O'Doherty papers, Box 47/125. Thomas O'Doherty would later succeed Thomas O'Dea as Bishop of Galway on 13 July 1923.
50 Memorandum by Patrick Hogan, 11 Jan. 1923, UCDA, Mulcahy papers, P7/b/96. Cited in O'Halpin, *Defending Ireland*, p. 31.
51 Cited in Ó Tuathaigh, 'The land question, politics and Irish society, 1922–1960', p. 172.
52 Maurice Moore to Richard Mulcahy, 9 May 1922, MA, A/3126. Cited in Terence Dooley, 'IRA veterans and land division in independent Ireland 1923–48', in Fearghal McGarry (ed.), *Republicanism in Modern Ireland* (Dublin, 2003), p. 91.
53 Copy of Hogan's 'Memorandum: seizures of land', 22 Dec. 1922, NAI, DT, S1943. Cited in Dooley, *'The Land for the People'*, p. 42.
54 Memorandum by Hogan, 11 Jan. 1923, UCDA, Mulcahy papers, P7/b/96. Cited in O'Halpin, *Defending Ireland*, p. 31.
55 O'Halpin, *Defending Ireland*, p. 33.
56 Denis Daly to Darley, Orpen & Synott, Solicitors, [no month recorded] 1922, NAI, DJ, H5/578.
57 Dooley, *'The Land for the People'*, p. 52.
58 William Murphy, 'Patrick Hogan', in James McGuire and James Quinn (eds), *Dictionary of Irish Biography*, vol. 4 (Cambridge, 2009), p. 747.
59 Cited in Anthony Kinsella, 'The Special Infantry Corps', *Irish Sword*, vol. 20, no. 82 (Winter, 1997), pp. 334–5.
60 *Ibid.*, p. 333.
61 Memo from Patrick Hogan to W. T. Cosgrave, 7 Apr. 1923, NAI, DT, S3192.
62 Supt. Burke, Garda Síochána, Roscommon, to O'Duffy, 11 Aug. 1923, NAI, DJ, H5/907.
63 *Western News*, 31 Mar. 1923.
64 James Mongan to Padraig Ó Máille, 20 Apr. 1923, NAI, DJ, H15/99.
65 Ó Máille to O'Higgins, 13 July 1923, *ibid.*
66 O'Friel to Ó Máille, 14 July 1923, *ibid.*
67 Canon McHugh to Ó Máille, 5 Aug. 1923, *ibid.*
68 Patrick O'Donnell, Carna Branch of the Irish Farmers' Union, to O'Higgins, 12 Aug. 1923, *ibid.*
69 Ó Tuathaigh, 'The land question, politics and Irish society, 1922–1960', p. 175; Mary E. Daly, *Industrial Development and Irish National Identity, 1922–1939* (Dublin, 1992), p. 13.
70 Minutes of the Standing Committee, 10 Oct. 1924, UCDA, Cumann na nGaedheal party minute books, P/39/MIN/1/439–41.
71 *Irish Independent*, 16, 17 July 1936; *Irish Times*, 17 July 1936; *Connacht Tribune*, 21 Jan. 1922, 18, 25 July 1936; Joan M. Cullen, 'Patrick J. Hogan, T.D., Minister for Agriculture, 1922–1932: a study of a leading member of the first government of independent Ireland', PhD thesis, Dublin City University, 1993, p. 21; Mary E. Daly, *The First Department: A History*

of the Department of Agriculture (Dublin, 2002), p. 117; Murphy, 'Patrick Hogan', *Dictionary of Irish Biography*, pp. 747–9.

72 O'Halpin, 'Politics and the state, 1922–32', p. 113.

73 Ó Tuathaigh, 'The land question, politics and Irish society, 1922–1960', p. 175.

74 *Ibid.*, p. 176. Meenan would later become president of the Royal Dublin Society.

75 George O'Brien, 'Patrick Hogan: Minister for Agriculture 1922–1932', *Studies*, vol. 25 (Sept., 1936), pp. 355, 359.

76 For more on the establishment of the Agricultural Credit Corporation in 1927, see Daly, *The First Department*, pp. 101, 133–8.

77 Daly, *The First Department*, p. 102.

78 Lee, *Ireland 1912–1985*, p. 115.

79 Varley, 'Irish land reform and the west between the wars', p. 214.

80 Lee, *Ireland 1912–1985*, p. 114.

81 Daly, *The First Department*, p. 157.

82 *Connacht Tribune*, 19 May 1928.

83 Daly, *Industrial Development and Irish National Identity, 1922–1939*, p. 14; Patrick Lynch, 'The social revolution that never was', in T. D. Williams (ed.), *The Irish Struggle, 1916–1926* (London, 1966), p. 52.

84 Lynch, 'The social revolution that never was', p. 53.

85 Daly, *Industrial Development and Irish National Identity, 1922–1939*, p. 17.

86 Speech by Hogan in Gort on 14 Jan. 1928. Cited in *Connacht Tribune*, 21 Jan. 1928.

87 Dooley, 'The Land for the People', p. 56.

88 *Ibid.*, p. 10; Daly, *The First Department*, p. 116; Varley, 'Irish land reform and the west between the wars', p. 213.

89 Report by Publicity Branch of the Department of External Affairs on the progress made by the Department of Lands and Agriculture since the establishment of the State, Jan. 1925, NAI, Department of Agriculture (hereafter AG), AG1 92/3/852.

90 DE, vol. 2, 5 Jan. 1923.

91 Lee, *Ireland 1912–1985*, p. 71.

92 DE, vol. 3, 28 May 1923. Cited in Dooley, 'The Land for the People', p. 19.

93 DE, vol. 10, 26 Mar. 1925. Cited *ibid.*

94 Dooley, 'IRA veterans and land division in independent Ireland 1923–48', p. 93.

95 Patrick Hogan, 'The Irish land question and its future', *Manchester Guardian*, 10 May 1923. Cited in Rumpf and Hepburn, *Nationalism and Socialism in Twentieth Century Ireland*, p. 53.

96 DE, vol. 13, 4 June 1925. Cited in Daly, *The First Department*, p. 117. For another of Hogan's speeches on the scarcity of land, typical of the minister's abhorrence of cant, see DE, vol. 13, 26 Nov. 1925.

97 Varley, 'Irish land reform and the west between the wars', p. 220.

98 Dooley, 'The Land for the People', pp. 65–6.

99 O'Higgins to O'Friel, Sec. Dept. of Justice, 19 Feb. 1926, NAI, DJ, H5/734.
100 *Connacht Tribune*, 10 July 1926.
101 Resolution passed by Ballinasloe Rural District Council, 18 Oct. 1924, GCCA, Ballinasloe RDC minute books, G00/6/20.
102 Dooley, *'The Land for the People'*, pp. 20–5. Access to the files of the Land Commission is still not permitted.
103 *Ibid.*, p. 94; Varley, 'Irish land reform and the west between the wars', p. 215. 1 acre = 0.405 hectares; 330,825 acres = 133,984 hectares; 133,499 acres = 54,067 hectares. 1 hectare = 10,000m².
104 Return showing purchase proceedings under the Land Acts 1923–7 in respect of tenanted and untenanted land at 31 March 1929, DE, vol. 29, 17 May 1929.
105 Report of the Land Commission on the recommendations of the Gaeltacht Commission, 29 Apr. 1927, NAI, DT, S7440/A. For details of the administrative mechanisms of the Commission, its insufficient resources, internal factions, disputes among commission officials over the desirability of prioritising the relief of congestion in the west of Ireland and the inevitable delay in the vesting of land, see Dooley, *'The Land for the People'*, pp. 95–8; Varley, 'Irish land reform and the west between the wars', pp. 221–5; J. Anthony Gaughan (ed.), *Memoirs of Senator Joseph Connolly (1885–1961): A Founder of Modern Ireland* (Dublin, 1996), ch. 23.
106 Varley, 'Irish land reform and the west between the wars', p. 216.
107 Seamus Mac an Iomaire to Kevin O'Higgins, 21 Jan. 1925, NAI, DJ, H15/99.
108 Cited in Varley, 'Irish land reform and the west between the wars', p. 215.
109 DE, vol. 19, 24 Mar. 1927; *An Phoblacht*, 29 Jan. 1926.
110 Cited in Ó Tuathaigh, 'The land question, politics and Irish society, 1922–1960', p. 182.
111 DE, vol. 2, 5 Jan. 1923.
112 DE, vol. 3, 28 May 1923.
113 Patrick J. Sammon, *In the Land Commission: A Memoir 1933–1978* (Dublin, 1997), pp. 12–13.
114 Report of the Land Commission on the recommendations of the Gaeltacht Commission, 29 Apr. 1927, NAI, DT, S7440/A.
115 William Nolan, 'New farms and fields: migration policies of state land agencies 1891–1980', in William J. Smyth and Kevin Whelan (eds), *Common Ground: Essays on the Historical Geography of Ireland* (Cork, 1988), p. 308.
116 W. T. Cosgrave, 'Policy of the Cumann na nGaedheal Party', 1927, NAI, DT, S7440/B.
117 For further details on this new movement, see Nolan, 'New farms and fields', p. 309.
118 In 1935, twenty-seven families from Galway (totalling 177 persons) migrated to Rathcairn, Co. Meath, the first Gaeltacht colony to be established. For a description of the families leaving Connemara on that 'wet

spring morning' on four specially arranged Coras Iompair Éireann buses, see Dooley, *'The Land for the People'*, p. 146; Sammon, *In the Land Commission*, pp. 157–8.

119 Sammon, *In the Land Commission*, p. 158.

120 Dooley, *'The Land for the People'*, p. 143.

121 Cited *ibid.*; DE, vol. 20, 23 June 1927.

122 Dooley, *'The Land for the People'*, pp. 145–6, 148–9.

123 *Meath Chronicle*, 8 May 1937. Cited in Nolan, 'New farms and fields', p. 311.

124 Nolan, 'New farms and fields', p. 315.

125 Translation of interview of Colm Seoighe with Máirtín Ó Fhlatharta, Radio na Gaeltachta, 13 Apr. 1985. Cited *ibid.*, p. 316.

126 Máire Cruise O'Brien, *The Same Age as the State: The Autobiography of Máire Cruise O'Brien* (Dublin, 2003), p. 92.

127 Translation of interview of Colm Seoighe with Máirtín Ó Fhlatharta, Radio na Gaeltachta, 13 Apr. 1985. Cited in Nolan, 'New farms and fields', p. 316.

128 Cullen, 'Patrick J. Hogan, T.D., Minister for Agriculture, 1922–1932', p. 208.

129 Cited in Dooley, *'The Land for the People'*, p. 99.

130 'Statement of Views of Coiste Gnotha relative to the political aspect of the present situation', Oct. 1924, UCDA, Cumann na nGaedheal party minute books, P/39/MIN/1.

131 Cosgrave, 'Policy of the Cumann na nGaedheal Party', 1927.

132 Report of the Land Commission on the recommendations of the Gaeltacht Commission, 29 Apr. 1927, NAI, DT, S7440/A.

133 Cited in *Connacht Tribune*, 25 July 1936.

4

Poverty and the Irish language

Land purchase alone would not afford an adequate solution to the poverty prevalent in parts of County Galway. Even if all of the land in the Free State available for the relief of congestion was used for the resettlement of the people of the west, the plain fact was it would still not be sufficient for the purpose. The problem that the Cumann na nGaedheal government faced was an economic one. The new state's beginnings had opened with reports of famine-like conditions in parts of Connemara and each year brought a recurring pattern of poverty and distress to many parts of the region.[1] In particular, the appalling weather conditions and incessant rain that fell in 1923 and 1924 resulted in poor harvests and a shortage of turf that left many small farmers in considerable difficulty. In January 1924, Dr Casey, medical health officer for the Clifden district, reported that

> Bad weather, unemployment, and actual poverty are causing great suffering among the poorer families, and many cases of actual want of food and clothing have come under my notice … I have no hesitation in stating that at no time in my experience has poverty and unemployment been greater.[2]

In February, the Clifden Rural District Council passed a resolution calling on the government to come to the assistance of the people by obtaining for the poor the necessary quantities of seed potatoes and seed oats.

> We would remind the Government that it is their duty to do so … we call upon the Government also to open up relief works so that the present pressing need might be staved off. It surely is the function of a Government to look after its people.[3]

The government, this time a native Irish one, was criticised for its slow response in providing the necessary assistance and charged with paying eloquent lip service to the economic problems of the west. However, the Cumann na nGaedheal administration had inherited the contradictory strains of 'widespread popular expectations of state assistance and a civil service to whom this was anathema'.[4]

Distress in the west

In 1925, following on the previous poor seasons, the harvest failed in many parts of Connemara. The season of floods caused great shortages in many parts of the county, but conditions in the more isolated villages of Connemara were particularly desperate. Writing to Joseph Walsh, diocesan secretary of Tuam, John Dignan, Bishop of Clonfert,[5] remarked

> I know that many of my people are in great need: numbers have little or no fuel and many suffered through the flooding of their lands and hundreds of sheep have perished. I realise however that the need of Clonfert is not comparable with the need existing in the West of the County and by the sea board of the Province.[6]

On 20 January, Mary Monnelly, local inspector for the National Society for the Prevention of Cruelty to Children (NSPCC), sought the committal of five children to Letterfrack industrial school. She reported that the father of the household had no cattle; his land was flooded; he had no money and he, his wife and eight children were living in a one-roomed cabin. They did not have the means to light a fire and their bed and bedding consisted of hay and a few old rags. The children were ill-nourished, poorly clad and thin. The previous week the roof had fallen in on them and 'their sole diet for some time past had consisted of black tea and a little bread made from water'.[7] Mounting cases of severe distress forced the government to take steps to provide immediate relief. An initial grant of £25,000 was issued to meet the shortage of fuel in areas where turf-saving had failed and thousands of tons of coal were distributed at a nominal charge of six pence per hundredweight (cwt).[8] In the more affected areas seed potatoes and seed oats for the next crop were dispensed at considerably reduced prices (usually five shillings per cwt); schemes of relief works (predominantly road- and bridge-building) were established, giving payment in return for work; and assistance was offered for the provision of school meals to those children most in need.[9] Writing in the *Connacht Tribune*, Violet Connolly, a member of the Save the Children Fund stated,

> I have visited most of the schools in the Clifden, Recess, Letterfrack, and Roundstone parishes, where school-feeding has now begun. The whole success of these meals depends upon the willing cooperation of the teachers, as owing to the limited facilities of most of these school-houses, the teacher has to keep his eye on a kettle or huge black pot while instructing his little flock before their meal. When the water is boiling, cocoa is made in big mugs (bought in large numbers by the Emergency Committee in Dublin),

sweetened with sugar and Irish condensed milk, and given to the young-
sters, with a generous ration of bread (½ lb) and butter ... Many of the
teachers remark upon the increased vitality of their pupils since they have
been provided with this midday lunch.[10]

Alongside the government schemes, supplementary aid was provided
by the Catholic Church to meet the aggravated distress. Relief efforts were
coordinated by Thomas Gilmartin, Archbishop of Tuam, whose episcopal jurisdiction encompassed many of the most affected areas. Outlining
his scheme for the distribution of assistance, Gilmartin wrote:

> Let me say first of all that three years ago when acute distress existed along
> the sea-board, relief was given by means of local committees. The experi-
> ment did not prove successful: many of the people became demoralised,
> and some who were not really poor tried to get relief. After going fully into
> the question I have decided on this occasion to have all relief distributed
> quietly making one or two persons of trust responsible for the distribution
> in each centre. Before any money is paid from here, vouchers of expenditure
> must be sent: and in all cases I will try to get work of public utility done for
> the money, so as to prevent demoralisation.[11]

The scheme was particularly effective. A Connemara Distress Committee
was formed and vouchers issued by the Committee were signed by the
local priests, the merchant who supplied the goods and the recipient of
the goods. The value and description of the items were recorded and the
receipt was sent to Joseph Walsh, who secured payment of the bill. On
24 April 1925, Fr Mark Curley, Recess, Connemara, submitted receipts
for food supplied to fifteen families in the district. The bill, he explained,
was £45 – 'you advised me to spend £40 but when I got started I could
not help it'.[12] In a similar letter, Fr Healy of Carraroe, Connemara,
wrote:

> I am sending you on today receipts for the clothing of school children. The
> amount comes to £28 16s 6d. My reason for expending so much relief money
> on clothing was to enable the children to attend school so that they could
> avail of the food given daily through the government. Through this they are
> enabled to get one good meal daily which is a good thing for them.[13]

Two representations of the type of relief tickets issued by the Connemara
Distress Committee are supplied below (Figure 4.1). In these instances
the goods were supplied by T. Naughton, Recess, Connemara.[14]

Subscriptions to the distress fund established by Gilmartin were wide
and varied. On 26 January 1925 he received a donation of 2,000 guineas
(£2,100) from the Bank of Ireland. On 2 February the directors of the
Hibernian Bank Ltd contributed five hundred guineas, allocating 300

Goods supplied to P. Joyce Bill £2.15		Goods supplied to Mary Greene Bill £2	
	£.s. d.		£. s. d.
1 lb tea & 4 lb sugar	6.4	6 loaves bread	3.6
4 lb bacon	6.0	1 tin cocoa	0.8
2 lb butter	5.0	1 can condensed milk	1.3
Soda C. tarter	0.9	2 lb butter	5.0
2 cans condensed milk	1.3	1lb tea & 4 lb sugar	6.4
1 lb butter	2.6	6 lb bacon	9.0
4 loaves bread	2.4	2 lb soap	1.0
1 large tin cocoa	1.6	4 oz cream tarter	0.8
Candles	0.2	Candles	0.7
2 lb soap	1.0	3 sts oatmeal	12.0
½ lb tea & 2 lb sugar	3.2	Total	£2.0.0
Total	£1.10.0		
2 blankets	£1.05.0		
Total	£2.15.0		

Figure 4.1 Relief tickets, 1925

guineas to Gilmartin, 100 guineas to the Bishop of Raphoe (Donegal) and 100 guineas to the Lady Dudley's Nursing Association. On 16 February, the National Bank Ltd, London, donated 1,200 guineas and on 4 March Ulster Bank Ltd, Belfast, sent Gilmartin a draft for £105. A donation of $100 was provided by the San Antonio Texas branch of the Ladies' Auxiliary of the Ancient Order of Hibernians in America. Relief money was also received from religious organisations and charity groups in other parts of North America, Mauritius and France. In Britain, the United Irish League and the Irish Democratic League forwarded several cheques in aid of the distress. St Bede's College, Manchester, sent £500 from its parochial collections in February 1925 and offered further subscriptions in March and June. In South Africa, readers of the *Southern Cross*, Cape Town, donated £77. Individual donors enclosed cheques ranging in amounts from £1 to £20 to £600. Monica Rafferty of Torquay, UK, acknowledging that 'committees are slow things', wrote to Joseph Walsh advising him that she had sent two bales of clothes directly to Tuam in an effort to have them distributed quickly. The clothes, she wrote, 'are good, warm and clean and will be a help in this cold weather to the poorest people'.[15]

In March 1925, a sum of £4,629 donated from private sources (including Arthur Guinness Company Ltd, the 'New York World' and 'Chicago Citizens') was placed at the disposal of the government to aid its relief effort.[16] In the first instance, it was proposed by the Department of Agriculture that the sum be devoted to the districts where it had not been possible to establish relief works and where, owing to acute poverty, the people had been unable to avail of the facilities for obtaining supplies of seed. In such areas, seed oats and potatoes would be distributed either at a nominal fee or free of charge to those who were too poor to purchase them for themselves. However, the Department's scheme to distribute free seed was strongly opposed by members of the local clergy on the grounds that it counteracted the progressive self-help ethos they were trying to promote in their parishes. Communicating his thoughts to Joseph Walsh, Fr Charles White of Roundstone stated

> It came to my ears that on account of the earnest cooperation of many of the priests in the working of the seed and fuel scheme, the Department of Agriculture were about to give free grants of some tons of potatoes to some parishes. I at once wrote to Hogan the minister asking him for all sakes not to do it pointing out that it was that kind of thing that had ruined the Connemara man and he endorsed and agreed ... the people here are so demoralized that a man with £1,000 in [the] bank will come looking for relief as well and with more cheek than the man that is starving.[17]

In its place, it was decided that the assistance to the most distressed districts would be administered by the bishops of the dioceses concerned. Writing to Gilmartin on 10 March 1925, F. J. Meyrick, secretary of the Department of Agriculture, explained:

> You are, no doubt, aware of the steps already taken by the Government to relieve distress among the rural population of the congested districts by distributing seed potatoes and oats of approved varieties at a reduced price ... You will realise that if the Government were to give potatoes to the people free, or at nominal charges, it would have a very great pauperising effect, and would largely neutralise the good effects of the scheme which is already in operation, as well as giving rise to great discontent among persons who had had difficulty in raising the money to pay the prescribed prices for seed.[18]

Accordingly, the fund was handed over to the bishops, in proportion to the extent of acute distress in their diocese. Of the £4,629 available for distribution, Gilmartin received the largest allocation of £1,115 and £290 was sent to O'Doherty, the new Bishop of Galway.[19] It was suggested that the selection of applicants in each parish would be left to the parish priest who would, by means of an announcement at Mass, or other such suitable methods, take steps to ascertain the persons resident

in his parish in need of assistance. The parish priest would then com-
municate his requirements to the bishop who would at that time, with
the assistance of the Department's local agricultural overseer, organise
the distribution of the quantity of seed potatoes or oats required for
each parish. In this way, a clear distinction could be made between the
Department's scheme of seed distribution, in which applicants had been
required to pay at least half the cost of the seed, and the *new* charitable
scheme in which seed would be sold at a much reduced price, or in special cases distributed free of charge by the Church (not the government)
to those most in need of relief.

That conditions of aggravated distress and extreme poverty existed
in Connemara and other parts of the county in 1925 was unquestion-
able. However, sensationalist reporting of the crisis by the press, and
the painting of harrowing pictures of human suffering, caused some
resentment. Writing in the *Sunday Times* (London) Darrell Figgis
complained that

> correspondents, moved by the sincerest motives, but unfamiliar with con-
> ditions of life in the West of Ireland, have written of sights they have seen
> there in a way that has caused pain, and has even created anger. In consid-
> ering the distress that prevails there, it is perhaps necessary to remember
> that, if in some cases the people live herded in villages that do not allow the
> decencies of life, it is not at their election they do so. If cabins are poor, none
> too comely, or weather-proof, and if cattle are to be found in them together
> with human beings, the fault lies in painful causes in history. One does not,
> in desiring to help a friend to whom time has not been too kind, insist on
> drawing attention to his frayed cuff.[20]

From the Aran Islands, Fr S. J. Walsh protested: 'We are not so badly
off as the *Connacht Tribune* makes us, though goodness knows we are
bad enough ... I have written a strong letter to the [*Irish*] *Independent*
contradicting the utterly false and unjust statements contained in it.'[21]
Another commentator contended that

> some of the sensational accounts published in London were from the pens of
> correspondents who arrived by train, were driven by motor to see selected
> hard cases, and returned to London straightaway to write up 'the famine',
> as if these cases were general and normal. There is apparently a design in
> the extreme Tory press to work up 'the famine' spectre as another stark spot
> in the outlook of the Free State.[22]

In America, Irish-American newspapers were reporting that the west of
Ireland was threatened with conditions more severe than in 1847. On
29 January, the editor of the *New York Evening World* cabled Cosgrave
stating: 'Reports here of widespread famine in West [of] Ireland. Many

dying, starving, freezing ... Would appreciate cable at once, 500 words, our expense, on exact conditions. Is assistance needed?'[23] On 30 January, Professor Timothy Smiddy, Minister Plenipotentiary in Washington DC, notified the government that 'Papers here carry statements of famine in Connemara, Kerry and Fermanagh. Thousands imperilled. Crisis worst since 1847.'[24] On 3 February, he wrote, 'Substantial help suggested from this side. Do you wish to accept? Am of opinion it will not help credit of Saorstat here.'[25] The conflict of testimony as to the extent of the distress in the west was causing a great deal of confusion. Cosgrave was quick to respond, stating: 'No famine in [the] ordinary sense exists and comparisons with black forty seven made by certain newspapers [are] absurd.'[26]

The concern of the government for the reputation of the Irish Free State abroad is significant. (It is also evident in Cosgrave's Saint Patrick's Day broadcast to the Irish in America in 1931, where he claimed that the Free State had remained 'relatively unaffected' by the world economic crisis.[27]) In 1925, the government was eager to assure prominent Irish-Americans that the situation was in hand. The newly independent Irish state was not to be portrayed as a mendicant nation, perpetually sending round the hat in America.

The combination of church and state relief measures established control over the immediate crisis in the west, but the schemes provided only temporary relief. As long as the region remained in this condition, the occurrence of another poor harvest would result in further distress and privation, the pattern of poverty would repeat itself once more, and special relief measures would be an annual necessity. If they were to remain on the land, the uneconomic small holders in the poorest districts would have to have their income supplemented by other industries.

In 1925, Cumann na nGaedheal was commended for its effective action in dealing with the crisis, but the appalling economic condition of the western districts was a severe problem and, in the words of the Minister for Agriculture, 'a blot on the country'.[28] Successive Galway County Councils had expressed their despair of ever coping with the Connemara problem and declared it to be a matter for the national government. The reality was that while the people might not have been starving, many were simply surviving. Writing to Cosgrave in 1926, Maura Ostyn, the abbess of Kylemore Castle in Connemara, described the hopeless destitution and malnutrition that continued to occur in her locality. Advising the President that these 'instances are not cited as exceptional cases but rather as types, and by no means exaggerated ones, of the distress which prevails over the whole area of Connemara', she described the primitive housing she encountered. The principal and often the only room in the dwelling of these people, she wrote,

> is a kitchen, unsanitary and dirty. The manure heap is frequently the prom-
> inent object outside the door. The cabin itself is built of un-mortared stones,
> with no ceiling, no wooden floor. The ground is as the ground was when the
> covering was put over it. At one end is the large wooden four poster bed,
> and at the other an abiding place for the fowl ... And this shelter passes as
> the habitation where father, mother and nine or ten young children eke out
> an existence. Their food is in accordance with their miserable surroundings.
> It is a feast when a mackerel or a herring is cooked at the smoky fire.

In another cabin she described how a woman suffering from typhoid fever was lying on a straw bed and covered over with some rags. In the next cottage a young girl of eighteen years was wasting away in the last stages of phthisis. In the fourth cabin, the one and only room of the house was shared by an old fisherman with his two daughters, a sick calf, a donkey, a pig and some hens.[29] Describing similar instances of poverty, Bartley O'Beirne, Tuberculosis Officer for County Galway, reported that in one case a man in Letterfrack was stretched beside the fire dying of consumption, his four children sat a little distance away in the kitchen, behind the door his wife was confined and the family had nothing to eat.[30]

The economic problem of the west was a problem of brutal facts. The hard reality was that the land was poor and barren, the proportion that was arable was very small and it was with difficulty the people wrested a crop from it. There was a grave over-dependency on the land, many of the holdings were too small to be economic, and when the crop failed the people were little removed from destitution. The two main supple-mentary industries – fishing and kelp-burning[31] – had declined. Housing was inferior except in the case of a few newly built cottages, the priest's house, the doctor's house and the teacher's house. In some instances, the condition of the dwellings impaired the health of the occupants. Cases of typhoid and typhus fever (for the most part attributable to impure water supply) continued to be reported by the medical health officers, many people lived from hand to mouth, and in recent years the heavy rains had resulted in poor harvests and saturated practically all of the turf supplies. These people, as Douglas Hyde contended, had 'been for generations fighting with the sea, fighting with the weather, fighting with the bogs, [and] fighting with the mountains'.[32] They constituted some of the poorest to be found in the country.

Incidents of distress, however, were not confined to west Galway. At a meeting of the Home Assistance Committee in January 1925, Monnelly (local NSPCC inspector) described the conditions under which a number of families in Galway city were living. In the Claddagh district, she believed the people were willing to do without sufficient food supplies if they could get enough fuel. During the recent bad weather several families had been flooded out. She visited one woman with a family of ten children who were all now living in a single room with the woman's mother-in-law.[33] In June 1927, the Claddagh was certified as an 'unhealthy area' by the medical health officer, Dr Michael McDonagh, compelling the Urban District Council to obtain a clearance order for the area.[34] One resident described his house as being 'too small for a good henhouse'.[35]

The housing shortage was a particular problem in many parts of the city. Although the overall population of the county continued to decline, the number of people living in Galway city rose from 14,227 in 1926 to 18,285 in 1936. This increase, primarily due to the steady drift of people from the rural areas, imposed a severe strain on the housing accommodation of the city.[36] One (although possibly intentionally exaggerated) application submitted to the Urban Council by Patrick Smith, Bohermore (Galway city), read:

> I appeal to you to give me a house about to become vacant in St Bridget's Terrace. I am at present living under the most miserable conditions in a thatched house of one room, and five of us are sleeping in one bed. One night last week I had to dig a hole in the floor of the room to let out the water. This house was condemned by the sanitary officer as unfit for human habitation.[37]

In 1930, residents of a tenement in Middle Street had to be removed because of the dangerous condition of the building. In 1932, in his annual report to the Galway Board of Health, Dr Seamus O'Brien noted that the tenements, especially in No. 1 dispensary, were not only a danger to health but in many cases a danger to life.[38] Outside of the city the demand for new housing was equally vocal. Reports from the local dispensary doctors referred to one inhabitant who had built a new house that was in an unsafe and unhealthy condition. The walls were unable to support the roof and the roof leaked so much that lime-washing was a waste of time. In a case in north Galway it was reported that after the roof of one man's house had blown away, the father was compelled to house his children in a shed and diphtheria ensued.[39]

During the 1920s the Department of Finance restricted local authority access to funds because the available capital was needed for other schemes. When the local authorities were finally granted access to the Local Loans Fund in 1926, loans for housing, which made up the majority of their capital requirements, were excluded.[40] However, notwithstanding the financial stringencies of the 1920s and 1930s, a number of public housing schemes were carried out both privately and by the local councils. Between 1922 and 1944, 731 houses were built by the

Urban Council in Galway city, particularly in the areas of Bohermore, Shantalla and the Claddagh (the main portion of the old Claddagh was demolished in the early 1930s). In the same period, 305 houses were built in Tuam and 174 were constructed in Ballinasloe. In addition, 1,332 rural cottages were built with the assistance of the County Board of Health.[41] Nevertheless, there was still a critical shortage of adequate housing across much of the city. Commenting on the situation in 1932 the *Connacht Sentinel* wrote

> The record of the Urban Council in building houses for the poor has, on the whole, been a creditable one, having regard to the difficulties to be met with and the post-war money stringency; but how far it falls short of the need of the people is proved by the scores of applicants who clamour for every new cottage before it becomes vacant, and by scores more who are destined to live in crowded and ill-equipped tenement slums.[42]

Overcrowding was prevalent not only in the houses but also in a number of the county's national schools. In February 1931, a correspondent for the *Connacht Tribune* reported that in a school he visited in Ballinasloe the students had to be overflowed into a hat and cloak room. The room, which was formerly the porch of the Town Hall, was without a fireplace and without a window. There were some families in the town, he noted, whose 'children needed meals in school as much as any children in Connemara'.[43]

In 1929, the Housing (Gaeltacht) Act introduced £80 building and £40 improvement grants as well as small outhouse grants for Irish-speaking areas.[44] The supply of healthy, weather-proof dwellings for the people and suitable outbuildings for their livestock was a critical necessity. Nonetheless, the substitution of slate houses for thatched cabins in the congested areas did not alter the fact that without satisfactory land redistribution, the small patches of land on which the new dwellings were built were unable to support the occupier. As Padraig Ó Máille argued, in his capacity as Gaeltacht Inspector in 1933, congestion, whether in a slate house or a thatched cabin, was still congestion, the only difference being that the slated houses made it more permanent.[45] The instance of poverty in the west of Ireland was one of the most intractable among the problems of the Saorstát.

The Gaeltacht Commission and the Irish language

For the Cumann na nGaedheal government, the revival of the Irish language was, as Oliver MacDonagh has suggested, a more desirable and attainable touchstone of its commitment to Irish nationalism than the delivery of an Irish republic. Such a commitment to the Irish language also served to counter republican claims that they were the sole custodians of national ideals. Furthermore, three key ministers of the Cumann na nGaedheal government, Ernest Blythe (Finance), Eoin MacNeill (Education, until the end of 1925) and Richard Mulcahy (Defence, until March 1924 and Local Government from June 1927), were all zealots in the cause of the revival.[46] Additionally, although far from satisfactory, the Irish language, as a result of the earlier campaigns of the Gaelic League, had secured a foothold within the education system.[47] On 27 January 1925, the Executive Council appointed a Commission, under the chairmanship of Mulcahy, to examine the conditions of the Gaeltacht 'in the hope that proper inquiry will lead to a clear and definite national policy in respect to those districts and local populations which have preserved the Irish language as the language of their homes'.[48] The Commission's terms of reference were threefold: first, to define what constituted an Irish-speaking area; second, to inquire into the preservation of the Irish language; and third, to investigate the solution to the economic problems of the Gaeltacht. Besides the government's dependence on the children of the nation to restore the language, it was the native speakers of the Gaeltacht who were relied upon to recover Pearse's vision of a Gaelic Ireland. However, it was the government's recognition, that any attempt to preserve the language in the Gaeltacht districts would be futile without the economic recovery of those areas, which was so important to the west of Ireland. In County Galway, the Gaeltacht region encompassed many of the areas most associated with abject poverty in Connemara in the 1920s. Reacting to the establishment of the Commission, Fr Malachy Brennan (thus far a stalwart Cumann na nGaedheal supporter and a member of the party's National Executive) declared: 'The way in which the Government handles this national question should be for all Irish-Irelanders who have supported the Government up to the present the main factor in determining their future attitude to it or to any other Government claiming their support.'[49] Cumann na nGaedheal could not hope to preserve the language if the Gaeltacht continued to lose its native speakers. Without effective economic intervention, survival and not revival would remain the focus of the people.

According to the 1926 census, the number of Irish speakers as a percentage of the total persons in each of the seven Gaeltacht counties was Galway 47.4 per cent, Mayo 36.8 per cent, Donegal 34.4 per cent, Kerry 33.0 per cent, Clare 30.4 per cent, Waterford (excluding the County Borough) 30.0 per cent and Cork (excluding the County Borough) 21.1 per cent. Nationally, the number of people who could speak Irish had increased by 24 per cent from 1911, but these speakers were practically confined to children of school age, many of whom would inevitably lose the language once they left school. The gain of one Irish speaker in this group, it was argued, would not compensate for the loss of one Irish speaker in the Gaeltacht.[50] And the Gaeltacht was losing its Gaeilgeoirí. The number of Irish speakers in the Fíor and Breac Gaeltacht regions of Galway decreased from 82,311 in 1911 to 67,022 in 1926. While County Galway still retained the highest number of Irish speakers in the Free State, the figure of 47.4 per cent represented a decline of 6.7 per cent from 1911. More ominously, it was also the first occasion where non-Irish speakers exceeded the number of Irish speakers in the county.[51]

Locally, some dissent was raised at the expenditure of vital funds on such an inquiry. For instance, Fr MacAlinney, parish priest of Spiddal, refused to co-operate with the Commission, stating that 'Coimisiún na Gaeltachta now sitting at leisure on "the language and economic problems in the Gaeltacht" is the last word in costly inefficiency and do-nothingness, so characteristic of most such bodies'.[52] The Gaeltacht Commission presented its report to the Executive Council on 14 July 1926. It was published on 23 August 1926. Yet a series of delays meant that Cumann na nGaedheal's official statement of government policy on the recommendations of the Commission was not issued until 1928. Part of the delay was due to the fact that the Commission was not required to provide a financial estimate for putting its recommendations into practice. Therefore, the Executive Council had to wait for each state department to submit its own observations on the practicality and feasibility of the Commission's recommendations before it could submit its official response.[53]

The Commission's economic report read almost like a stocktaking of the Gaeltacht. Its recommendations included the implementation of comprehensive schemes of afforestation, arterial drainage and land reclamation; the protection and promotion of the fishing industry; the introduction of a special system of loans and grants for the improvement of houses; the re-development of the kelp industry and the renewal of local rural industries. While the report bore every sign of having been carefully and sympathetically considered, with an understanding of the social and economic difficulties presented by the Gaeltacht, its recommendations were nothing new to the affected communities. Notwithstanding the significant investment made by the Congested Districts Board for the past thirty years, there had been a continual clamour for comparable, more permanent solutions. Nonetheless, despite the fact that the suggestions of the Commission were perhaps well-worn, the likely implementation of at least some of these schemes raised great expectations in County Galway.

Apart from tackling the land question, the three key components for the economic revival of the Gaeltacht, outlined in the report, were the fisheries, rural industries and education. Along the western seaboard, the fishing industry had provided a vital additional means of livelihood for small farmers. However, in recent years it had regressed. In 1918 Irish herrings prices averaged 27s per cwt at port of landing. In 1919 they averaged 15s 7d; in 1920, 13s; and in 1925, 10s. In the same period, Irish mackerel prices dropped from 21s per cwt in 1918 to 10s in 1920 and 9s 7d in 1925.[54] Mounting loan debts, the scarcity of fish and irregular migration patterns of herring and mackerel, the collapse of the markets, bad weather, the political disturbances of 1920–23 and the lack of reliable transit facilities, worn out equipment and the incursion of foreign trawlers were key factors in the decline in local fishing. In 1920 west Galway's herring catch was worth £4,658. Three years later it had declined to £625, while Donegal's catch amounted to £75,732.[55] In 1923, the former Congested Districts Board loan scheme, which had supplied fishermen with motor vessels and the necessary equipment, was suspended owing to the inability of the fishermen to meet their loan repayments. In 1924, in an address to the Gaelic Society in Trinity College Dublin, Padraig Ó Máille TD remarked that

> With its extended coastal line, one would expect to find a strong fishing industry in the West of Ireland. But it does not exist. Here and there small communities do endeavour to support themselves and their families on the proceeds of the industry but fishing on a big commercial scale must wait on the introduction of modern methods and much improved transport by road and rail.[56]

The development of deep sea fishing would demand considerable government capital to furnish the large class of boats and equipment required, but commenting on the total estimate of £25,318 allocated to his department in 1924, Fionán Lynch, Minister for Fisheries, acknowledged that it was scarcely possible with that amount to carry out the old fishery functions of the Congested Districts Board.[57]

In the Aran Islands, on account of the particularly poor quality of the soil, the exposed nature of the landscape and very low crop yields, the people had little economic outlook save the sea. For the majority of this community, sea fishing was their sole livelihood. In his statement to the Gaeltacht Commission in 1925, Fr S. J. Walsh, Aran Islands, wrote:

> Many of the older inhabitants will tell you that they have never seen worse economic conditions that those prevailing at present. This is entirely due to the continued almost complete failure of fishing. No other industry can take its place here. The younger people, after waiting in vain for five or six

years for revival are, therefore, leaving for America in as large numbers and as fast as they can get there. Those at home are depending largely on the American cheques to provide the necessaries of life ... The shopkeepers, to do them justice, have stood loyally by the people, hoping every day the revival of fishing would enable them to get back their own. But they must of necessity soon stop credit.[58]

Cumann na nGaedheal had introduced some initiatives such as the 'Eat more fish' campaign and encouraged diversification in fishing methods. But, as Ó Fathartaigh has argued, the government focused on fostering domestic markets rather than providing the equipment and instruments of production required for a successful fishing industry.[59]

In its report the Commission recommended the establishment of a Fishery Technical School that would offer courses of instruction on navigation and modern fishing methods; the habits of the common marine fish; the driving and care of motor engines; the mounting, mending and preservation of nets and gear; and the handling, curing and preparation of fish for the market. In addition, it supported the continuation of government loans for large boats and equipment and proposed a new scheme in which the remaining vessels in the hands of the Department of Fisheries should be kept in commission, under a captain employed by the Department, and manned by efficient local crews.[60] The government's response was measured. The setting up of a Fishery Technical School would be the subject of departmental consideration; the granting of loans without insisting on solvent personal sureties would not be endorsed; but, realising the exceptional conditions of the Gaeltacht, the Department of Fisheries was instructed to attempt to find a method of overcoming these difficulties.[61] However, few innovative initiatives were forthcoming. Reacting to the slow pace with which the government began the revision process, Walsh claimed in 1927 that 'The continued failure of the fishing industry left the people of the islands and seaboard no other alternative between starvation and wholesale emigration ... Any government deserving the name paternal would make the protection of its deserving poor its first care ... The whole history of the Ministry of the Fisheries might be written in that one word, "failure".'[62] In 1928, a comparative study of sea fishing between Denmark and Ireland, commissioned by the Irish Fishermen's Association, revealed that between 1927 and 1928, while Denmark was spending £340,000 on fishing development and protection, the Irish Free State was spending £37,175. Where the Danes authorised £30,000 in loans in 1927, Fionán Lynch sanctioned £7,000.[63]

Just as the fishing industry was depended on to supplement the income of many small farmers along the west coast, and as the sole basis of revenue for others, local rural industries were also relied upon to reduce

the dependence on agriculture. In the Gaeltacht, the small rural industries of hand spinning, weaving, knitting and lace-making provided the
basis of livelihood for a small number of people who would otherwise
be compelled to emigrate. Yet many of these traditional industries and
handicrafts established in the 1890s by the Congested Districts Board,
titled ladies and religious orders were not in fact traditional industries at
all.[64] W. L. Micks noted that among the problems which these employers
initially faced was 'the difficulty of training to fine needlework, or lace
and crochet work, hands that had been hardened by various kinds of
rough out-of-door work in which they were engaged, including agriculture, saving turf for fuel, and in many localities gathering seaweed for
manure or for kelp-burning'.[65] In recent years, the homespun industry,
because of a failure to keep abreast of modern techniques and changes
in fashion, was in decline and confined to the local demand.

The Commission made four recommendations for the recovery of the
rural industries: that a small number of experts be employed to organise the homespun industry and provide instruction; that a state stamp
for clothes of particular quality be introduced; that loans be provided
for the establishment of carding and finishing mills; and that a central
depot be founded for the marketing of the products produced in the
Gaeltacht.[66] Endorsing the Commission's belief that local rural industries could be revitalised, the government did appoint an expert in the
textile industry to ensure that the products of the local looms would be
more suited to modern demands than was the case at the time. But until
sufficient success in this instance was achieved, steps towards establish-
ing a state stamp or central depot were deferred.[67]

In supporting the economic development of the Gaeltacht, the government promoted the idea of making goods by the people of the Gaeltacht
for the people of the Gaeltacht. Such a vision of small self-sustaining
industries reflected the long-standing nationalist image of rural society
and the protection of its rural values. Yet, in their present form, small
rural industries would remain little more than a sop to the greater problem of land congestion. In 1927 Dr Seamus O'Brien, medical health
officer, argued that putting money into the development of these industries was simply 'money thrown away'. Another factor against any rural
industry, he contended, was that the young people would not stay in the
countryside. They must and would go to the towns. Instead of supporting stopgap rural industries, O'Brien proposed, as a more permanent
solution, the gradual progress of Galway into a manufacturing town.
'We are all familiar with the odour from Messrs. McDonogh's chemical
factory', he argued, 'but even the most sensitive of us would not dare
suggest the closing down of the factory to get rid of the odour.' The

congested districts would provide a readily available work force and the migration of the people to the city would see the gradual disappearance of the Gaeltacht crux.[68] O'Brien's vision of a thriving manufacturing city, however, was at odds with the government's desire to solve the problem of the Gaeltacht in the Gaeltacht. An infusion of state capital and the permanent establishment of profitable rural industries might have helped relieve the pressure on the land, but the industrialisation of the region in the modern sense was neither anticipated nor desired.

One initiative to provide additional employment, and help spread a fluent knowledge of the language, was the recommendation to create resident training schools of domestic economy for the purpose of training young Irish-speaking girls as nursery maids and domestic servants. Here, the Commission suggested that free scholarships for girls desirous of becoming nursery maids be provided annually for suitable girls from the Gaeltacht. The course would last ten months and instruction would be given in hygiene; the washing, care and mending of children's clothes; the feeding of infants and young children; simple cooking; recreation (such as stories and first lessons); the study of child mentality and the treatment of sick children. Similar scholarships would be offered to suitable girls wishing to become domestic servants. Both courses would be run in a joint institution that would be established in Dublin, where the demand for persons so trained would be the greatest. Irish-speaking nursery maids and domestic servants who could propagate the language by teaching or speaking it to the children would be particularly sought after, the Commission argued, by families who wanted to make their children fluent Irish speakers.[69] Consideration of the proposal, however, was postponed until the Commission on Technical Education reported to the government.

If the conservation of the Irish language and its spread throughout the country were to be sincerely contemplated, let alone achieved, systematic arrangements had to be made to quell the exodus of Irish speakers from the Gaeltacht and find employment for the people at home. It was a matter of education, economic growth and development. However, the intrinsic value of the local education structure, in part dictated by the economic condition of the region, did not support or open the necessary avenues of advancement. Summarising the education system in the Gaeltacht, the Commission wrote:

> the only type of education available to the Irish Speaking child is Primary education. Intrinsically, this Primary education is defective; either the child gets it in English, which is not his natural language, or he gets it in Irish through teachers who, for the most part, have received their own education through the medium of English, and who have been trained entirely in English Speaking

Institutions. Furthermore, in the latter case, the child is instructed by means of unsuitable books, and with school equipment which has no pertinence to his language, with the result that in the child's mind his own language is given the brand of inferiority. The Irish Speaking child in an Irish Speaking District has little opportunity for Higher education in any language. Through the medium of his own language he has no such opportunity at all. Broadly speaking, the education he gets leads nowhere, except to emigration or to unskilled drudgery at home. It makes no contribution to the solution of the local economic problem, nor to the economic problem of the boy or girl who has to leave his or her native district to find a living outside.[70]

Thus, very few young Irish speakers of the Gaeltacht, for instance, went on to become teachers. The poverty of many families dictated that parents considered it necessary for their children to work the land and supplement the family income from the age of twelve years onwards. As a result, few children remained in the primary schools up to the age of fourteen years and fewer still attended secondary school and obtained the level of education required to enter the Teacher Training Colleges. Similarly, given the fact that the minimum standard required for entrance into minor clerical appointments in the civil service was the Intermediate Certificate – the obtaining of which implied that a boy or girl had spent at least two years in a secondary school receiving higher instruction – only a select few could carve out careers in the commercial life of the country. In an effort to promote further education (and accordingly the spread of the language) the Commission recommended the establishment of free secondary schools in the Gaeltacht. Cumann na nGaedheal, however, rejected the proposal on the grounds that, owing to the pressing economic circumstances of the region, it would be difficult to persuade parents to send their children to secondary school and the scheme 'would not produce results commensurate with the cost'. When 'the parents show desire for such Secondary Education', the government argued, facilities would be provided in advanced classes of the existing primary schools.[71]

Positive discrimination in favour of native speakers in the teaching, policing, army and civil service professions failed to fill the number of places made available by the government. In response to the Gaeltacht Commission's recommendation that at least one army brigade of Irish speakers be formed, the Minister for Defence, Peter Hughes, wrote

It is true that in 1923 when the special recruiting appeal was issued to native speakers the activities of the irregulars and the generally unsettled conditions which then prevailed may have been to a considerable extent responsible for the failure of that appeal but since that date the number of suitable candidates from the Gaeltacht has been disappointingly small. The fact is that if native speakers are to be recruited in the proportion (75%)

recommended by the Commission the educational qualifications demanded from recruits, low as they are at present, would require to be considerably lowered if not almost entirely abolished.[72]

Attempts to gaelicise the newly established police force, An Garda Síochána, met with similar difficulties. The setting aside of 500 places for Irish-speaking recruits in 1923 had received practically no response. As Commissioner of the force, Eoin O'Duffy (despite his own lack of proficiency in the language) advocated the formation and promotion of a bilingual force. One initiative adopted by the government was the introduction of a Linguaphone scheme in 1930. Under the scheme each guard was to receive a self-study Irish language text book, a Linguaphone machine was to be purchased for every station and a set of Linguaphone records were to be shared among groups of three or four stations.[73] Station members were to spend one hour per day learning Irish together and practising everyday conversation and each guard was to devote one full day per week to the study of the language. In addition, the arrival of newly recruited native speakers from the Gaeltacht areas would assist in the instruction of Irish in the stations. If they stuck to the task, O'Duffy was confident that after a period of two or three years' study the members of the force would be competent in the language.[74] However, his later declaration that the acquisition of Irish was no longer a matter of patriotic choice 'but one of stern necessity for those who intend to remain in the Garda' provoked much resentment among some members of the force now compelled to study the language and threatened with dismissal if they were unable to master it.[75] As the 1930s and 1940s wore on, the Linguaphones, as Comerford put it, began to gather dust.[76]

Notwithstanding O'Duffy's claim that 'there are hundreds of men in the guards today who would not have the remotest chance of admission were it not for their knowledge of Irish',[77] according to McNiffe's figures the number of native speakers admitted to the force between 1923 and 1932 represented only 5 per cent of the total number of recruits.[78] Despite a general feeling of goodwill towards the language, the shortage of Irish-speaking guards in the force led to fluency in the language becoming associated with banishment to remote areas to staff the Gaeltacht stations with little hope of transfer. In 1927, one guard stationed in Connemara wrote:

> The áras [station] is four miles from the nearest church, eight miles from the nearest railway station, twenty miles from the nearest doctor, nineteen miles from the nearest District Court, thirty three miles from the nearest District H.Q. ... thirty six miles from the nearest Divisional H.Q. [and] 99 per cent of the people speak no English at all. There is no field for hurling or football.[79]

When the Galway West division of the Garda Síochána was designated an all-Irish division in 1934, Eamon Broy, the new commissioner, wrote to the Department of Justice requesting that a special bonus of 10 per cent be added to the salary of each member transferred to the new Division. Explaining his reasons for advocating such a financial inducement, Broy stated:

> As these Gaeltacht stations are for the most part situated in backward areas devoid of social amenities, facilities for study or opportunities of earning reward or promotion, it will be readily understood how a knowledge of Irish has come to be regarded as a 'one-way ticket to professional stagnation'. If the new Division is to be a success, the members allocated there must not be victimised or penalised on account of their knowledge of Irish. Only a bonus such as that suggested will ensure this.[80]

In the end the Department agreed to a bonus of 7½ per cent, to be terminated on a guard's transfer from the Division. However, within the force, notwithstanding the fact that it had become a prerequisite for promotion, the development of a sound working knowledge of the language was often seen to be more of a hindrance than a help.

The prestige of the Irish language was low. As Cosgrave readily admitted, it had become 'in the minds of many a badge of poverty and backwardness'.[81] In his statement to the Commission, Fr S. J. Walsh described how one would-be emigrant from the Aran Islands was recently turned back from Cobh 'because he didn't know English, and he was quite an intelligent boy otherwise'.[82] Seán Ó Ceallacháin, Secretary, Galway Chamber of Commerce, in his evidence stated that

> A doctor with a large practice, much of it in the Gaeltacht, told me that though he could speak Irish fluently, he never used it among the Irish-speaking population. When asked why, he said that if he spoke Irish the people would never again have any respect for him, that they would look upon him as being as bad as themselves. He said that the Irish speaker had great respect for those who spoke English, but none for those who spoke Irish.[83]

English remained the language of business, the language of politics, the language of the courts and the language of America. 'Irish is dying', the Department of Education contested, 'because the people of the Gaeltacht think that Irish and poverty, Irish and social inferiority are inextricably connected. They will continue to think so until the Government proves conclusively, not merely by its words but by its acts, its appointments, salaries, use of Irish as a real language, etc., that Irish is the superior language socially and economically, in other words that Irish pays.'[84]

Without the financial provision for adequate economic regeneration, Cumann na nGaedheal's scheme for the education, recruitment and expansion of the Gaeltacht and its Gaeilgeoirí was completely unviable. While the government supported the Commission's recommendations for implementing the use of Irish in the official administration of the Gaeltacht districts, in reality, the lack of Irish experts throughout the state departments at a senior level greatly impeded their successful introduction. According to Ó Tuathaigh, as late as 1959 'over one-third of the Civil Service had little or no Irish, while in Gaeltacht areas almost half the public servants were incompetent in Irish'.[85] Thus, placing its reliance for the linguistic recovery on the children of the country, their teachers and the Gaeltacht poor was hopelessly ambitious. 'It was a wild innumerate dream.'[86] Recognising this fact, the Department of Education, in its report to the Executive Council, wrote:

> When all is said and done there can be little doubt that the problem of the Gaeltacht is at root an economic one and that the Gaelicising of officials and even of teachers and schools will be but a superficial remedy for the decay of Irish if the economic problem remains unsolved and emigration continues to deplete the Irish speaking areas at the present fatal rate ... If this should happen and the Gaeltacht population continues to disappear by emigration at the present rate it is clear that this century will see the death of the Irish language as a real living tongue in spite of the utmost efforts that can be made by the Department of Education to save it in the Schools.[87]

That the use of Irish should be made more general in every phase of Irish business, social, political and intellectual life was a prerequisite of the revival. Where priest, guard and shopkeeper led, so the logic went, others would follow. The essential hypocrisy of the government's policy, as Lee argued, 'occurred less in the area of compulsory Irish in the schools than in the failure to provide opportunity, or obligation, for the regular use of Irish subsequently'.[88] Irish as the school language would never be sufficient for revival. A commercial, material interest in the language had to be fostered. It had to be elevated to a position of economic rather than nationalistic or cultural importance in Irish society. Yet as long as English remained the language of government officials – pension officers, medical officers, engineers, Land Commission officials, agricultural and fishery instructors and inspectors and the like – as long as it remained the language of business, commerce and, particularly, employment, the gradual flow and spread of Irish from the Gaeltacht to the surrounding areas could not be achieved.

The position of Galway city was a classic case in point. It was one of the few urban areas in the Free State in which Irish was commonly used and which had a large Gaeltacht area at its doorstep. As an important administrative, educational and commercial centre, the city, as the Commission recognised, had a unique opportunity 'for becoming an intellectual rallying ground for the language'.[89] The influence of state policy was felt to some degree in the city with the establishment of an Irish-speaking battalion of the army, and the foundation of an Irish-language theatre, An Taibhdhearc, by Micheál MacLiammóir in 1928. However, Irish was seldom used by the officials of the local political bodies. In 1925 only five members of the higher staff of Galway County Council were capable of conversing in Irish.[90] In 1928, the defeat of a proposal by Councillor John Burke, at a meeting of the Urban District Council, that the name of Galway be changed to the original Irish name of Gaillimh prompted one reader of the *Connacht Tribune* to ask: 'Does Galway detest Irish so much that it will not have the Irish rendering of the name?'[91] The principal objection among the council members was that the language was not considered sufficiently modern to justify its revival. In 1929 an article in the *Nation* criticised what it saw as the failure of Galway County Council to promote the Irish language, on account of its members' own lack of proficiency.

> Galway is one of the capitals of the Gaeltacht. Seven years ago the machinery of Government in the Twenty-Six Counties came into the hands of men who were so imbued with the Gaelic spirit that they could only sign their names, to proclamations and decrees and what not, in Gaelic. The Gaelicising work of these men was illustrated at a meeting last week of the Galway County Council. 'Is anyone on the staff capable of doing the correspondence through the medium of Irish?' asked Mr. Gerald Bartley, one of the members. 'I think not,' said the Assistant Secretary. That the Council which maintains itself by the rates gathered from Irish speakers should at this time of the day be an anglicising influence is surely the last word in irony.[92]

One important suggestion made by the Gaeltacht Commission was its recommendation that steps be taken to develop University College Galway (UCG) as an Irish-speaking university.[93] In 1925, at a conference attended by representatives of the Governing Body of the College and the Department of Education, the important service that UCG could render to the revival of the Irish language, if it were developed into an Irish-speaking centre of university education, was already recognised. However, the exclusion of the college from the University Education (Agricultural and Dairy Science) Act 1926 led to accusations of unfair discrimination by the government against the western college. Under the new act the Faculty of Agriculture in University College Dublin (UCD) was extended, the College of Science was amalgamated with UCD and a Faculty of Dairy Science was established at University College Cork (UCC). No provision was made for UCG, and while substantial grants were approved for Cork and Dublin no additional funds were allocated to Galway. In June 1926 a large representative meeting was held in the

Town Hall, Galway, to protest against the omission of UCG from the Act; to appeal for better financial provision for the maintenance and development of the college; to press the claim for equal treatment with the Dublin and Cork colleges; and to demand that the permanency of UCG be definitely assured.[94] Objecting to the perceived financial neglect of the college, the *Connacht Tribune* questioned whether the people of Galway should be satisfied with the 'few crumbs of consolation' that were occasionally being thrown their way.[95] Addressing the meeting Patrick Hogan TD declared:

> I do not want to see University College, Galway closed down. I am not going to stand for its closing down. I will give Dr Anderson, President of the College, my personal assurances that I know of no intrigues against University College, Galway, nor of any wire-pulling behind the scenes in connection with it, and I assure him that there was not and is not any intention of closing it down.[96]

Despite Hogan's assurances that there was no foundation to the allegations that the government intended to downgrade the college or abolish any of its Faculties, in the Dáil T. J. O'Connell, Labour TD for Galway, protested: 'it seems to be the policy that if Galway College is a poor college, and if its resources are limited, then it must remain so. It is "to those who have much, much shall be given" – that seems to be the policy of the Government with regard to the constituent colleges.'[97]

In his evidence to the Gaeltacht Commission, Liam Ó Briain, Professor of Romance Languages, UCG, an advocate of the Irish language and later Chairman of An Taibhdhearc, Galway, discussed in detail the proposal that the College had submitted to the Department of Education in 1925 for the development of an all-Irish university. Ó Briain explained that the ability of the college to grow into a completely Irish-speaking institution would depend on the progress of the development of the use of Irish in the schools and the number of Irish-speaking students proceeding to university studies. However, as the teaching of Irish progressed in the schools, the college would be willing to keep pace with the increasing number of students anxious to attend their lectures in Irish. Nonetheless, if UCG was to become an all-Irish college it would be necessary to acquire an Irish-speaking staff. Despite having a number of Irish language enthusiasts in the college, the current position, according to Ó Briain, was that of the twenty or so academic staff members 'six or seven know Irish more or less, but most of these would not be good enough to do anything in regard to the language'; only a small percentage of students coming in to the college were native speakers; and the bulk of staff members were 'middle-aged men and engaged in their avocations', and it was believed that if they could not teach through Irish now they would never be able to do so.[98] Additionally, until the development of teaching subjects through Irish in the schools was brought to such a standard that Third Level students would wish to be taught through Irish, the numbers of students for such courses would be small. In all likelihood, as Ó Briain explained, the probability was that Irish-speaking lecturers, having being hired, would have no classes to teach for some time. When questioned on whether a professor who had no classes to teach would continue working at his subject, Ó Briain responded: 'There is no compulsion like that. There is only a pious hope at the time of his appointment.' On the suggestion that the new teaching assistants could be required to provide textbooks, Ó Briain answered: 'No university compels a man to write a book.'[99]

In presenting his evidence, Ó Briain also argued that the efforts towards extending the use of Irish in the official administration of the Free State were too scattered and haphazard to be effective. To resolve this problem he recommended the establishment of an institute at UCG where the work of translating and preparing texts could be coordinated and an official language developed and practised. The institute would group a number of students and workers together who, aided by the Celtic Studies Faculty, would be trained in the use of Irish in intellectual work. In addition, the Irish-speaking staff could form a body of language specialists, prepare students for civil service examinations, and assist the Faculty of Education in training national teachers to teach in Irish.[100] In effect, the college, as well as providing instruction through Irish, could be made a centre for the scholastic study of the language.

Despite the recommendations of the Gaeltacht Commission, Minister for Finance Ernest Blythe was not convinced of the commitment of the staff of UCG to remodel the organisation and workings of the college to carry out the functions of an Irish-speaking university. Speaking in the Dáil, he declared,

> I am not satisfied that it [the college] really cares a great lot about the Irish language at all … there is no 'down' on University College, Galway, but the facts of the situation must be realised. As it stands, it is not an institution of the importance of University College, Dublin or University College, Cork.[101]

Attacking the pace of change proposed by the university, Blythe contended that the only thing the Governing Authorities of the College were in earnest about was getting money and labelled the university a 'toy' college. Reacting to the minister's comments, Alexander Anderson, President of the UCG, stated that 'if anyone thinks that a sudden and radical change of this kind is practicable at present, he must be the victim of educational hallucinations'.[102]

UCG was the smallest of the three constituent colleges. In 1925–26 it had 242 registered students. This compares to a figure of 534 students in UCC and 1,209 students in UCD. However, by 1930–31 the number of students in UCG had risen to 555 compared to 617 in UCC and 1,684 in UCD. In five years, the number of students attending UCG had more than doubled in size.[103] In 1929, under the University College Galway Act, the college was given special statutory responsibility for the provision of university instruction through Irish and its annual grant was increased from £12,000 to £28,000.[104] Nevertheless, it would take some considerable time and significant financial investment to establish even a partial Irish-speaking university. In 1933, a memorandum compiled by the Department of Education on the proportion of students conducting their studies through Irish in UCG stated that out of a total of 93 Arts students, 53 were educated entirely through English and 40 were taking at least one subject through Irish; all 39 Education Diploma students and 100 of 116 Higher Diploma students were taking subjects through Irish; and of the 69 Science students, 38 were educated through English and 31 were taking at least one subject through Irish. Facilities for the students of Commerce (156), Engineering (40), Medicine (82) and Law (6) to be taught through Irish had not yet been provided for.[105]

Despite some local protest at the requirement for the college to fulfil a special obligation before additional funding would be made available by the government, the 1929 Act safeguarded the survival of the Connacht college. In this respect the language did pay. But neither Galway city nor UCG emerged as an all-Irish-speaking urban centre of commerce and university education. Irish did become a working language of the college, but English remained the dominant medium. Additionally, some of the teaching staff were criticised for allowing academic politics to distract them from their efforts to promote the language. In February 1933, a disgruntled George Thompson (Seoirse MacTomais), UCG, informed Blythe that

> instead of working away quietly, providing textbooks and training their pupils well, most of them seem to prefer agitating and intriguing on the Academic Council – to get themselves the title of professor, to ban hockey, and the like. They don't understand the function of a University.[106]

However, such sentiments must be understood in the political context of the time and with an eye to the immediate political purposes they were meant to serve.

Addressing the socio-economic concerns of the Gaeltacht was fundamental to safeguarding the region as a reservoir of the Irish language. Nonetheless, while the government endorsed the main body of the Gaeltacht Commission's report, the heavy expenditure involved in giving effect to the suggested recommendations impeded the implementation of many, if not most, of the schemes. Additionally, the benefit of these measures was not felt for a considerable time in the distressed areas. Ultimately, they proved insufficient to stem the tide of emigration. In effect, the language remained a symbol of cultural triumphalism. In the 1930s, the vision of Seán MacEntee, Fianna Fáil Minister for Finance, of developing UCG into an 'Irish-speaking Oxford' and cultivating Galway city into an 'Irish-speaking Heidelberg' was fanciful to say the least.[107] Without the determined financial backing of the state, the incongruity of the description becomes manifest. Perhaps Ó Briain's whimsical suggestion to the Commission that an incentive be offered to parents to teach Irish to their children at home, or that adults should be offered money to go into the schools to talk Irish to the children, or better yet that the government give back the one shilling to old age pensioners on condition that they teach the language to their children, might have had more impact! Perhaps, as Frank Fahy sardonically reflected, the best thing the government could have done to revive the Irish language was to ban it.[108]

Within Irish society, there was an obvious sympathy for the economic plight of the west and the depopulation of the Gaeltacht areas. Yet there was also a clear sense of social detachment. In an article in October 1929, the *Nation* wrote

> Here on the Atlantic, the dwindling remnant of the Gael carried on the unequal struggle against Nature, against the very elements. We are aghast at the sight. Soon we forget, we are far away. And so the Gaeltacht is lonelier than ever, further away than ever … Hence, it is that the Gaeltacht is far nearer to New York, to which it is bound by every tie of affection, than it is to Dublin. A fishing disaster, or an outbreak of fever, recalls to us the existence of this silent forgotten quarter of a million of our people. So silent it is, the officials in Dublin scarcely hear its heart beating. The heart of the Gaeltacht beats for America, towards which its children's eyes are turned from birth.[109]

At the Cumann na nGaedheal party Árd Fheis in 1927, Cosgrave declared: 'We realise that it is a national duty to assist this area to raise itself to an economic level.'[110] However, remuneration as well as patriotism was needed to rouse the west, and regional expectations exceeded national performance.

Notes

1 *Connacht Tribune*, 18 Feb. 1922.
2 Report by Dr Casey to Clifden Rural District Council on 16 Jan. 1924. Cited *ibid.*, 19 Jan. 1924.
3 Minutes of Clifden Rural District Council, 16 Feb. 1924, GCCA, Clifden RDC minute books, G01/7/14. Such sentiments may not have met with the approval of certain members of the Cumann na nGaedheal government. See, for instance, the oft-cited remarks of Patrick McGilligan, Minister for Industry and Commerce, in the Dáil in 1924 that 'People may have to die in this country and die of starvation.' McGilligan it must be stated, did not desire this outcome, but he also argued that 'it is not the function of the Government to provide work'. DE, vol. 9, 30 Oct. 1924.
4 Daly, *Industrial Development and Irish National Identity, 1922–1939*, p. 177.
5 John Dignan was appointed Bishop of Clonfert on 24 March 1924. The vacancy arose when Thomas O'Doherty, previously of Clonfert, succeeded Thomas O'Dea in the Galway diocese.
6 John Dignan to Joseph Walsh, 21 Feb. 1925, TAA, Gilmartin papers, Box 178, B4/8-ii/28.
7 *Connacht Tribune*, 24 Jan. 1925.
8 NAI, DT, S4278/A. A hundredweight (cwt) = 112 lb or 50.8 kg. '£. s. d.' signifies pounds, shillings and pence in 'old money' (pre-1971). There were twelve pence to the shilling and twenty shillings to the pound: 1 shilling (s) = 12 pence (d); 1 pound (£) = 20 shillings (s) or 240 pence (d).
9 The Roger Casement Relief Fund had been responsible for providing warm meals for school children in the Gaeltacht for a number of years. In 1925, government assistance and further charitable relief efforts helped maintain the scheme whose funds were wholly inadequate to deal with the level of distress. In 1930, the School Meals (Gaeltacht) Bill introduced a £5,000 annual subvention for the Galway Board of Health to allow bread, cocoa, condensed milk, jam and sugar to be given daily to school children in much of west Galway. Cited in Ó Fathartaigh, 'Cumann na nGaedheal, the land issue and west Galway 1923–1932', p. 168.
10 Letter from Violet Connolly to the editor of the *Connacht Tribune*, 21 Mar. 1925. The Save the Children Fund (London) established a relief centre in Clifden to distribute food and clothing to children under school age.
11 Letter from Gilmartin to the Manchester and District Irish Distress Fund, 8 Feb. 1925, TAA, Gilmartin papers, Box 178, B4/8-ii/23.
12 Fr Curley to Joseph Walsh, 24 Apr. 1925, *ibid.*, Box 178, B4/8-ii/32.
13 Fr Healy to Joseph Walsh, 30 Mar. 1925, *ibid*.
14 TAA, Gilmartin papers, Box 178, B4/8-ii/32. Note that the prices of similar items, for example the price of milk, vary from bill to bill. One possible explanation may be that the cans of milk differed in size. Another possibility may be the even nature of the bills submitted. The supplier may have

rounded his figures either up or down to provide a neat, even bill – note how the total amounts for the bills above come to two pounds fifteen shillings and two pounds even.

15 Letters received by Gilmartin and Walsh confirming donations to the distress fund, *ibid.*, Box 178, B4/8-ii/23.

16 'Disposal of fund subscribed from private sources for the relief of distress in the west of Ireland 1924–25.' Memo from F. J. Meyrick, Sec. Dept. of Agriculture, to W. T. Cosgrave, 23 Sept. 1925, NAI, DT, S1693.

17 Fr White to Joseph Walsh, 29 Mar. 1925, TAA, Gilmartin papers, Box 178, B4/8-ii/29.

18 F. J. Meyrick to Gilmartin, 10 Mar. 1925, *ibid.*, Box 178, B4/8-ii/25.

19 'Disposal of fund subscribed from private sources for the relief of distress in the west of Ireland 1924–25.' Meyrick to Cosgrave, 23 Sept. 1925, NAI, DT, S1693.

20 *Sunday Times*, 15 Feb. 1925, NAI, DT, S1693.

21 Fr S. J. Walsh (PP, Inis Mór) to Joseph Walsh, 11 Feb. 1925, TAA, Gilmartin papers, Box 178, B4/8-ii/29.

22 *Irish Truth*, 14 Feb. 1925, NAI, DT, S1693.

23 NAI, DT, S1693.

24 *Ibid.*, DT, S4278/A.

25 *Ibid.*

26 *Ibid.*

27 *Irish Times*, 18 Mar. 1931.

28 Speech by Hogan in the Town Hall, Galway, Jan. 1927. Cited in *Connacht Tribune*, 29 Jan. 1927.

29 Letter from the abbess of Kylemore Castle, Connemara, forwarded by R. J. Duggan (Turf Accountant) to W. T. Cosgrave, 11 Nov. 1926, NAI, DT, S7440/A. The Public Health Act 1874 prohibited the keeping of animals in residential dwellings, but it was very difficult to enforce. For details of the Act see Caitriona Clear, *Social Change and Everyday Life in Ireland, 1850–1922* (Manchester, 2007), p. 94.

30 *The Commission on the Gaeltacht: Minutes of Evidence* (Dublin, 1926), evidence of Dr Bartley O'Beirne, recorded on 3 June 1925, pp. 4–5.

31 Kelp burning was a labour-intensive commercial industry of varying fortunes that involved the cutting, drying and burning of seaweed to obtain the ash known as kelp. The calcined ashes were a source of alkali first used to make soda for soap, then utilised in glass manufacturing and later sold to manufacturers of iodine.

32 Supplement of *An Claidheamh Soluis (Fáinne an Lae)* Dec. 1926, NAI, DT, S7439.

33 *Connacht Tribune*, 24 Jan. 1925.

34 James P. Murray, *Galway: A Medico-Social History* (Galway, 1994), pp. 142–3. The main portion of the village was demolished between 1932 and 1934.

35 *Connacht Tribune*, 25 Feb. 1928.

36 Murray, *Galway: A Medico-Social History*, p. 142.

37 *Connacht Tribune*, 15 Aug. 1925.

38 *Ibid.*, 1 Oct. 1932.

39 *Ibid.*, 23 Aug. 1930.

40 Mary E. Daly, *The Buffer State: The Historical Roots of the Department of the Environment* (Dublin, 1997), pp. 142, 144.

41 Murray, *Galway: A Medico-Social History*, pp. 142–3.

42 *Connacht Sentinel*, 12 Jan. 1932.

43 *Connacht Tribune*, 14 Feb. 1931.

44 Ó Fathartaigh, 'Cumann na nGaedheal, the land issue and west Galway 1923–1932', pp. 167–8.

45 Report by Padraig Ó Máille and Maitú de Buitleír, Gaeltacht Inspectors, on 'Condition of the Gaeltacht', 20 Sept. 1933, NAI, DT, S7447.

46 Oliver MacDonagh, *States of Mind: A Study of Anglo-Irish Conflict 1780–1980* (London, 1983), pp. 117–19.

47 M. A. G. Ó Tuathaigh, 'The state and the language since 1922', *Irish Times*, 19 Apr. 1977.

48 Letter from W. T. Cosgrave to Richard Mulcahy, 4 Mar. 1925. *Report of the Commission on the Gaeltacht* (Dublin, 1926), p. 3. For more on the structure and composition of the Commission, see Neil Buttimer, 'The Irish language, 1921–84', in Hill (ed.), *A New History of Ireland, vol. VII: Ireland 1921–84*, p. 545.

49 Cited in *Connacht Tribune*, 29 Jan. 1927.

50 *Census of Ireland 1926*, General Report, vol. X, p. 130.

51 *Ibid.*, Irish Language, vol. VIII, pp. 4, 5, 8. Fíor Gaeltacht refers to Irish-speaking districts where more than 80 per cent of the population is Irish-speaking. Breac Gaeltacht refers to partly Irish-speaking districts where 25 to 79 per cent of the population is Irish-speaking. Together they constitute the Gaeltacht.

52 Cited in *The Commission on the Gaeltacht: Minutes of Evidence*, evidence of Frank Fahy, TD, recorded on 16 June 1925, p. 16.

53 The Department of Local Government and Public Health, the Department of Industry and Commerce and the Department of the Fisheries submitted their reports by the end of 1926. However, the Department of Finance and the Department of Agriculture did not complete their reports until January 1927; the Department of Education not until 25 February 1927; and the Department of Justice and the Land Commission not until April 1927. NAI, DT, S7440/A.

54 *Report of the Commission on the Gaeltacht*, p. 47.

55 Micheál Ó Fathartaigh, 'Cumann na nGaedheal, sea fishing and west Galway, 1923–32', *Irish Historical Studies*, vol. 36, no. 141 (May, 2008), p. 77.

56 Cited in *Connacht Tribune*, 8 Mar. 1924.

57 Cited in Ó Fathartaigh, 'Cumann na nGaedheal, sea fishing and west Galway, 1923–32', p. 82.

58 *The Commission on the Gaeltacht: Minutes of Evidence*, evidence of Fr S. J. Walsh, recorded on 20 Aug. 1925, p. 1.

59 Ó Fathartaigh, 'Cumann na nGaedheal, sea fishing and west Galway, 1923–32', pp. 80–1.

60 *Report of the Commission on the Gaeltacht*, pp. 46–50.

61 *Statement of Government Policy on the Recommendations of the Commission* (Dublin, 1928), p. 26.
62 Speech by Fr. S. J. Walsh in the Town Hall, Galway, Jan. 1927. Cited in *Connacht Tribune*, 29 Jan. 1927.
63 Ó Fathartaigh, 'Cumann na nGaedheal, sea fishing and west Galway, 1923–32', p. 85.
64 John Cunningham, *Labour in the West of Ireland: Working Life and Struggle 1890–1914* (Belfast, 1995), p. 77.
65 William L. Micks, *An Account of the Constitution, Administration and Dissolution of the Congested Districts Board for Ireland from 1891–1923* (Dublin, 1925), p. 67.
66 *Report of the Commission on the Gaeltacht*, pp. 51–4.
67 *Statement of Government Policy on the Recommendations of the Commission*, p. 27. In 1930, the Department of Finance sanctioned the establishment of a 'Gaeltacht industries depot' at the old military barracks at Beggar's Bush in Dublin. Buttimer, 'The Irish language, 1921–84', p. 552.
68 Lecture by Dr Seamus O'Brien to the Galway Chamber of Commerce, 1927. Cited in the *Nation*, 14 Jan. 1928.
69 *Report of the Commission on the Gaeltacht*, p. 55.
70 *Ibid.*, p. 11.
71 *Statement of Government Policy on the Recommendations of the Commission*, pp. 8–9.
72 Report of the Department of Justice on the recommendations of the Gaeltacht Commission, submitted on 16 Apr. 1927, NAI, DT, S7440/A.
73 Report of the Department of Justice, 23 June 1936, *ibid.*, S9303.
74 Liam McNiffe, *A History of the Garda Síochána* (Dublin, 1997), p. 128.
75 Fearghal McGarry, *Eoin O'Duffy: A Self-Made Hero* (Oxford, 2005), pp. 144–5; McNiffe, *A History of the Garda Síochána*, p. 128.
76 R. V. Comerford, *Ireland* (London, 2003), p. 146.
77 McNiffe, *A History of the Garda Síochána*, p. 124.
78 *Ibid.*, p. 125.
79 Cited *ibid.*, p. 127.
80 Statement from Eamon Broy to Sec. Dept. of Justice, 7 June 1934, NAI, DT, S5975/A.
81 Cosgrave to Mulcahy, 4 Mar. 1925. *Report of the Commission on the Gaeltacht*, p. 3.
82 *The Commission on the Gaeltacht: Minutes of Evidence*, evidence of Fr S. J. Walsh recorded on 20 Aug. 1925, p. 3.
83 *Ibid.*, evidence of Seán Ó Ceallacháin, recorded on 1 Sept. 1925, p. 11.
84 Memo from Eoin MacNeill, Minister of Education, on 'The Gaelicising of Ireland', 1924, NAI, DT, S3717.
85 M. A. G. Ó Tuathaigh, 'Language, literature and culture in Ireland since the war', in J. J. Lee (ed.), *Ireland 1945–70* (Dublin, 1979), p. 114.
86 MacDonagh, *States of Mind*, p. 122.
87 Report by the Department of Education on the recommendations of the Gaeltacht Commission, 25 Feb. 1927, NAI, DT, S7440/A.

88 Lee, *Ireland 1912–1985*, p. 135.
89 *Report of the Commission on the Gaeltacht*, p. 58.
90 *The Commission on the Gaeltacht: Minutes of Evidence*, evidence of Dr Bartley O'Beirne, recorded on 3 June 1925, p. 1.
91 *Connacht Tribune*, 4 Feb., 7 Apr. 1928.
92 *Nation*, 19 Oct. 1929.
93 *Report of the Commission on the Gaeltacht*, p. 27.
94 *Connacht Tribune*, 26 June, 3 July 1926.
95 *Ibid.*, 5 June 1926.
96 *Ibid.*, 3 July 1926.
97 DE, vol. 16, 9 June 1926.
98 *The Commission on the Gaeltacht: Minutes of Evidence*, evidence of Liam Ó Briain, recorded on 24 June 1925, p. 9.
99 *Ibid.*, p. 10.
100 *Ibid.*, pp. 8–10.
101 DE, vol. 16, 9 June 1926.
102 *Ibid.*; Alexander Anderson to the Executive Council, 11 June 1926, NAI, DT, S2407.
103 Memo compiled by Department of Education, 24 Apr. 1933, NAI, DT, S10856/A. John Coolahan lists the number of students attending UCD as 1,105 students in 1925–26 and 1,542 students in 1930–31. Coolahan, 'Higher education in Ireland, 1908–84', in Hill (ed.), *A New History of Ireland, vol. VII. Ireland 1921–84*, p. 766.
104 University College Galway Act, 1929, NAI, DT S2368. The Act also stipulated that when making staff appointments, once the candidate was declared suitable, provided there was suitability in all other respects with regard to the other candidates, it was the duty of the College to appoint the person who was most competent to discharge his or her duties through Irish.
105 Memo compiled by Department of Education, 24 Apr. 1933, NAI, DT, S10856/A.
106 George Thompson to Ernest Blythe, 8 Feb. 1933, UCDA, Blythe papers, P24/1552.
107 Letter from Seán MacEntee to Eamon de Valera, 22 Aug. 1935, NAI, DT, S9303.
108 *The Commission on the Gaeltacht: Minutes of Evidence*, evidence of Liam Ó Briain, recorded on 24 June 1925, pp. 12–13, and evidence of Frank Fahy, TD, recorded on 16 June 1925, p. 17.
109 *Nation*, 19 Oct. 1929.
110 'Policy of the Cumann na nGaedheal Party', 1927, NAI, DT, S7440/B.

5

Crime, security and morality

Agrarian discontent with the slow and ineffective progress of the Land Commission provided certain possibilities for mobilisation behind republican opposition to the Irish Free State, if the leaders could convincingly demonstrate that the redress of such grievances hinged upon a rejection of the Cumann na nGaedheal government. However, Liam Mellows did not inspire a successor in Galway, or at least not one that would successfully harness the potential for agrarian and political upheaval in Galway as he had done in 1915–16. Neither Sinn Féin nor the IRA managed to exploit the obvious social tensions to effectively mobilise anti-government support or challenge the authority of the state. Sticking to its policy of abstention, Sinn Féin failed to provide a constructive social or economic strategy that might galvanise the local community. The party's weakness was emblematic of the ebb and flow of the power structure within Irish society where control of the Irish revolution had continually oscillated between the politicians and the army. The IRA could have emerged as a central organ of resistance. As Hanley has argued, 'a major part of the IRA's attraction was its paramilitary nature but its real importance lay in its role as a force for opposition to the Irish states rather than in its prospects of actually overthrowing them'.[1] By the end of the civil war, however, the local IRA was in a poor, disorganised condition. The Twomey papers clearly delineate the feeling of dry rot that had set in after the military engagements of the war. The post-civil war IRA was emotionally and militarily punctured.[2] Yet despite military defeat, it still proclaimed its defiance of the new state.

Crime and security

In the districts around Ballinasloe during 1923–24, a group of republicans under the leadership of John (Jack) Keogh and John Downey continued to mount small-scale operations against the state. Keogh was a dominant figure in the anti-treaty IRA in Ballinasloe and had escaped from Athlone barracks in January 1923. The following examples were typical of their campaign. In February 1923 the Civic Guard station at Ahascragh was attacked. Reporting on the incident, the Garda journal wrote that five guards under Sergeant Rodgers had since occupied temporary premises but were visited again by twenty armed men who seized all their private property. A bomb was also thrown at the guards' quarters but it did not cause any damage.[3] On 20 March the Civic Guard station and a large Co-operative store at Laurencetown were burned out. On 7 April a mail car at Laurencetown was robbed, the village of Ahascragh was held up and six RIC pensioners were ordered to leave the district. On 9 April a deputation of traders from Ahascragh informed John Gallagher, District Justice, Ballinasloe, that unless they got protection from the state against raids and looting, they would refuse to pay any further rates or taxes to the government. On 12 April a point-to-point race meeting, due to take place at Redmond Hill, Eyrecourt, was proscribed by Keogh. When the Race Committee (made up of local gentry, large graziers and shopkeepers) realised the race meeting was banned, they sent a deputation to Keogh to request a permit for the running of the event. Their application was refused. On 23 April two guards were held up near Kilconnell. On 25 April the public house of Ellen Killeen in Toher was raided and quantities of money, tobacco, cigarettes, whiskey, chocolate and five suits of clothes were stolen. On the same night the Civic Guard station in Ahascragh was attacked once more, the guards were beaten, and their uniforms and bedding were set alight. A second assault on the Civic Guards took place at the railway station, Ballinasloe. On 22 May the Munster and Leinster Bank, Athenry, was held up and £500 stolen. In June the post offices at Gurtymadden and Tynagh were raided and the ticket money from a dance held at Cappataggle was taken. On 22 September Ballygar station was raided (the items stolen included three truncheons, three sets of handcuffs, five coats, four tunics, six pairs of trousers, two suits of clothing, five suit cases, two watches, three pocket books, two velour hats, a camera, three sets of underwear, a razor, a cardigan and £3 17s 6d in cash). In October the Bank of Ireland, Mountbellew, was held up and £1,020 stolen. On 9 and 17 October the station at Killimore was attacked.[4] Recalling the incident, Sergeant Michael Kealy stated that Keogh 'struck me on the head with his clenched fist ... Downey was at this time standing alongside with a revolver in his hand. Keogh then told me to go to my room to dress as he was going to do a Noel Lemass on me.'[5] Writing to the Criminal Investigation Department (CID), Henry O'Friel demanded that the issue of Keogh's arrest be dealt with as a matter of urgency as his conduct in the locality was creating an impression that the government was powerless to interfere with him.[6] Keogh was eventually captured by the military in Ennis in November 1923. He was sentenced to ten years' penal servitude. He escaped in 1926. Downey was arrested in Aughrim in June 1924.

In east and south Galway, the actions of Keogh's unit underlined the government's lack of practical authority in parts of the county. The courageous strategy of unarmed policing from the autumn of 1922 (originally in the form of the reconstituted Civic Guard and afterward as the remodelled Garda Síochána from mid-1923), paid off in terms of winning public acceptance for the guards.[7] However, as an unarmed force, they were powerless to combat republican armed activities. Guards stationed in more isolated barracks were especially helpless in the face of intimidation and provocation where a significant portion of the population was sympathetic to the republican campaign. One member of the force, burned out repeatedly in a little station in Connemara, wrote to O'Duffy asking:

> How long more am I going to be left in this God-forsaken place? Am I like Dumas's prisoner in the Bastille, to be left here to rot and grow grey in the service, surrounded by squalor and poverty, rocks and bogs, cut adrift from all social amenities and the things that make life worth living?[8]

Despite O'Higgins's own admission in 1924 that soldiers 'make bad policemen' the military had to be relied on to restore law and order. The new police force were neither sufficiently trained nor organised enough to deal with political crime or subversion.[9] However, as residual republican attacks on the state receded, O'Higgins was anxious to remove the continuing presence of the National army from the local towns. If the new state was to progress, it had to demonstrate its capacity to function without the expedients of 'internment without trial, intrusive domestic political surveillance, and the use of the army to dispense justice'.[10] Nevertheless, the gradual withdrawal of the troops exposed the limitations of the police force to cope effectively with armed crime. Writing to O'Higgins on 13 March 1924, Gallagher (District Justice, Ballinasloe) informed the minister that 'the Bank of Ireland in Mountbellew will close down, unless afforded military protection, and the Manager of the National Bank, Ballygar, also informs me that his directors will close down unless the military post is re-established there'.[11] Ultimately, the army would continue to act as a 'surrogate police force' in the fight against political crime until the establishment of the Special Branch of the Garda Síochána in 1925.[12]

Nonetheless, O'Duffy's superb use of propaganda and well-publicised speeches in which the Commissioner extolled the bravery, valour and

resistance of the defenceless police force in the face of IRA armed raids
won public sympathy, stiffened the morale of the force (who often found
themselves billeted in makeshift, unsuitable and substandard accommodation) and elevated the prestige of the guards in the local towns and
villages as the unarmed servants of the people.[13]

In imposing ordinary law, the gradual move to civilian policing was
far more effective. The local guards were particularly active in enforcing
licensing laws, securing prosecutions against publicans and clamping
down on the illegal poitín trade which had expanded during the civil
war. The vigilant policing of the circulation of alcohol in the county
reflected not only the temperance drive of the Commissioner, but also
the concerns of both the government and the Catholic Church over the
alleged dearth of sobriety in rural Irish society. Yet, in the west of Ireland,
the distillation and distribution of poitín was a vital source of income
(a factor that seemed to have been ignored by the government). In one
raid on 1 June 1923, thirty-five bottles, ten one-gallon cans, seven petrol
tins and eight barrels of poitín were uncovered in Cashel, Connemara.[14]
Poitín distilled in the isolated districts of Connemara was also easily
transported to other localities. Commenting on the trade in east Galway,
Gallagher reported:

> Poteen is not manufactured anywhere in the area, but large quantities
> are brought in turf boats from Connemara to Kinvara, Newquay and
> Oranmore where Area 13 skirts the eastern shore of Galway Bay, and
> from these places it is sold in Craughwell, Ardrahan, Gort and Athenry. I
> have instructed the Civic Guard at or near these places to do their utmost
> to catch publicans or others dealing in the poteen trade, and if any of these
> are brought before me I am determined to inflict fines that will operate as
> a deterrent to the carrying on in future of this demoralising and degrading
> business.[15]

District Justices in County Clare insisted that the guards put a watch on
the coast line from Galway to Ballyvaughan to prevent the distribution
of the illicit spirit from Connemara.[16] Prosecutions and the infliction
of heavy fines had a sharp effect. For the six months from 1 March to
31 August 1923, forty-one prosecutions and thirty-two convictions for
illicit distillation were made in County Galway. This compares to a figure of eighty prosecutions and fifty-three convictions in County Donegal
for the same period.[17] The higher figure, however, may not necessarily
imply a stronger trade in Donegal but perhaps a weaker aptitude for
avoiding detection.

Similarly, the guards were successful in curbing opportunistic criminality and made a number of prosecutions for acts of larceny. Particular

attention was paid to the recovery of items looted from local RIC barracks, Coast Guard stations, Civic Guard stations, big houses and abandoned residences during the war of independence and the civil war. For instance, investigating the location of furniture stolen from Oliver St John Gogarty's burned-out residence in Renvyle, Connemara, H. J. Keegan, Chief Superintendent, Galway, discovered in the less salubrious surroundings of a small house owned by Mrs Ruddy in Tully, a few miles from Renvyle, an oval-backed, gold-framed armchair and four dining-room chairs crafted by Woods of Dublin, the value of which the occupier could not have afforded and whose matching counterparts were among the pieces of furniture saved from the fire at Renvyle House.[18] In north Galway, it was reported that carts could be seen night and day taking away personal effects from Castlegrove House. Subsequently, in a number of searches of private premises in Tuam, the guards recovered a deer's head, two fox heads, an oval mirror and a motor car.[19] In another case, valuable furniture had been stolen from the lodge at Doohulla, Clifden. Reporting on their attempts to retrieve the appropriated items in 1924, Inspector Twomey, Garda Síochána, Clifden, claimed that the looted property appeared to have been thrown into the sea, as during searches made by the guards they found a sofa and part of a mahogany table on the beach.[20]

The guards were also directed to curtail the running of local unlicensed dance halls, described by O'Duffy as 'orgies of dissipation'.[21] In this they were fervently supported by Thomas O'Doherty, Bishop of Galway. A police report of a country dance held on the top floor of a barn in Monivea (east Galway) is an illustration of the type of dances publicly denounced by the bishop.

> I visited the place at about 11 p.m.; the dance was in full swing at this time, there being about fifty couples present. The charge for admission was 1s for gentlemen and 6d for ladies ... The loft where the dance was held is an oblong building about 20 feet by 45 feet. It is on the top floor of a barn and entry is by means of a trap door up a rather shaky ladder. Only one person can go up or come down at a time. This is the only entrance or exit. The floor is held up by means of props underneath. There is no ventilation or sanitary accommodation of any kind attached to the place.[22]

In 1924 O'Doherty declared that these types of public dances, frequently held on Saturday nights, were 'an abomination and a moral danger to the whole community'.[23] In 1925 he forbade the organisation of such dances in the diocese.

> In 1924 I was hopeful that a public protest from the bishop of these dioceses would suffice to end the evil. As my hopes have been somewhat

disappointed, I now formally forbid every Catholic in these dioceses to organise or take part in these Saturday night dances. My reasons you already know, and they have the approval of every right-minded man and woman. Should this formal prohibition be ignored I shall make the offence referred to a reserved sin, in the first place; and if this is not sufficient I shall use further powers which Christ and His Church have placed in my hands. For I must protect the people committed to my care from the ravening wolves who would make havoc of their souls.[24]

As has been well documented, it was not simply the dance hall, but the accompaniments associated with it – drinking, company-keeping, the motor car and late night ramblings – that, in the eyes of the Church, proved the greatest threat to sexual morality. Commenting on the dangers of the motor car, parked in the vicinity of the dance hall in badly lighted streets or on the dark country roads, O'Doherty warned that 'evil men ... come from outside the parish and outside the city ... to lure girls from the town to go for motor drives into the country, and you know what happens ... it is not for the benefit of the motor drive. It is for something infinitely worse.'[25] Dancing and the rural dance hall became 'a classic terrain of fantasy projection and pseudo-knowledge involving a potent brew of alleged sources of evil and degradation'.[26]

In the 1930s, when applications for dance hall licences were coming before the courts, Thomas Gilmartin, Archbishop of Tuam, urged his parish priests to try to ensure that certain limitations be imposed by the local District Justices before a licence was granted. Such restrictions included a closing hour of 11 p.m.; that no dances be permitted on Saturday nights or on the eve of holidays; that no all-night dances be allowed under any circumstances; that no occasional alcohol licences be granted; that dance halls be restricted in number according to the needs of the locality; that no licence be given for a hall reported by the guards to be lacking in sanitary accommodation or in hygienic requirements; that no girls under eighteen years be allowed to attend licensed dance halls; that the parking of motor cars in the immediate vicinity of dance halls be prohibited; and that attendance at a licensed dance hall be restricted to persons from the parish or from a given locality.[27] Their efforts met with limited success. In 1933 Monsignor Edward D'Alton, Tuam, requested that provision be made in the impending Public Dance Halls legislation to allow the clergy and the parents of local girls to enter and inspect the dance halls during the time of the dance. His request was refused by the Minister for Justice, P. J. Ruttledge, who responded that 'it would be most unusual to confer such powers on anyone except a servant of the State, or of a local authority'.[28]

Moral power

Galway society's occasions of sin were no different from those of the rest of the country. They included indecent company-keeping, mixed bathing, immodest dress, suggestive dancing, bad reading and sinful intercourse. What emerged in particular from the early 1920s was the belief strongly evident in the bishops' pronouncements on sexuality that 'the real threat to chastity and sexual morality resided in the bodies of women'.[29] Speaking in 1924, O'Doherty attested:

> Let there be no mistake about it. People talk a lot of nonsense about innocent girls, and about seduction and this and that and the other. The blame lies upon the girls themselves. I will say that from what I know and from what I have heard. Talk of innocent girls! Those wretches who fall, unfortunate people that they are, they are not innocent and they were not misled.[30]

If it were not for 'the purity of our Irish boys', he continued, 'there would be far more scandals than there are to-day'. He then advised fathers of disobedient girls to 'lay the lash upon their backs'.[31] Of course not all Galway girls were regarded as 'wretches'. There were, naturally, many 'fine girls' who rather than frequenting cold, rough and often dirty dance halls were encouraged to sit in at night with a good book.[32] If their attraction to dancing was physical exercise, O'Doherty recommended that they 'go out and skip'.[33] Thomas Gilmartin, in his 1924 Lenten pastoral, wrote that 'when girls make themselves cheap, boys will value them accordingly. Boys become disillusioned about girls that make toys of themselves. As people easily get tired of toys, too much unlawful pleasure ends in disgust.'[34] These girls, he contended, by offering such inducements to sensuality, were keeping the young men of the diocese from getting married.[35] Responding to similar pronouncements made by the archbishop in 1931, *An Phoblacht* argued that the vast majority of the people had resisted this demoralisation and complained that such denunciations constituted 'a disgusting slander on Irish womanhood'.[36] Diarmaid Ferriter's research of the Circuit Court archive for this period also reveals how, particularly with regard to sexual crime, it was 'invariably girls and women rather than boys and men who were seen as the sexual deviants'.[37]

Women's adherences to modern fashions were also threatening to upset the moral social order.[38] From the altar, Gilmartin declared:

> There was a time when the face of a woman was the focus of her attractiveness, including not only her natural beauty, but her Christian modesty. How much this is changed by some of the modern hideous fashions I feel ashamed

to say. I am glad to know that in this diocese a great number of girls have joined the national crusade in favour of modesty in dress. I hereby impart my most cordial blessing to all who conform to the rules of this crusade, which, if successful, will restore dignity, and decency, and gracefulness.[39]

This campaign to restore the purity of Irish womanhood, led to the establishment of organisations such as the Modest Dress and Deportment Crusade. Following the lead of Catholic Action groups in Italy, the movement campaigned for the abolition of extravagant fashions, scantiness of attire and immodest deportment and aimed to restore national prestige by setting up 'a standard of modesty in keeping with national traditions'.[40] These women of 'Mary's militia' were instructed not to wear dresses less than four inches below the knee; or cut in a suggestive style; or sleeveless; or with a neck lower than an inch below the collar bone or of transparent material, unless a non-transparent slip was worn underneath. Members were forbidden to assume postures that were not in accordance with modesty such as loud talking, boisterous laughter, irreverent language and smoking in public. Suggestive dancing, immodest bathing, the taking of alcohol and the viewing of improper cinema films were also prohibited.[41] In one of its pamphlets titled 'Ireland's noble crusade', the editor pronounced:

> Women of Ireland, the men of Ireland have done their part in fighting for Irish nationality. Will you do your part now? Will you join in a mighty crusade to drive King Jazz and his fashions out of our land and replace the latter by that modesty in attire and deportment which won for your forebears world-wide respect and admiration?[42]

The influence of modern fashion on the women of Ireland did not escape the attention of political leaders either. At a Fianna Fáil rally in Galway in 1926, de Valera advised the crowd that while 'Paris fashions may be very attractive' they 'did not look good sometimes in the mud of our roads'.[43] Adopting a more light-hearted tone, the *Tuam Herald* printed the speech of the Scottish peer Lord Dewar, who, commenting on the fashion trends in London, remarked that 'the dresses today begin anywhere and leave off abruptly. There is more latitude than longitude about them. There is many a safety pin that carries more responsibility than the chairman of a bank.'[44] Yet in the minds of the bishops such tempting fashions, suggestive dancing, seductive dress, excessive drinking, inducements to sensuality and mixed bathing on the coastal beaches of Galway could only lead to scandal, ruin and moral degradation. In a sermon delivered at Saint Joseph's Church in May 1931, O'Doherty proclaimed:

> There are … some people who go to Barna strand and indulge in mixed bathing, where people lie in groups practically naked. Are these occasions

of sin? Ask yourselves in your hearts are not these [the] things that lead to foul thoughts, foul desires, and foul acts?[45]

While the declarations of the local bishops against occasions of sin and unlawful pleasure seem at times to have been regarded as a sort of annual trumpeting, the perceived degeneration of social morality and insobriety and the increase in sexual crime did offer the Catholic Church an occasion to re-establish its sense of social power, restore its position of political neutrality and re-assert its moral authority over local society. Unlike the political authority of the state, which was contested by the republicans, the Catholic Church was recognised as a legitimate pastoral power, it was acknowledged as a provider of welfare services, and its influence underpinned the conservative structures of local society.

Anti-state activities

Nationally, the upsurge in IRA activity in the late 1920s, the intimidation of jurors and witnesses in political trials, the production of seditious material and the increase in illegal drilling unnerved both the church and the government. Locally, disillusion, emigration and low morale restricted IRA activity to minor opportunistic actions carried out by small detached groups. For instance, in November 1925 the cinema reel of the popular First World War film *Zeebrugge*, which had attracted large crowds at the Empire Theatre in Galway city, was seized and burned by the local IRA.[46] In June 1930, during the Irish Omnibus Company national dispute, local strike-breaking buses were hijacked and ambushed. Overall, however, the steady consolidation of the new state, the establishment of a constitutional republican party in the form of Fianna Fáil in May 1926 and the popular rejection of militant republicanism as a source of effective political action limited the appeal of the IRA in Galway. The campaign against the payment of land annuities was an important case in point. Amounting to £3 million annually, the annuities were payments made by Irish farmers to the British government to repay the loans they had secured during the late nineteenth and early twentieth centuries to buy their farms. By the late 1920s many local impoverished farmers were in arrears with their payments. In November 1928 Galway County Council (now under the chairmanship of Fianna Fáil's Eamonn Corbett, a strong supporter of the non-payment campaign) declared that the land annuities were 'neither legally nor morally due to the British treasury' and that the exportation of such large sums of money was prejudicial to the financial stability of the state.[47] Such an emotive, popular, economic issue could have been utilised by the IRA as a vehicle for assertive ordered opposition against the state. Yet attempts to rally the small landholders of the west never approached anything like an organised, resolute resistance. Forceful parliamentary agitation, as Fianna Fáil demonstrated in the 1930s, effected a much wider appeal, despite the fact that the party merely advocated retention of the annuities by the Irish government and not the outright abolition of the payments.

In 1929, the activities of the radical cleric Fr John Fahy, in promoting the non-payment of land annuities in east Galway, gave the local republican campaign a greater prominence and more publicity than its strength indicated. An avowed republican, Fahy was transferred to Bullaun, near Loughrea, in the diocese of Clonfert in 1926. The pronouncements in his pamphlet 'The Oath and the Annuities', for example, are an indication of the intemperate rancorous harangues of the curate: 'Personally, I would not execute those who stand for the Oath by either hanging or shooting. I would disembowel them slowly and then saw their heads off with a cross-cut.'[48] In a letter to Mary MacSwiney he declared 'I believe ... that National feeling is stirring once again, that the evil spell of awe and fear that stunned and paralysed the spirit of our people for the past seven years is breaking, and that the Free State nightmare will disappear like a dark cloud before a storm. Courage is returning.'[49] In January 1929, on the occasion of the tenth anniversary of the establishment of Dáil Éireann, he read the Declaration of Independence from the altar and exhorted his listeners to join the local IRA.[50] In the course of another sermon he urged his parishioners to keep the land annuities in the village and use the money to build a curate's house rather than send it to the British government.[51]

After the collapse of Peadar O'Donnell's land annuities struggle in Donegal in 1928, Fahy invited O'Donnell to join his campaign in Bullaun. O'Donnell, a strong proponent of social radicalism, accepted the invitation, savouring the opportunity, as he put it, 'to light a fire on Paddy Hogan's doorstep'.[52] On 25 February 1929, Fahy rescued two cattle from the Sheriff's bailiff, Peter Whelan, who had seized the cattle from the farm of Bridget Nevin, Bullaun, for failure to pay land annuities. Fahy protested that he had no objection to seizures being made for a lawful debt, but that he would not permit the execution of decrees in his parish for the non-payment of land annuities. He was served with a summons on 11 March to appear in Loughrea District Court a week later. He refused to attend and on 16 April he was arrested at his home and conveyed to the courthouse. In conducting his own defence Fahy declared that he had been brought by force into 'an unlawful assembly' without the permission of his ecclesiastical authorities; he held that those responsible were accountable for 'the greatest of national crimes in bringing a citizen of a Free country into an enemy court and holding that court on Republican territory'; and he accused them of 'being guilty of high treason'. Arguing that his act was one of 'justice and charity', he refused to recognise the legality of the court, declined to accept bail and was lodged in Galway jail for six weeks until his trial in Galway Circuit Court on 3 June.[53]

Wary of the national publicity the arrest of a priest might gain, District Justice Cahill had warned O'Friel that Fahy's arrest would give a false importance to his actions and an exaggerated idea of the strength of the land annuities movement.[54] Additionally, John Dignan, Bishop of Clonfert, had requested Superintendent Doyle, the senior guard handling the case, to write to his authorities to establish that if Fahy publicly apologised for his actions (which Dignan ordered him to do), and the amount of the decree for which the seizure was made was paid (£7 14s 10d), the matter could be allowed to rest. Accordingly, on 30 March O'Friel travelled from Dublin to discuss the case with Dignan. However, no concordat was reached. O'Friel reported to O'Higgins that 'owing to Fr Fahy's eccentricity and intractability the bishop was not in a position to give the necessary assurance'.[55] Dignan, on the other hand, citing the most recent Code of Canon Law (1917) on juridical matters, was irritated by the fact that the government had issued a warrant for Fahy's arrest without seeking his prior approval and was particularly incensed at O'Friel's argument that the privilege of exemption for clergymen from trial by a secular court had no legal standing in British law in Ireland before 1921.[56]

Fahy was particularly fortunate that his bishop was an outspoken republican supporter. Dignan was the first bishop to publicly identify with the anti-treatyites.[57] After his consecration in Loughrea on 1 June 1924, he had delivered a rousing republican speech in response to the addresses of the local Sinn Féin clubs.[58] In it he proclaimed that 'morally, economically, even nationally', the Cumann na nGaedheal government was on 'an inclined plane, slipping gradually but surely into the abysmal pit of confusion and disorder'. 'I predict', he added, 'that the Republican Party is certain to be returned to power in a short time. Prepare for that day and do your best for its quick approach, while in the meantime you obey the law of the Free State, and subordinate your political [interests] to the national interests.'[59] Patrick Murray has recorded that on the bottom of his copy of the Sinn Féin address Dignan wrote the words 'Colourless, brainless, Cumann na nGaedheal'.[60] Writing to MacSwiney from Galway jail, Fahy affirmed that 'Dignan is in a position to do a very good act of patriotism. He stands very isolated unfortunately.'[61]

The six weeks Fahy spent in Galway jail was an embarrassment to the government. Opponents quickly fashioned a portrayal of an incarcerated priest awaiting trial, refusing to celebrate Mass, declining visitors and threatening (although never earnestly) to go on hunger strike in a county prison. The Fianna Fáil East Galway Comhairle Ceanntair condemned the action of the government in arresting and detaining Fahy; expressed their gratitude for the curate's 'fine example of heroism'; and commended him for 'defending the fundamental rights and liberties of the Irish people'.[62] On 1 May, Galway County Council adjourned their meeting in protest against Fahy's imprisonment.[63] In addition, the Council threatened to boycott the town's Catholic Emancipation centenary celebrations in June. Resolutions calling for Fahy's release were also passed by Tuam Town Commissioners (Galway), Wicklow County Council, Wexford Municipal Council and Tipperary, South Riding, County Council.[64] Writing in *An Phoblacht* Dignan deplored Cumann na nGaedheal's handling of the affair and laid the blame for the 'scandal and injury to religion' at the door of the government which had decided to appropriate the functions of a Bishop and to violate Canon Law.[65]

At his trial on 3 June, Fahy, in obedience to his bishop (and after close consultation with Michael Browne, Professor of Canon Law in Maynooth), expressed regret for his actions in the case; admitted that he seized the cattle from the Sheriff's officer; stated he was prepared to abide by the consequences and desired that the case be dealt with without a jury. Accepting this as a plea of guilty, Judge Wyse Power sentenced Fahy to six weeks' imprisonment to take effect from the date of his arrest. He was therefore immediately discharged. Fahy had broken the law, served a term in prison and publicly denounced the state, but the only ecclesiastical censure Dignan inflicted on his curate, after his release from jail, was a transfer within the diocese to his previous parish of Clostoken. He was also ordered to refrain from discussing matters of a political nature when two or more persons were present; a rather incredible request that he flagrantly disregarded.

At Clostoken, Fahy was joined in his small cottage by O'Donnell (when he was not in Dublin) and remained in close contact with prominent members of the local IRA. In 1931 he was accused of attempting to induce an Army reservist, Michael Tierney, to obtain machine guns for the IRA and of administering the oath to new members of the organisation.[66] Detailing his activities to O'Duffy, Sergeant Thomas Direen wrote:

> there is nothing to show that his activities in connection with the Irregular organisation are easing off of late ... I am inclined to think that Father Fahy is in a position to do serious damage, and is constantly going around on a motor cycle with [a] civilian cap and overcoat apparently organising for the IRA and other illegal movements ... I consider Father Fahy a danger in

so much as he is functioning as a Roman Catholic Priest and the fact that he is one of the local leaders of the Irregulars may be regarded by youths as sufficient moral sanction to continue in the movement.[67]

In 1931 there was an escalation in IRA violence. The shift in radical republicanism towards the left-wing doctrines of the newly founded socialist republican movement Saor Éire and the appointment of young officers energised the national organisation. At its debut congress in September, Saor Éire outlined the two principal objectives of its radical socialist policy: first, the achievement of 'an independent revolutionary leadership for the working class and working farmers towards the overthrow in Ireland of British Imperialism and its ally, Irish Capitalism'; and second, the organisation of 'the Republic of Ireland on the basis of the possession and administration by the workers and working farmers, of the land, instruments of production, distribution and exchange'.[68] In the columns of *An Phoblacht*, O'Donnell, a Saor Éire zealot, urged readers to 'beat the landlord out of life … smash the state machine [and] arm the workers'.[69] At a meeting in Galway, he exhorted his audience of farmers and labourers to organise to fight against capitalism.[70] Cumann na nGaedheal presented the adoption of the Saor Éire programme by the IRA general army convention as marking a definite union of the two groups, but traditionalists and the non-socialist elements of the IRA were less enthusiastic about the new political agenda and its engagement in class politics.

Local IRA activity remained small freelance affairs, carried out primarily in east and south Galway under the direction of John Joe Kennedy and Michael Sylver. In July 1931, for instance, at a meeting in Fahy's house in Clostoken, a plan was devised to assemble a firing party at the Garda sports day in Loughrea. The men were instructed to fire a volley of shots over the sports field in order to stampede the crowd. The plan was later aborted, however, when the venue of the sports day was changed to a different location. On 12 September the newly refurbished Garda station at Kilreekill, the home town of Patrick Hogan TD, was destroyed. In another incident, a school teacher in Clarenbridge named Glynn, who had allegedly taken a job from a local woman, was ordered to be 'driven out'. Glynn had already received a threatening letter telling him not to return to the school. Shortly after, he was held up by two armed men and ordered to leave the district. On 14 September, Kennedy led a raid on the offices of James Lynch, State Solicitor, Ennis. The purpose of the attack was to destroy decrees issued by the Land Commission. If the documents could not be found Kennedy ordered that the office was to be sprinkled with petrol and set alight. However, the party, despite being well armed, was unable to force its way into the house. Having fired several unsuccessful shots at the door locks and showered the house with gunfire (narrowly missing one of their own men), they abandoned the raid.[71]

Nonetheless, the growth in low-intensity violence and the visible strengthening of the IRA at a national level heightened Cumann na nGaedheal sensibilities. The depressing social and economic context at the turn of the decade and the conceivable threat of widespread radical activity alarmed the government. Reacting to the risk the professed alliance between the IRA and Communists posed to the security of the state, Cosgrave warned that 'a situation without parallel as a threat to the foundations of all authority has arisen'.[72] On Sunday 18 October 1931 the Catholic hierarchy, in its first joint pastoral since the civil war, denounced Saor Éire as being 'frankly Communistic in its aims'. It declared its policy of 'materialistic Communism' to be 'a blasphemous denial of God', the inevitable result of which would lead to 'class warfare, the abolition of private property and the destruction of family life'. It condemned both Saor Éire and the IRA (although not referring to the latter directly by name) as 'sinful and irreligious' organisations, and proclaimed that no Catholic could lawfully belong to either movement.[73] Two days later, Cosgrave implemented the Constitution Amendment Act, a stringent public safety act that sanctioned the establishment of a military tribunal with the power of the death penalty to deal with political crime and proscribed twelve organisations including Saor Éire, the IRA and the Workers' Revolutionary Party.[74] *An Phoblacht*, the *Workers' Voice* and other associated republican and left-wing publications were censored, and searches, raids and arrests of leading republicans began immediately. Opposing the passing of this new legislation, Galway County Council protested that 'those who dictate the policy of coercion to the Free State Government ... are evidently determined, even at the approach of the Eucharist Congress, to destroy the goodwill and harmony at present prevailing'.[75]

In February 1932, in what became an awkward case for the IRA, seven Galway men were put on trial at one of the convened military tribunals in Dublin. They were accused of membership of the IRA, participation in illegal drilling, possession of fire arms and partaking in armed raids. At his trial, John Burke, Loughrea IRA, confessed to his part in the abortive assault on the Garda sports day, the raid on Lynch's offices in Ennis, and the destruction of Kilreekill barracks. Michael Silke, Loughrea IRA, also admitted to his part in the Ennis and Kilreekill attacks. Burke and Silke described how the landmine they used to destroy the barracks was in an iron case about two feet long and eight inches in diameter, weighed about two stone, was bolted at the ends and fitted with a three to four foot fuse. They also provided details of how on the night of the attack they had carried it on their backs as far as the barracks, forced open the front door and put the mine into the fireplace in the kitchen. After lighting the fuse they ran across the fields and were about 200 yards away when the mine exploded.[76] More significantly (and most embarrassing for the IRA), all seven of the men on trial expressed a level of scepticism and hostility towards the doctrines of Saor Éire and claimed that since the passing of the Constitution Amendment Act and the Catholic Church's condemnation of it as anti-Christian they had resolved to have nothing further to do with the movement. Silke, for instance, stated: 'I was loyal and true to the IRA and I thought we were doing what was right until all the IRA men were brought into Saor Éire by John Joe Kennedy, Michael Sylver and Father Fahy. After all about Saor Éire came out, John Burke, my O/C, and myself thought things were wrong but we were kept in it by Kennedy and were afraid to try to get away.'[77] Silke agreed to give an undertaking that he would leave the IRA. Burke also subscribed to severing his connection with the IRA. Patrick Connaughton, Athenry IRA, stated that Kennedy 'told us that we would have a good way of living in the future and that the land and property would be taken from the rich people and given to the poorer people'.[78] Martin Fahy, Fianna Fáil County Councillor and local IRA officer, somewhat dubiously claimed he was lured into taking part in the raid on Lynch's offices by Kennedy but also pledged to have no future dealings with the organisation.[79] The Galway men were later denounced by the IRA as 'arrant cowards'.[80] Furthermore, the testimonies of Burke and Silke implicated Fr Fahy in the organisation and recruitment of local IRA units. Yet despite mounting police evidence, Fahy denied all of the allegations. On 12 February 1932, in the presence of his bishop, he signed a statement insisting that the declarations made about his activities in the IRA and Saor Éire before the military tribunal were utterly false and without foundation.[81] A rather sceptical Dignan, however, relieved Fahy of his duties as curate in Clostoken, temporarily suspended his parish ministry and transferred him briefly to the parish of Kilconnell. In September Fahy was given a new curacy in Ballinakill, where Dignan vainly hoped he would devote himself 'exclusively' to his work 'as a minister of God'.[82] The bishop's patience had snapped, but his overall treatment of his rebellious curate was notably lenient. In the Galway diocese, by way of contrast, Thomas O'Doherty warned his clergy that

> Any priest, secular or regular, in these Dioceses (Galway, Kilmacduagh and Kilfenora) who by word or writing or even signs, whether in Tribunali or outside it, expresses to any person the opinion that it is not gravely unlawful to be a member of the IRA or Saor Éire Organisations is 'ipso facto'

suspended, and absolution from this suspension is reserved to the Bishop or the Vicar-General, and will be granted only after the imposition of a grave, salutary penance. Membership of any of the societies mentioned is to be treated in Tribunali as in the case of any other mortal sin.[83]

State repression and episcopal condemnation successfully supressed the short-lived Saor Éire experiment, temporarily subdued the IRA and exacerbated internal tensions within the organisation. Despite the potential for social unrest, a socialist class struggle, as Richard English noted, 'was not a popular brand of politics in the contemporary Free State'.[84] Saor Éire's preference for land socializiation failed to resonate with a rural society whose social aspirations developed around small farm private ownership. Locally, it lacked public enthusiasm. Speaking at the Easter commemorations at Headford, north Galway, Dr John Madden complained that as far as he could see 'the only thing that could awaken any enthusiasm is the question whether they were going to have a non-Catholic librarian in Mayo or whether the "Daily Mail" is going to circulate in Galway'.[85] The Saor Éire orthodoxy did not reflect the collective Galway *mentalité*. Cumann na nGaedheal's fundamental miscalculation was its decision to use its anti-Communist crusade as the basis of its political assault on Fianna Fáil.

Notes

1 Brian Hanley, *The IRA, 1926–1936* (Dublin, 2002), p. 49.
2 Richard English, *Radicals and the Republic: Socialist Republicanism in the Irish Free State, 1925–1937* (Oxford, 1994), p. 112.
3 *Iris an Gharda*, 5 Mar. 1923. Cited in Conor Brady, *Guardians of the Peace* (2nd edn, London, 2000), p. 94.
4 NAI, DJ, Jus8/2007/56/002; DJ, H5/785; *Connacht Tribune*, 28 Apr. 1923.
5 Deposition of Sergt. Michael Kealy, NAI, DJ, Jus8/2007/56/002. Noel Lemass, elder brother by two years of Seán Lemass, was murdered in 1923. It was widely believed that the Criminal Investigation Department was responsible for his death. His mangled, mutilated body was found on Featherbed Mountain, County Dublin, on 12 October 1923.
6 O'Friel, Sec. Home Affairs, to Director General, CID, 14 Aug. 1923, *ibid.*, Jus8/2007/56/002.
7 O'Halpin, *Defending Ireland*, pp. 9, 63–4. Hastily established in February 1922, the Civic Guards did initially carry arms. However, the force's early difficulties, which included a mutiny in Kildare barracks in May, led the government to forsake the initial scheme for an armed force, akin to the RIC. See Gregory Allen, *The Garda Síochána: Policing Independent Ireland 1922–82* (Dublin, 1999), chapters 3, 4.
8 Cited in Brady, *Guardians of the Peace*, pp. 94–5.
9 O'Halpin, *Defending Ireland*, pp. 40–1.

10 *Ibid.*, p. 81.

11 Report from John H. Gallagher, District Justice, Ballinasloe, to O'Higgins, 13 Mar. 1924, NAI, DJ, H6/88.

12 O'Halpin, *Defending Ireland*, p. 41.

13 In 1925, for example, conditions in Milltown, north Galway, were so bad that Deputy Commissioner Coogan ordered an immediate evacuation of the force from their accommodation. Allen, *An Garda Síochána*, p. 82; McGarry, *Eoin O'Duffy*, pp. 124–5. In a report to O'Higgins in February 1923, O'Duffy stated: 'With its serious list of criminal offences it may be wondered why a hopeful view is expressed about Co. Galway. The reason is that it has been found that the County reacts to the operations of the Police Force.' Garda Síochána monthly report, Feb. 1923, NAI, DJ, H99/125.

14 Kinsella, 'The Special Infantry Corps', p. 340.

15 Report of the District Justices on the state of the district, 1923, NAI, DJ, H5/1307. Stephen Gwynn gave an interesting description of poitín after one of his visits to Connemara: 'Potheen [*sic*] I may observe, has the strongest imaginable peat flavour, and with cold water is downright nasty. But those who make and value it, never think of attempting this mixture – though they may drink a glass of water after the other glass taken neat. To my thinking it makes excellent punch. Yet many will be of Miss Edgeworth's opinion, who described it thus: "Of all the detestable tastes that ever went into my mouth, or smells that ever went under my nose, I think this was the worst – literally smoke and fire water." But then, she drank it with water, or without the other "materials".' Stephen Gwynn, *A Holiday in Connemara* (London, 1909), p. 89.

16 Report of the District Justices on the state of the district, 1923, NAI, DJ, H5/1307.

17 NAI, DJ, H67/23. According to the 1926 census, the population of County Donegal was 152,508. The population of County Galway, as noted earlier, was 169,366. *Census of Ireland 1926*, Population, Area and Valuation, vol. I, pp. 5–6.

18 Report of H. J. Keegan, C/Supt. Galway, to O'Duffy, 29 Jan. 1929, NAI, DJ, H112/34.

19 *Western News*, 14 Apr. 1923.

20 Report of D. Twomey, Inspector, Garda Síochána, Clidfen, to Keegan, C/Supt. Galway, 23 Mar. 1924; letter from Commissioner's Office to Sec. Dept. of Justice, 31 Mar. 1924, NAI, DJ, H5/1221. During the truce in 1921, the lodge at Doohulla was taken over by the local IRA captain, John McDonagh. The grounds were used as a training camp and the house was made into a dance hall, presumably to raise funds for the IRA.

21 Testimony of O'Duffy to the Carrigan committee. Cited in McGarry, *Eoin O'Duffy*, p. 159.

22 *Connacht Tribune*, 2 Jan. 1932.

23 Pastorals, Lent 1924, GDA, O'Doherty papers, Box 46/75.

24 Pastorals, Lent 1925, *ibid*.

25 *Irish Independent*, 7 May 1931.

26 James Smyth, 'Dancing, depravity and all that jazz: the Public Dance Halls Act of 1935', *History Ireland*, vol. 1, no. 2 (Summer, 1993). Cited in Diarmaid Ferriter, *Occasions of Sin: Sex and Society in Modern Ireland* (London, 2009), p. 178.

27 Letter from Gilmartin to the clergy, Sept. 1935, TAA, Gilmartin papers, Box 85, B4/2-ii/2.

28 Edward D'Alton to P. J. Ruttledge, 22 Dec. 1933; response from Ruttledge, 29 Dec. 1933, NAI, DJ, H290/19.

29 Maria Luddy, 'Sex and the single girl in 1920s and 1930s Ireland', *Irish Review*, no. 35 (Spring, 2007), p. 80.

30 Sermon by O'Doherty at a confirmation ceremony at St Patrick's Church, Galway. Cited in *Connacht Tribune*, 12 Apr. 1924.

31 *Ibid.*

32 Pastorals, Lent 1932, TAA, Gilmartin papers, Box 85, B4/2-i/1.

33 Sermon by O'Doherty at St Patrick's Church, Galway. Cited in *Connacht Tribune*, 12 Apr. 1924.

34 Pastorals, Lent 1924, TAA, Gilmartin papers, Box 85, B4/2-i/1.

35 *Ibid.*

36 *An Phoblacht*, 23 May 1931.

37 Ferriter, *Occasions of Sin*, pp. 7–8.

38 Luddy, 'Sex and the single girl in 1920s and 1930s Ireland', p. 81.

39 *Irish Catholic*, 18 Feb. 1928, TAA, Gilmartin papers, Box 175, B4/2-v/13.

40 Modest Dress and Deportment Crusade pamphlet, 'Its aim and spirit', TAA, Gilmartin papers, Box 175, B4/2-v/13. The organisation originated at Mary Immaculate Training College in Limerick and established branches all around the country. James S. Donnelly, Jr, 'Bishop Michael Browne of Galway (1937–76) and the regulation of public morality', *New Hibernia Review*, vol. 17, no.1 (Spring, 2013), p. 32.

41 Modest Dress and Deportment Crusade pamphlet, 'Children of Mary in name or in deed?', TAA, Gilmartin papers, Box 175, B4/2-v/13.

42 *Ibid.*, 'Ireland's noble crusade', *ibid.*

43 *Connacht Sentinel*, 2 Nov. 1926.

44 Cited in *Tuam Herald*, 29 June 1929.

45 Cited in *Connacht Tribune*, 16 May 1931. For more on mixed bathing in the 1960s in Salthill, see Donnelly, Jr, 'Bishop Michael Browne of Galway (1937–76) and the regulation of public morality', pp. 32–6.

46 Reporting on the incident, the *Connacht Tribune* described how on 29 November P. F. Pfonds, manager of the Empire Theatre, was returning to Galway from Athenry where he had shown the film that evening. His car was held up by four armed men who stated they had orders to seize propaganda films. The raiders searched the car, removed the transit box containing the *Zeebrugge* reel and a number of other films, and set them alight. The film reels had been hired from the Phoenix Film Company and the damage was estimated at £160. In a separate incident in Dublin, the Masterpiece Cinema was blown up after the film *Ypres* was shown and other theatre managers were warned by the IRA that if such films were put on they would be

'drastically dealt with'. Previously, in March 1923, the Dublin IRA had damaged the Carlton, Fountain, Grand Central, Pillar and Stella picture houses because the proprietors refused to obey an IRA order instructing them to close their doors to the public and observe 'a time of National mourning'. *Connacht Tribune*, 5 Dec. 1925; T. P. Coogan, *The I. R. A.* (5th edn, London, 2000), p. 46; NAI, DJ, H84/13.

47 Resolution passed by Galway County Council, 21 Nov. 1928, GCCA, Galway County Council minute books, GC1/4.

48 Cited in Jim Madden, *Fr John Fahy: Radical Republican and Agrarian Activist* (Dublin, 2012), p. 40.

49 John Fahy to Mary MacSwiney, 11 May 1929, NAI, DJ, Jus8/2007/56/113.

50 NAI, DJ, Jus8/2007/56/113.

51 Cited in Madden, *Fr John Fahy*, p. 41.

52 *Ibid.*, p. 40.

53 Pamphlet issued by Comhairle na Poblachta, May 1929, NAI, DT, S5864/B; *Connacht Tribune*, 20 Apr. 1929; letter from Fahy to MacSwiney, 11 May 1929, NAI, DJ, Jus8/2007/56/113. While in jail, Fahy applied for permission to be given assistance in cleaning his cell. The application was granted, with Fahy agreeing to pay one shilling per day for the service. Letter from Dept. of Justice to Sec. Executive Council, 20 Apr. 1929. Cited in Madden, *Fr John Fahy*, p. 52.

54 Cahill, District Justice, to O'Friel, Sec. Dept. of Justice, 28 Feb. 1929, NAI, DJ, Jus8/2007/56/113. In the letter Cahill described Fahy as 'a man of very little ballast'.

55 Cited in Madden, *Fr John Fahy*, p. 44.

56 NAI, DJ, Jus8/2007/56/113. For details on the interpretation of *privilegium fori*, which prohibited civil prosecution of a priest without ecclesiastical approval, see Murray, *Oracles of God*, p. 315.

57 Dermot Keogh, 'The Catholic Church and the Irish Free State 1923–1932', *History Ireland*, vol. 2, no. 1 (Spring, 1994), p. 48.

58 Murray, *Oracles of God*, p. 163.

59 *Connacht Tribune*, 7 June 1924; *Irish Independent*, 2 June 1924.

60 Cited in Murray, *Oracles of God*, p. 163. Another republican supporter in the Diocese of Clonfert was Fr Cawley, parish priest of Shanaglish. Described as 'a very enthusiastic republican' by his local sergeant, he was reported in 1931 for selling Easter lilies inside his church at the altar rails and for introducing the speaker at the local commemoration. NAI, DT, S5864/A.

61 Fahy to MacSwiney, 11 May 1929, NAI, DJ, Jus8/2007/56/113.

62 Cited in Madden, *Fr John Fahy*, p. 53.

63 The resolution, passed by 24 votes to 4 with four abstaining, read: 'That whereas the inviolability of a Nation's soil is a basic principle of Nationality; and whereas the lawful owners of the soil of Ireland are being robbed by the British Exchequer and by the remnant of the British Garrison in Ireland, we, the Members of the Galway County Council, adjourn this Council Meeting to-day to show our whole hearted sympathy with the patriotic action for which Father Fahy and our other comrades in Tirconaill and elsewhere are

behind prison bars and also to express our deep appreciation for the practical and heroic gesture which they have given to the enslaved and oppressed
farmers of Ireland. That, with great respect, we tender our congratulations
to Father Fahy the worthy comrade of the sainted Father Griffin.' Minutes
of Galway County Council, 1 May 1929, GCCA, Galway County Council
minute books, GC1/4.

64 NAI, DT, S5837.

65 *An Phoblacht*, 16 May 1929.

66 Statement of Michael Tierney to Garda Síochána, Loughrea, 19 Oct. 1931;
report by Sergt. J. Collins, Loughrea, to O'Duffy, 20 Oct. 1931, NAI, DJ,
Jus8/2007/56/113.

67 Memo from Sergt. T. Direen to O'Duffy, 20 Oct. 1931, *ibid.*

68 Pamphlet, 'Saor Éire: Constitution and Rules', 1931, NAI, DT, S5864/B. A
third objective was the restoration and fostering of the Irish language, culture and games. Additionally, in its rules and regulations Saor Éire set out
its strategy for the development of a socialist society in Ireland. For further
details on Saor Éire see English, *Radicals and the Republic*, pp. 124–60;
Murray, *Oracles of God*, pp. 317–25; Donal Ó Drisceoil, *Peadar O'Donnell*
(Cork, 2001), pp. 64–8.

69 *An Phoblacht*, 7 Feb. 1931. Cited in English, *Radicals and the Republic*,
p. 124.

70 Government memo, 1930, UCDA, Blythe papers P24/168. Cited *ibid.*,
p. 112.

71 Statements of John Burke, Patrick Connaughton, James Geoghegan, David
Callinan, Martin Fahy, Eddie Hynes, Michael Silke and Michael Skerry,
submitted to the Military Tribunal, Dublin, Jan., Feb. 1932, NAI, DJ,
Jus8/2007/56/143; Jus8/2007/56/148; *Irish Independent*, 13 Jan. 1932; *Irish
Times*, 11 Feb. 1932; Hanley, *The IRA*, p. 43.

72 Letter from Cosgrave to Gilmartin, 17 Sept. 1931. Similar copies were sent
to Cardinal Joseph MacRory, Primate of All Ireland, and the other bishops.
In addition, the government enclosed an extensive seventeen-page memorandum and appendices outlining the development of anti-state activities in the
state. The document was intended to convince the Catholic hierarchy of the
gravity of the situation and encourage them to use their influence to counter
the perceived threat of social radicalism. NAI, DT, S5864/B.

73 Pastoral Letter, Oct. 1931, NAI, DT, S5864/B; *Irish Catholic Directory*
(Dublin, 1932), pp. 622–5.

74 The Workers' Revolutionary Party had renamed itself the Revolutionary
Workers' Groups in November 1930.

75 Minutes of Galway County Council, 10 Oct. 1931, GCCA, Galway County
Council minute books, GC1/4.

76 Statements of John Burke and Michael Silke submitted to the Military
Tribunal, Dublin, Feb. 1932, NAI, DJ, Jus8/2007/56/148; *Irish Times*, 11
Feb. 1932.

77 Statement of Michael Silke, *ibid.*

78 Statement of Patrick Connaughton, *ibid.*

79 Statement of Martin Fahy, *ibid.* The Galway men were not the only ones to give undertakings to sever their connections with the IRA. For a list of other IRA men from Leitrim, Roscommon, Kerry, Waterford, Dublin and Kilkenny, see Hanley, *The IRA*, p. 39. All seven of the Galway men were released.
80 Cited in Hanley, *The IRA*, p. 43.
81 Statement signed by Fahy at St Brendan's, Loughrea, 12 Feb. 1932. Cited in Madden, *Fr John Fahy*, pp. 82–3.
82 Dignan to Fahy, 9 Sept. 1932, *ibid.*, p. 85.
83 Statement by O'Doherty to the clergy of Galway, Kilmacduagh and Kilfenora, 16 June 1933, *ibid.*, p. 88.
84 English, *Radicals and the Republic*, pp. 131, 148.
85 *Connacht Tribune*, 11 Apr. 1931.

Part III
Politics

6

Conservative revolutionaries:
1923–32

Party orientation

Finding himself somewhat politically adrift after his release from jail in July 1924, de Valera was by the summer of 1925 realigning his political thinking on Sinn Féin's self-imposed exile from the Dáil. The formal split with Sinn Féin came in March 1926 and Fianna Fáil, 'the Republican Party', was officially launched at the La Scala Theatre in Dublin on 16 May.

The party's organisational success was instantaneous. According to Dunphy's figures, within six months Fianna Fáil had established 460 branches at national level. By the spring of 1927 this figure had risen to 800. By the summer of 1927 there were more than a thousand affiliated party branches in Ireland and a group of twenty-five speakers was available to tour the country to mobilise support and educate the electorate on party policy. Its approach to party organisation and building an alternative power base was dynamic and modern.[1] Fianna Fáil adopted the model of the old IRA networks, but it also successfully imitated the root and branch parish-based organisational technique developed by the Irish Parliamentary Party and further advanced by Sinn Féin in 1917 and 1918. In fact, in many ways, the party blended the IRA method of organisation with the old Sinn Féin and United Irish League practice of using the party clubs as a source of entertainment as well as a forum for political harangues. It was an approach that was particularly successful in rural Ireland where participation in these bodies, as Fitzpatrick suggested, was in part 'a barricade against boredom' affording a welcome social outlet and variety of life for many people whose life experience was concentrated within a few miles of their home.[2] In 1929, Seán Lemass and Gerry Boland told the Fianna Fáil party Árd Fheis that 'everything should be done to counteract the tendency in recent years to concentrate exclusively on purely political matters, and members should realise that work done to foster Irish language, games and customs was useful work for the Fianna Fáil movement'.[3]

To some republican irreconcilables de Valera's declared intention of entering the Dáil once the oath was removed was anathema. In their mind Fianna Fáil had betrayed the ideal of the Republic even more comprehensively than Cumann na nGaedheal.[4] Nonetheless, the new party attracted into its ranks most of the more moderate Sinn Féin adherents. In Galway its strong performance in the 1927 general elections resonated with a less radical electorate who wished to work the institutions of the Free State to secure an Irish Republic. Yet it was the appeal of the party's ambitious promise of economic development and social reform that won it its most faithful supporters. As the impact of the economic depression swelled the chorus of opposition to government policies, Fianna Fáil's 'choice of social lures' allayed electoral uncertainty.[5] In the general economic malaise of the early 1930s the clear contradictions and air of unreality inherent in the party's programme of further land redistribution, economic self-sufficiency, increased social services, reduced public expenditure and greater profits were deliberately ignored. For instance, at a most basic level, if the right of private property was accepted as fundamental and if the party was loath to seize acreage from the richest graziers, where would the new land that was to benefit the small farmers come from?[6] Cumann na nGaedheal had grappled with the same dilemma for almost ten years.

The genius of the party, as Dunphy has argued, lay in its ability to project the interests of an emergent national bourgeoisie as 'universal', in the process 'building an enduring cross-class electoral bloc which included urban workers, small farmers, those dependent on welfare payments, and so on'.[7] De Valera's personal appeal was also significant in securing Fianna Fáil's rise to political dominance. For the depressed farmers of the west of Ireland, de Valera may not have been the champion of their interests but he was certainly looked upon as the champion of their rights.[8] This mentality was crucial to the Fianna Fáil appeal in rural Ireland. The people might be poor, but de Valera would never let them starve. The carefully cultivated portrayal of Fianna Fáil as a paternalistic party, as a party whose policy, Seán T. O'Kelly declared, 'was the policy of the plain people'[9] and the perception that it was making the poor and the distressed their first care were fundamental to its sustained success in the west.

On the other hand, within Cumann na nGaedheal Cosgrave was determined to create an organisation that would appeal, as he put it, to 'the best elements of society'.[10] A circular prepared by the party's organising committee on 21 June 1923 issued instructions to each organiser to try to enlist the support of local notables and influential people in the towns.[11] As Regan wrote, 'where doctor, merchant and lawyer would lead, so the logic went, patient, customer and client would somehow follow'.[12] For Patrick Hogan, the old school network he had established at his time at Garbally College, Ballinasloe, was of significant import-ance when it came to his successes at the polls. His former classmates included many future Galway lawyers, doctors, merchants and large farmers who formed a local network of considerable influence.[13] Unlike the new brand of Fianna Fáil politics, there were fewer local Cumann na nGaedheal branches and less emphasis was placed on canvassing, fund-raising and fostering a grassroots party organisation. Reflecting in later life, Richard Mulcahy spoke of a deliberate effort in 1924 to wind down the party organisation in the country. The theory was 'that branches throughout the country were a source of inconvenience and annoyance and demand on the government'.[14] One contemporary supporter in the 1920s claimed that 'government ministers felt no urgency about door-to-door canvassing, or speaking on cold and wet platforms at church gates, or appealing for funds'.[15] Ernest Blythe, commenting later on Cumann na nGaedheal's proposed merger with the Army Comrades Association (ACA or 'Blueshirts' as they became known), remarked that he saw an organisational benefit in joining up with the ACA – it would 'never be possible to get responsible business men, middle-aged farmers or busy professional people' to do the arduous and tedious local work for the party, but the 'young men and boys' of the ACA would be ideally suited to undertake these chores.[16] Cosgrave's 'best elements' showed little enthusiasm for knocking on doors at election time.

Frustrated by the party's lacklustre electoral machine, in 1924 Eoin O'Duffy complained: 'There are no meetings, no speakers, no explana-tions, no correction of false rumours, no political machinery of any kind, and, to make matters worse, the expenses of the last elections are not yet paid.'[17] On a specific and salient issue, the local county council elections of 1925 and 1928, Cumann na nGaedheal's decision not to contest the election on party political lines was a strategic error in terms of build-ing and moulding a strong, disciplined local organisation. Outlining the party position in an address to the east Galway branch of Cumann na nGaedheal in April 1925, Seán Broderick TD stated

> Cumann na nGaedheal are not running candidates as they do not want to make the County Council a political body. They do not want political resolutions. Every day they had men going in to make political speeches delivered for the Press, and such members then go away from the meeting and take no part in the business beyond that.[18]

While Cumann na nGaedheal supporters were encouraged to contest the local elections, the capture of the local bodies was of less importance to the party once the business of these boards worked in harmony with the constitutional authorities of the state. At the party's Annual Convention in May, W. T. Cosgrave declared that

> The meeting of the local authority is not the place for discussion of political issues. In the past these questions were indeed obtruded – to the disadvantage of local administration, but there was an excuse in the absence of a national assembly where they could properly be dealt with. The Oireachtas, the sovereign assembly of the nation, is now available to settle such matters. It is the only place they can be effectively considered. Henceforth they have no place in the local councils.[19]

Cumann na nGaedheal's determination to de-politicise local government was a creditable, if optimistic, ambition for a country divided by civil war.[20] At least in the case of Galway County Council, its decision was vindicated by the smooth operation of the council during its term of office, but it was a blow to local party development.

Local elections were an occasion to test the party machine and promote the party creed. In Galway they were particularly important as no by-election contests took place in the county between 1922 and 1932. They also provided a platform on which local republican councillors, eager to carry on some form of action, could exercise a degree of political influence. Sinn Féin, in contrast with their attitude towards the legitimacy of the Dáil, continued to recognise the authority of the local councils (Appendix A.5 and A.6). More significantly, for the Fianna Fáil party, searching for a means to achieve political power, the 1928 election provided it with an opportunity to demonstrate its ability to tackle the task of day-to-day local administration (sanitation, public health, rates, housing, drainage, road building and so on). Moreover, the contests facilitated the identification and promotion of prospective candidates for the national elections. While Cumann na nGaedheal stressed that national economic rehabilitation should be put before local political considerations, Fianna Fáil grasped the chance to campaign on party lines, rouse its supporters, publicise its alternative party policy and fly the party flag. The Cumann na nGaedheal elite prioritised running the country over expanding the party. Born into office, it did not regard the party organisation as an instrument for winning or retaining power.[21] It was otherwise for Fianna Fáil. De Valera's new party was thoroughly orientated towards winning elections from the outset.

Yet that is not to say that Cumann na nGaedheal did not prioritise electioneering at the national (Dáil) elections. Here, its methods, as Meehan maintained, were at times both more modern and more innovative than Fianna Fáil's. Between 1927 and 1933, for instance, Cumann na nGaedheal's efforts included the use of an aircraft to drop election pamphlets over a Dublin constituency during a by-election, and the production of a film of W. T. Cosgrave that was shown in several parts of the country. In Britain, Cumann na nGaedheal's September 1927 election campaign (in which the party hired the services of advertising agency O'Kennedy-Brindley Ltd) was viewed 'as a model to be replicated'.[22] The party allocated and invested large sums of money into its campaign. But its strategy was flawed. Cumann na nGaedheal's 'Safety First' message did not resonate with a depressed west.

Class divisions

Various writers on Irish politics have commented on the class dimension to the Sinn Féin split in 1922–23, the significant socio-economic conflict underlying the treaty divide, and the way in which subsequent party political support separated into those who had an interest in the status quo and those who harboured 'egalitarian expectations of economic betterment as an inherent part of the realisation of radical nationalist aspirations'.[23] In short, it is suggested that pro-treaty Sinn Féin won the support of the conservative, propertied classes, the large farmers, the leaders in industry and commerce and the professional men, and that anti-treaty Sinn Féin, by contrast, drew its support from the lower middle class and the workers, the small farmers, shopkeepers, artisans and labourers.[24]

In 1933 Moss argued that it was the poorer elements of Irish society, the unskilled labourers and the small farmers of the west, who initially supported the anti-treaty side.[25] Pyne, too, described a western bias and rural proclivity to anti-treaty Sinn Féin. He identified links between party support and areas of overcrowded housing conditions, high emigration, low land valuation, and districts that had a tradition of radicalism. Anti-treaty Sinn Féin, he suggested, was not the party of 'city dwellers, university graduates, non-Catholics and large farmers'. Its supporters were the 'rural lower middle class, the owner-occupiers and small shop-keepers and traders' – those who were most affected by the economic ills of Irish society and had less to lose if a Republican government came to power. However, Pyne also acknowledged that the party drew supporters from all sections of society and that 'a purely socio-economic interpretation of Republican support' was not altogether satisfactory.[26] Rumpf presented a similar assessment, arguing that the barren wilderness and economic backwardness of the small farmers of the west of Ireland not only preserved their traditional Gaelic outlook, but sheltered them from the worldly pressures which inclined other parts of the country to take a more practical view.[27] The difficulty with some of these proposals, however, lies with the authors' interpretation of the west. Some parts of County Galway were suffering from severe destitution. To suggest, as Rumpf does (and indeed Mellows and de Valera did), that this community would prefer the romantic idealism of republicanism, rather than support the pragmatism of the Free State, fails to take into consideration the social and economic condition of this region. Although the anti-treatyites received their greatest share of support from the west and south-west, in 1922 and 1923 the majority of Galway society voted for pragmatism over radicalism.

In the late 1920s and the early 1930s, the political and, particularly, the economic policies of Fianna Fáil attracted the support of the rural small farmer. However, as Sinnott has illustrated in his cartographic analysis of the Fianna Fáil vote between 1927 and 1933, while there was an obvious east–west variance in Fianna Fáil support in Ireland, the spatial contrast in party support was at first glance more apparent than real. At each general election Fianna Fáil consistently increased its support across the whole country. As the party grew in the west of Ireland, so too did it rapidly expand outside of the rural periphery. But because support for Fianna Fáil was initially stronger in the west and was therefore growing from an already established support base, the proposition that Fianna Fáil was a party of the periphery can be formulated. Yet it is a difficult argument to sustain. As Sinnott noted, the spatial spread of the party vote outside the western region was equally comprehensive.[28] While increasing its pronounced rural support, Fianna Fáil's blend of ideological pragmatism and republican rhetoric saw the party quickly develop into a successful catch-all national organisation.

Hence, the evidence of a marked social cleavage between the two sides of the treaty divide is, as Gallagher emphasised, 'at best impressionistic'.[29] Kissane suggested that there was almost 'something superficial' about the treaty split.[30] Thus, although general trends in party support have been established at national level, a clear distinction in County Galway's voting pattern is difficult to detect in the first decade of the Free State. Garvin has also identified a link with lower land valuation and support for anti-treaty Sinn Féin. Rumpf's cartographical analysis of the anti-treaty vote in 1923 confirms this, but again as Sinnott points out, there is no matching evidence to indicate the converse – 'the Cumann na nGaedheal vote does not show a corresponding positive relationship to high levels of land valuation'.[31] In County Galway the quality of land was generally rather poor, but there was an east–west variance where land in the east of the county was of a higher valuation than that in the west. For example, in 1926 the land valuation of Ballinasloe Rural District (east Galway), an area of 121,343 acres, was £60,126 compared to that of Clifden Rural District (west Galway), an area of 193,692 acres, which had a land value of £19,253. Similarly, the land valuation of Loughrea Rural District (east Galway), an area of 198,917 acres, was valued at £77,544 compared to that of Oughterard Rural District (west Galway), an area of 173,438 acres, which had a land value of £16,906.[32] The difficulty in Galway was obtaining land. And the issue of land congestion was as widespread in the east of the county as it was in the west. For those already on small holdings a few more acres meant the ability to keep an extra cow, which in turn provided additional income and perhaps the chance to keep one more family member at home rather than see him or her emigrate. For those without land, the acquisition of a small holding gave them the capacity, if only at a very basic level, to provide for themselves. The income of tillage farmers was more secure, but additional land provided extra work and more work increased the prospects of keeping another son on the land. The pertinent question is did the voters of east Galway, with slightly better holdings on slightly better land, support Cumann na nGaedheal in greater numbers than the more impoverished farmers of west Galway? The ability to answer such a question, however, is restricted by the single constituency characteristic of the county and the lack of appropriate data recorded at the local polling stations.[33] What we are left with is an impression of the county in general, but not of the regions and voters that defined it.

With such limitations in mind, McCracken examined the occupations of Dáil deputies in an effort to ascertain whether the occupation of a particular deputy was a possible indicator of the support of that class in his constituency. His analysis demonstrated that there was 'no profound difference in the occupational composition of the two main parties'.[34] His findings are mirrored at a local level. In September 1927, of the nine Galway deputies elected to the Dáil, Cumann na nGaedheal supporters returned a solicitor and farmer (Hogan); a merchant (McDonogh); a building contractor and IRA veteran (Broderick); and a hotel proprietor and farmer (Mongan). Fianna Fáil supporters elected a medical doctor and IRA officer (Tubridy); a teacher, barrister, Gaelic League activist and IRA veteran (Fahy); a shopkeeper, farmer and IRA officer (Killilea); a teacher and IRA officer (Powell); and a bootmaker, Town Tenants' League activist and IRA veteran (Jordan). A more useful indicator, given the geographic and economic variances of the county, may be to delineate the areas of the county with which the elected TDs were most associated. Yet, this line of enquiry does not set out clear pockets of strong party support in one area over another. The four Cumann na nGaedheal deputies were associated with Loughrea (Hogan), Athenry (Broderick),

Connemara (Mongan), and Galway city and Connemara (McDonogh). The five Fianna Fáil deputies were connected to the same areas – Loughrea (Fahy), Athenry (Jordan), Connemara (Tubridy), Galway city (Powell) and North Galway (Killilea). Neither the occupations nor the regional identities of the local TDs mark a clear-cut class distinction or regional discrepancy in party loyalty.

At the national elections, County Galway, as noted, served as a single constituency. It was otherwise, however, at the local government elections where the county was divided into five electoral areas – Galway city, Oughterard, Tuam, Ballinasloe and Loughrea. Yet while the return for the Oughterard division in 1928 indicated a pocket of Fianna Fáil support in west Galway, the rate-paying electorate in each of the other divisions returned a mix of candidates, reflecting the regional trend of voters at the national elections.[35] On the whole, County Galway was not a special stronghold of one party over another. Both Cumann na nGaedheal and Fianna Fáil drew support from widely scattered areas throughout the county. The local political ground was decidedly malleable. Galway elections, as will become evident in the next chapter, expressed a mix of localism, personal loyalty and party voting.

Cumann na nGaedheal tensions

Cumann na nGaedheal was complacent in its attitude towards the relationship between the government and the party organisation. Whether this stemmed from a degree of elitism (see for instance Hogan's speech quoted in Chapter 7 that one needed 'breeding' to govern) or whether it was the natural reaction of an organisation that was in the difficult position of having become a government before it ever became a party is open to question. But the perceived autocratic nature of the party elite was a source of growing frustration in local Cumann na nGaedheal circles. In theory, the main function of the local branch, along with maintaining the necessary machinery for contesting elections, was to keep the central organisation informed of local sentiment.[36] In practice, such interaction was nominal. Local branches were often unaware of the affairs of central government. In December 1923 Eoin MacNeill warned the party that

> It was a most dangerous policy to adopt the position of the old Parliamentary Party, i.e. that its only duty was to support the Government, leaving it entirely to the Government to initiate and carry through measures to deal with the big issues as they arise.[37]

Cumann na nGaedheal's vision of high politics was at odds with local Irish politics where grass-root networks determined the votes. In May

1924 Padraig Ó Máille (CNG), emphasising the need for closer consult-ation between the government and the party organisation, complained that the party had very little to contribute to legislation, 'which was usually presented to them ready-made by the Executive Council, to be accepted or rejected'.[38] A strong party organisation should have been a means of testing public opinion. However the Galway deputies regu-larly complained that they and the local branches were not being kept informed or given adequate explanation of the policy-making decisions being taken in Dublin.

A particularly difficult situation arose for the party in August 1924, when the military garrison was withdrawn from Tuam in north Galway and the bodies of the six men executed during the civil war were exhumed from the workhouse grounds and reinterred in Athlone bar-racks. Considerable public feeling was aroused over the government's decision not to release the remains to the relatives of the deceased men. Writing to Cosgrave, George Nicholls (CNG) complained that their actions had alienated many of the party's most consistent supporters.

> It is the opinion of those, and I may say of all our friends in County Galway, that once it became necessary to evacuate Tuam it would have been a grace-ful act to hand the remains over to the relatives for burial among their own people ... There would undoubtedly be big demonstrations for propa-gandist purposes but these demonstrations would, in my opinion, do far less harm than the transfer to and retention of the remains in Athlone ... The funeral demonstration would be merely a three day wonder and the Government would gain in popularity by reason of taking the bold course and handing over the remains.[39]

The Executive Council, however, despite the protests of the Galway TDs, stood by its decision. In September, a statement from the Coiste Gnótha, the organising committee of Cumann na nGaedheal, protested that the actions of the Department of Defence had produced indignation among its members and was regarded as nothing short of an atrocity.[40] On 4 November 1924, the bodies were exhumed from Athlone barracks and handed over to the relatives for burial.

Similarly, a succession of enactments, including the revision of the old age pensions, O'Higgins's intoxicating liquor legislation, the abolition of the Rural District Councils and the devolution of the county health scheme, proved politically unpopular with government supporters. Criticising the removal of the Union Hospital from Portumna, the *Galway Observer* described the plight of one sick woman who had to be carried for a mile on a stretcher by six men through fields and over ditches to the public road, from where the ambulance could then bring her to Galway Hospital, a distance of forty-five miles from where she resided.[41]

The government's proposal to abolish the local Rural District Councils was condemned as a 'retrograde step' by the Loughrea RDC.[42] Clifden RDC claimed the action to be 'subversive of democratic Government' and tantamount to disfranchising the ratepayers and giving them no control over their finances.[43] Under the Local Government Act 1925, the Rural District Councils were dissolved and their functions transferred to Galway County Council, which was expanded in number from twenty to forty members to meet its new responsibilities. Reacting to the passing of the bill, the *Connacht Tribune* stated:

> To hold that the entire business of a county like Galway can be performed by the County Council, or even that the County Council, no matter how representative, can be fully aware of the needs of all the people, is the veriest [*sic*] nonsense.[44]

It was argued that if the government believed that these local bodies were inefficient and worn out, they should not have postponed the local elections. Modification, not whole-scale abandonment was required. Again, the *Connacht Tribune* wrote

> If the voter had been permitted to do his work, it would have been found that his instinct would have been as right now as it invariably is, and that these decrepit bodies would have long since been swept out of existence. New blood would have been substituted and efficient and business-like local government would have been speedily restored.[45]

Such an argument was overly simplistic, but Cumann na nGaedheal's increasing centralisation of local government, its parsimonious approach to public spending, its reform of the local appointments process, and the paring down of local authority autonomy, antagonised some of its supporters. The Cosgrave party's reforms raised the quality of local government, but they did not necessarily win votes.[46]

Galway County Council, needless to say, was not immune from criticism. In November 1925, for instance, the council voted against the adoption of the Public Libraries Act. By that stage the Carnegie Library scheme had been in operation for over a year in County Galway and more than 20,000 books had been issued to over 4,700 registered readers in eighty-seven centres. Fiction led in popularity with 12,823 adults and 3,650 juveniles borrowing books of this genre. After fiction, but a long way behind, were the subjects of history, geography, travel and biography, in which 1,930 books were issued. Following these were literature (1,147), useful arts (662), social science and mythology (637), natural science (471), fine arts (150), religion (95), languages (80) and philosophy (61).[47] It can be easily imagined what the popularity and utility of the scheme meant in silent companionship and learning for many a lonely soul. Under the terms of the agreement, provided that the scheme was working satisfactorily, the running and financing of the library would be taken over by the County Council after two years. The council, by a margin of twenty votes to fifteen, decided, on the grounds of economy, not to introduce a rate of one halfpenny in the pound to continue financing the scheme. Two weeks later, in the wake of a public backlash and accusations of returning Galway back to the 'dark ages', it rescinded its decision.[48]

The matter of public service appointments was another contentious issue, and in Galway the local authorities challenged the selection or discharge of several candidates whether foisted on them by Cumann na nGaedheal or Fianna Fáil (post-1932). In 1925 Dr John O'Shea, physician at Galway Hospital, refused to sign the declaration of allegiance to the state as required under the Local Government Act (1925). The local Board of Health, however, continued to support his appointment until a threat of legal action by the Department of Local Government forced his resignation in September.[49] In a more publicised case in 1932, demonstrations were held in Loughrea against the Local Appointments Commission's decision to assign Dr M. F. Daly to the position of medical officer for the district ahead of the local candidate, Dr Charles Ryan, son of the late dispensary doctor who had served in the area for thirty-five years. When Seán Lemass visited Loughrea in September to address a meeting of the Fianna Fáil party, a large banner stretching across the street revealed the words 'Loughrea wants Dr Ryan'. When Daly arrived to take up his new position in November a section of the waiting crowd broke through the cordon of guards drawn across the road and attacked his car with stones and other missiles. He resigned his post in December 1932.[50]

In national affairs, Cumann na nGaedheal rowed through a number of political storms including the Army Mutiny of 1924 and the rivalries it exposed within the party; the lack of consensus within the government on socio-economic policies, exposed most clearly in the differences between Patrick Hogan's commitment to free trade and the protectionist views of J. J. Walsh; and the Boundary Commission fiasco of 1925, the dashing of nationalist expectations, the subsequent defection of party members and the hatching of break-away political groups. However, the self-denying ordinance of the republicans until August 1927 debarred de Valera and his supports from acting in parliament. Thus the ability to expose the uneasy fusion of conflicting elements that made up the Cumann na nGaedheal party was lost. The lack of a strong coherent opposition in the Dáil dictated that Cosgrave's majority was not politically threatened. In this the government was particularly fortunate, and there is a certain merit in the proposition that such an artificial state of affairs compounded the self-righteous attitudes and moral superiority of the party elite.

Cumann na nGaedheal supporters were advocates of Griffith's 'living nation' argument, and they were supporters of an Irish government shaping Irish policy, but the marginalisation of the ordinary people became a source of mounting discontent in the west. An editorial in the *Connacht Tribune* read:

> The simple truth is that the Government has ceased to consult the people. It prides itself that it knows better than the people themselves what the people want ... It is a well-recognised and understood fact that the party in power always yields a certain amount of patronage, but that patronage should not be abused because all who have wished the Government well have been slow to criticise it in view of the dangers and difficulties with which it was faced and the rare courage it demonstrated.[51]

Cumann na nGaedheal's considerable achievements in state-building and external affairs did not galvanise the local electorate. It was criticised for being arrogant, for failing to consult with its local representatives, for not prioritising the building up of a grassroots party organisation, and for ignoring local concerns. The constant criticism from the west of Ireland was that the national government had forgotten its poorest people. Yet the Cosgrave party could be excused for neglecting local issues. As Daly has pointed out, the civil war and the Sinn Féin split ensured that security and status dominated the political platform at the expense of socio-economic concerns.[52] A young, inexperienced government, engaged in creating and safeguarding the apparatus of the new state, was not going to be concerned if one man got more land than another, so long as the land was being divided and the threat of social anarchy checked. However, Cumann na nGaedheal also struggled to retain its nationalist credentials. By the late 1920s and early 1930s, de Valera, not Cosgrave, was seen by many people to be the one pursuing Collins's stepping-stone approach towards the constitutional dismantling of the treaty. But based on an uneasy coalition of moderates, radicals and stepping-stone republicans, drawn together by their support of the treaty, the nature and alignment of the Cumann na nGaedheal party was always likely to shift as the party searched for its own distinctive political identity – an identity that was forged and crystallised by its response to the challenges of governmental power in the aftermath of a bitter civil war. Kevin O'Higgins's statement in December 1923 that 'old friends would be lost but new ones would arise' was as much realistic as it was prophetic.[53] The challenge for Cumann na nGaedheal was striking a balance between prioritising state-building and national government and maintaining local popular support and the confidence of the electorate. The political, economic and public safety challenges it faced in the first decade of independence, coupled with the wide variety of views encompassed in the party, made it a difficult undertaking. By the 1930s the inherent conservatism and sober rectitude of the party was unpalatable to some supporters. Its drift from treatyite republicanism alienated others. In March 1930, Liam Ó Briain (UCG), a firm Cumann na nGaedheal supporter, in an article in the *Star*, criticised the government's shedding of its revolutionary nationalist commitment to an Irish Republic. The 'aspiration towards it', he wrote, 'will remain and must be allowed ... I was and am a doctrinaire Republican, a naïve one still I suppose. I wonder are there any others in Cumann na nGaedheal? I bet there are, and many of them, and I cannot see why they should not proclaim it occasionally.'[54] The Cosgrave party's revolutionary past was being eclipsed. A party sprung from the separatist movement, it became the party of the conservative elements of local society, the propertied classes, large farmers, big businessmen and the professional elite, many of whom had looked askance at Sinn Féin during the Irish revolution.[55] Cumann na nGaedheal failed to recognise the importance of retaining popular appeal and, broadly speaking, it lost more friends than it gained in the west of Ireland.

The case of Labour

Given the fact that the constant criticism coming from the west was that the government was neglecting and ignoring local vital issues, why did the party that attempted to focus on the socio-economic concerns of the people fail to advance its position in Galway? Why did the party that should have done well fail to broaden its electoral appeal? There is, as Ó Tuathaigh noted, more than a grain of truth in the argument that emigration and the departing feet of the men and women of no property defused potentially disruptive social tensions and deprived the Labour Party of a large part of its potential support.[56] In addition, the underlying social infrastructure of a conservative, possessor ethic, agricultural society did not reflect the traditional working-class support base of the party. Furthermore, on a national level, although the elected Labour deputies proved themselves to be capable parliamentarians in the Dáil, internal party divisions and the splintering of the trade union movement during the mid-1920s hindered Labour's ability to win significant political appeal.

In June 1922, as already established, Labour gained 13.2 per cent of the first preference vote in Galway. In August 1923 its vote dropped to 5.97 per cent. However, the sudden decrease in party support was more reflective of the peculiar circumstances of the Collins–de Valera pact than it was of a positive beginning that suddenly went wrong.[57] Between 1923 and 1932 the local Labour vote oscillated between 5.97 per cent and 3.88 per cent (Appendix A.1 and A.2). While the party held on to its one Dáil seat at the August 1923 and June 1927 general elections, it did not attract new supporters. Significantly, it also failed to make an impact at the local elections, winning only one of the forty seats available in 1925 and in 1928 (Appendix A.5 and A.6). Commenting on the composition of the new County Council in 1928, the Labour councillor Gilbert Lynch pronounced his position to be 'something like that of a lost lamb'.[58]

Favouring social stability and fearing class politics, the parliamentary party pursued a cautious approach to social reforms. As Lyons reflected, Labour never allowed its enthusiasm for James Connolly to morph into a living socialist faith.[59] What was needed was stability. And while this very much reflected the conservatism of Irish society and its support of democratic practices, it earned the party the enmity of social radicals. Moreover, constrained somewhat by a lack of party funds, Labour failed to nominate a sufficient number of candidates to present a credible political alternative for government.

Given the economic distress prevalent in parts of the community and the widespread social discontent over land distribution, socio-economic issues should have impinged on the Galway election debates. However, the national question, particularly in view of the fact that the political authority of the state was not recognised by a sizeable minority of republicans, dominated domestic politics at the expense of pressing local concerns. The problem of poverty might have been expected to become political. Yet the rhetoric of speeches made in a political and non-political context differed significantly, and an inexperienced electorate was unaccustomed to voting for sectional over national interests. Once the lines of division in the general elections remained political rather than social, and once the debate continued to centre on the Free State versus the Republic divide, Labour's appeal would, and did, become marginalised in the west of Ireland. Of the five electoral constituencies in Connacht, only Galway (August 1923 and June 1927) and Mayo South (June and September 1927) returned a Labour deputy to the Dáil (see Table 7.1 in Chapter 7). By 1932, the difficulty for Labour was that if the party could identify with the socio-economic policies of Fianna Fáil, there was no reason why their supporters could not do so also.[60]

Notes

1 Richard Dunphy, *The Making of Fianna Fáil Power in Ireland 1923–1948* (Oxford, 1995), pp. 75, 82.
2 Fitzpatrick, 'The geography of Irish nationalism 1910–1921', p. 131.
3 Dunphy, *The Making of Fianna Fáil Power in Ireland 1923–1948*, p. 78.
4 Foster, *Modern Ireland 1600–1972*, p. 542.
5 Alvin Jackson, *Ireland 1798–1998: Politics and War* (Oxford, 1999), p. 288.
6 Dunphy, *The Making of Fianna Fáil Power in Ireland 1923–1948*, p. 108. For a broader discussion on the contradiction within Fianna Fáil policy, see *ibid.*, pp. 108–13.
7 Richard Dunphy, 'The enigma of Fianna Fáil: party, strategy, social class and the politics of hegemony', in Cronin and Regan (eds), *Ireland: The Politics of Independence, 1922–49*, p. 69.
8 Rumpf and Hepburn, *Nationalism and Socialism in Twentieth Century Ireland*, p. 100.
9 *Irish Times*, 12 Jan. 1932.
10 *Freeman's Journal*, 28 Apr. 1923.
11 Circular letter signed by Patrick Ryan, 21 June 1923, UCDA, Cumann na nGaedheal party minute books, P/39/MIN/1/324.
12 Regan, *The Irish Counter-Revolution 1921–1936*, p. 307.
13 Cullen, 'Patrick J. Hogan, T.D., Minister for Agriculture, 1922–1932', p. 24.
14 Ronan Fanning, *Independent Ireland* (Dublin, 1983), p. 102; Dunphy, *The Making of Fianna Fáil Power in Ireland 1923–1948*, pp. 82–3.
15 Cited in Diarmaid Ferriter, *The Transformation of Ireland, 1900–2000* (London, 2004), p. 297; Thomas J. Morrissey, *A Man Called Hughes: The Life and Times of Seamus Hughes, 1881–1943* (Dublin, 1991), p. 69.
16 Cited in Regan, *The Irish Counter-Revolution 1921–1936*, p. 339.
17 Report from Eoin O'Duffy to the Executive Council, 8 Sept. 1924. Cited in McGarry, *Eoin O'Duffy*, p. 139. In July 1927 the Cumann na nGaedheal Standing Committee stated that local party structure in the constituencies required thorough reorganising. UCDA, Cumann na nGaedheal party minute books, P/39/MIN/1/516–18.
18 *Connacht Tribune*, 25 Apr. 1925.
19 Cumann na nGaedheal Annual Conference, 12 May 1925, UCDA, P24/616. Cited in Daly, *The Buffer State*, p. 118.
20 Daly, *The Buffer State*, p. 118.
21 Fanning, *Independent Ireland*, p. 101.
22 Ciara Meehan, *The Cosgrave Party: A History of Cumann na nGaedheal, 1923–33* (Dublin, 2010), pp. 118–19; David M. Farrell, 'Before campaigns were "modern": Irish electioneering in times past', in Tom Garvin, Maurice Manning and Richard Sinnott (eds), *Dissecting Irish Politics: Essays in Honour of Brian Farrell* (Dublin, 2004), p. 180; J. L. McCracken, *Representative Government in Ireland: A Study of Dáil Éireann 1919–48* (London, 1958), p. 83.
23 Sinnott, *Irish Voters Decide*, p. 280.

24 Maurice Manning, *Irish Political Parties: An Introduction* (Dublin, 1972), p. 112; Cornelius O'Leary, *Irish Elections 1918–77: Parties, Voters and Proportional Representation* (Dublin, 1979), p. 18; McCracken, *Representative Government in Ireland*, p. 114.

25 Warner Moss, *Political Parties in the Irish Free State* (New York, 1933), p. 19.

26 Pyne, 'The third Sinn Féin party: 1923–1926', vol. 1, no. 2, pp. 229–42.

27 Rumpf and Hepburn, *Nationalism and Socialism in Twentieth Century Ireland*, p. 62.

28 Sinnott, *Irish Voters Decide*, pp. 122–3. For a comparison of Rumpf's original cartographical analysis and Sinnott's revised maps (where he redraws Rumpf's maps to a consistent scale), see *ibid.*, pp. 120–1, 124–5.

29 Michael Gallagher, 'Electoral support for Irish political parties, 1927–1973', *Contemporary Political Sociology Series*, vol. 2 (London, 1976), p. 7.

30 Bill Kissane, *Explaining Irish Democracy* (Dublin, 2002), p. 223.

31 Sinnott, *Irish Voters Decide*, p. 131.

32 *Census of Ireland 1926*, Population, Area and Valuation, vol. I, p. 27.

33 Prior to the pact election in 1922, County Galway had been divided into five and then four electoral constituencies. Between 1922 and 1935 it was a single constituency. Under the terms of the Electoral (Revision of Constituencies) Act, 1935, the county was divided into two smaller constituencies and ever since County Galway has fluctuated between two and three constituencies with the constituency boundaries not always reflecting the county boundary.

34 McCracken, *Representative Government in Ireland*, pp. 114–16.

35 In 1928, the Galway city division returned two Fianna Fáil, two Sinn Féin, one Cumann na nGaedheal, one Farmers' Party, one Independent and one Labour Party councillor. Ballinasloe returned three Ratepayers' Association, two Cumann na nGaedheal, one Fianna Fáil and one Independent councillor. In Tuam, the distribution was five Cumann na nGaedheal, two Fianna Fáil, one Sinn Féin and one Independent councillor and Loughrea returned three Fianna Fáil, two Cumann na nGaedheal, two Farmers' Party and one Independent councillor. In Oughterard the eight candidates, including six outgoing deputies, were returned uncontested and five Fianna Fáil, two Cumann na nGaedheal and one Independent councillor represented the area. *Connacht Tribune*, 7 July 1928. For the distribution of candidates in the 1925 election, see *ibid.*, 24 July 1925.

36 McCracken, *Representative Government in Ireland*, pp. 110–11.

37 Conference of Standing Committee with Executive Council, 3 Dec. 1923, UCDA, Cumann na nGaedheal party minute books, P/39/MIN/1/376. 'Executive Council' was the term used for the cabinet.

38 Minutes of the Standing Committee, 30 May 1924, *ibid.*, P/39/MIN/1/411.

39 Nicholls to Cosgrave, 25 Aug. 1924, NAI, DT, S1884. Padraig Ó Máille (CNG) in a separate letter to the President added that if the government handed over the remains, there would not be any difficulty in distinguishing

the men as identification discs were placed on each of the coffins. Ó Máille to Cosgrave, 27 Aug. 1924, *ibid.*

40 Letter from Sec. Coiste Gnótha, Cumann na nGaedheal, to Cosgrave, 16 Sept. 1924, *ibid.*

41 *Galway Observer*, 7 May 1927.

42 Minutes of Loughrea Rural District Council, 1 Mar. 1924, GCCA, Loughrea RDC minute books, G01/8/14.

43 Minutes of Clifden Rural District Council, 10 Oct. 1923, *ibid.*, Clifden RDC minute books, G01/7/14.

44 *Connacht Tribune*, 8 Nov. 1924.

45 *Ibid.*

46 Daly, *The Buffer State*, p. 153.

47 The report and statistics of the Carnegie Libraries for County Galway for year ended 31 Aug. 1925. Cited in *Connacht Tribune*, 3 Oct. 1925.

48 For details on the public reaction to the Council's decision, see *Connacht Tribune*, 7, 14, 21 Nov. 1925. Between 1926 and 1927 over 55,000 books were issued to Galway readers. *Ibid.*, 15 Oct. 1927.

49 *Ibid.*, 26 Sept. 1925.

50 *Ibid.*, 1 Oct., 26 Nov. 1932; *East Galway Democrat*, 17 Dec. 1932.

51 *Connacht Tribune*, 29 Nov. 1924.

52 Daly, *Industrial Development and Irish National Identity, 1922–1939*, p. 13.

53 Minutes of conference between the Executive Council and the Standing Committee, 3 Dec. 1923, UCDA, Cumann na nGaedheal party minute books, P/39/MIN/1/376.

54 Cited in *Connacht Tribune*, 22 Mar. 1930.

55 O'Leary, *Irish Elections 1918–77*, p. 18.

56 M. A. G. Ó Tuathaigh, 'The historical pattern of Irish emigration: some labour aspects', in Galway Labour History Group, *The Emigrant Experience* (Galway, 1991), pp. 24–5.

57 Sinnott, *Irish Voters Decide*, p. 53.

58 *Connacht Tribune*, 7 July 1928.

59 F. S. L. Lyons, *Ireland since the Famine* (2nd edn, London, 1973), p. 525.

60 Enda McKay, 'Changing with the tide: the Irish Labour Party, 1927–1933', *Saothar*, 11 (1986), pp. 27–38; Sinnott, *Irish Voters Decide*, p. 54.

7

Elections: 1927–32

June 1927

After five years of self-government (1922–27), the people had more time to reflect on the administration's perceived neglect of the west and register its verdict. The plethora of small parties and interest groups that contended the June 1927 general election indicated a growing dissatisfaction with the economic and social conservatism of the Cosgrave regime. In Galway, twenty-two candidates stood for election and the campaign was characterised not by the voters' desire to elect a strong Cumann na nGaedheal government, but by the opportunity it presented to the electorate to return an effective opposition that would look after its vital interests in the Dáil. Commenting on the developing maturity of the local electorate, the *Connacht Tribune* wrote:

> The people to-day are much more critical than they were in 1923. They are also more alive to their own interests. A period of poverty that has been the common lot of all European countries since the war has made their senses much more acute, and has correspondingly lessened the influence of the mere 'tub thumper' or of the village politician. What is wanted is not self-interest or sonorous phrases of little meaning, but capacity and, where it is obtainable, experience.[1]

The complexion of the main political parties had changed considerably since the last election. Locally, of the four Cumann na nGaedheal deputies elected in August 1923, Patrick Hogan and Seán Broderick once more stood for Cumann na nGaedheal; George Nicholls retired, but acted as the party's election agent; and Padraig Ó Máille, having left Cumann na nGaedheal in 1925, ran as a Clann Éireann candidate. Of the three sitting Sinn Féin deputies, only Barney Mellows stood again for Sinn Féin; Frank Fahy joined Fianna Fáil; and Louis O'Dea, who did not run for re-election, acted as election agent for Fianna Fáil. James Cosgrave, the former independent deputy, ran for the new Irish National League Party and T. J. O'Connell, the outgoing Labour deputy, contested the Mayo South constituency. He was replaced in Galway by Gilbert Lynch (Figure 7.1). Additionally, in keeping with W. T. Cosgrave's desire to appeal to the best elements of society, Cumann na nGaedheal approached two influential figures to represent the party – prominent merchant Martin (Máirtín Mór) McDonogh, and Thomas Kenny, editor of the *Connacht Tribune*. McDonogh dominated the commercial life of the city as the largest employer in the region, and although by then sixty-seven years of age, he accepted the nomination.[2] Kenny, unwilling to divide his interests in light of the recent expansion undertaken by his newspaper, declined.

In Fianna Fáil, Cumann na nGaedheal now faced a sophisticated, energetic and disciplined party machine. A circular letter, issued from Fianna Fáil headquarters, informed local officials that the party's mottoes should be painted all over the constituency; that party flags should be displayed from committee rooms, club premises and the houses of supporters; and that telegraph poles should be kept covered with literature and posters.[3] Moss noted that

> Fianna Fail was given little newspaper support but its ample funds from America permitted the party to buy advertising space which it used to describe, on the one hand, the decline of the country's economic welfare and, on the other hand, the salaries of Cumann na nGaedheal leaders and the increasing cost of government.[4]

Commenting on the party's local campaign, the *Connacht Tribune* acknowledged that Fianna Fáil had the best organisation of any party from the point of view of advertisement, transport and the assistance that it was able to summon.[5] Nationally, it was the only opposition party to put forward enough candidates to form a single party government. In Galway it nominated six candidates, the same number as Cumann na nGaedheal, to contest the nine seats.

Nonetheless, despite its split with Sinn Féin and its rejection of violent republicanism, Fianna Fáil was still an abstentionist party. While recognising that the functioning political machinery of the state represented the most effective path to achieving political power, the party's refusal to take the oath prohibited its members from entering the Dáil. Moreover, Fianna Fáil's exchange of physical force republicanism for the experiment of Free State politics, while signalling a separation of the aims and strategies of both organisations, did not represent a complete break with the IRA. Three of the four Fianna Fáil candidates elected in Galway (Powell, Killilea and Tubridy) were IRA officers and 'it was some time before all those who followed de Valera into Fianna Fáil actually severed their connections with the IRA'.[6] On 4 June the party placed a half-page advertisement in the *Connacht Tribune* under the heading 'Fianna Fail is going in'. The crucial question was did 'in' mean into the Dáil?[7]

Locally, the Fianna Fáil candidates went to the restless electorate promising to abolish the oath, lower administration costs, reduce taxation, protect local industries and end emigration. Claiming that the ministers had lost touch with the people, they attacked the government's failure to ease the distress in Connemara; to protect agriculture and the fisheries from foreign competition; and to respond to and implement the findings of the Gaeltacht Commission. One election pamphlet critical of the government's expenditure in light of the cuts in old age pensions read: 'Is it any wonder that these officials, with their salaries and allowances, chauffeurs and aide-de-camps, talk of "Prosperity"? They have it.'[8] A more persuasive slogan was 'Vote for Fianna Fáil and put in a government which will give the poor and the struggling a chance to exist'.[9]

In addition to Fianna Fáil, Cumann na nGaedheal also faced competition from two other new parties, the National League and Clann Éireann. The National League was established in September 1926 under the leadership of William Redmond, son of the former Irish Parliamentary Party leader John Redmond. The party ambitiously ran four candidates in Galway, including two former Irish Party members, James Cosgrave, MP for east Galway 1914–18, and William Duffy, MP for south Galway 1900–18. Cosgrave's successful election as an independent candidate in August 1923, as suggested earlier, demonstrated a reservoir of old IPP support in east Galway and the appeal of returning a candidate with parliamentary experience. In 1927 the League attacked the government on the grounds of incompetence, profligacy and autocracy.[10] Opening the party's campaign in Kilconnell (east Galway), despite a downpour of rain, William Duffy outlined their position:

> In some respects the Government have done well ... but the people cannot afford to give them a fresh period of office unless they took advantage of the opportunity which now offers at this election to send to the Dáil a body of men who will act in a critical and constructive capacity to watch over and critically examine the people's interests in the Dáil.[11]

Emphasising its continuity with the Irish Party, James Reddington reminded those gathered that times had changed and the people were beginning to realise that 'the old Party was not a bad Party. They got the only thing you can claim to be owners of at the present moment – your own land.'[12] In resurrecting the rhetoric of the Land League and the United Irish League, the new party looked to seize upon the growing discontent over the failure of the Land Commission to satisfy the demands for land division in the county. Furthermore, it sought to present itself as the voice of sectional interests, the town tenants and the licensed trade.

If the National League could claim, as it did, to be a party that stood outside the Sinn Féin split, Clann Éireann, on the other hand, was very much a product of the unstable coalition of personalities that constituted the Cumann na nGaedheal party. Led by William Magennis, Professor of Metaphysics in UCD, Clann Éireann included several members of the 'National Group' who had left the Cosgrave party in 1924. Padraig Ó Máille TD (Galway), who defected from Cumann na nGaedheal over the Boundary Commission crisis in 1925, also joined the new party, along with Senator Maurice Moore and Wicklow TD Christopher Byrne. In essence, Clann Éireann was a treatyite protest party. First, it protested against the government's failure to implement a constitutional revision of the treaty in keeping with Collins's stepping-stone interpretation of the agreement. Secondly, it denounced what it perceived to be the imperialist nature of the government and the failure of the Boundary Commission and its intended (and leaked) report. And thirdly, while supporting the legitimacy of the Free State, the party contested the validity of the oath of allegiance and advocated its abolition. Speaking at a meeting in Spiddal (west Galway), Ó Máille argued that 'no obstacle like the oath ought to be imposed that would debar the elected representatives of the people from taking their place in the legislative councils of the nations'.[13] Responding to questions at Headford (north Galway) two weeks later he professed: 'I hated to take the oath. I bear allegiance to only one country and that is Ireland ... Every man is entitled to sacrifice himself in the cause of the nation. That is the reason I accepted the Treaty.' Yet he also advocated clemency. 'I was shot in Dublin', he told the crowd, but 'I have no griev-ance against the men who did that act. I took what I got, and bore it like a man ... There were rotten things done on both sides during the civil strife.'[14] Ó Máille's campaign focused on the government's neglect of the west of Ireland. The cardinal fault of the government, he argued, 'is that they regard every question with a Dublin rather than with a National outlook, with the result that Connacht is neglected, Galway is neglected and Connemara is left last of all'.[15] The policies of Clann Éireann bore a strong resemblance to those of Fianna Fáil, whose entry into the pol-itical fold undoubtedly caused the charismatic War of Independence veteran and former Leas-Ceann Comhairle of the Dáil to lose his seat. Magnanimous in defeat, Ó Máille told those gathered at the Town Hall that 'he thought he was as right in the attitude he had taken up as he was when he carried a rifle over the hills and glens of his native Connemara'.[16] The short-lived Clann Éireann party was wiped out in June 1927. Its national record made poor reading. The party ran eight candidates in the general election, none of whom were elected, and seven lost their depos-its. Seán Broderick's (CNG), portrayal of 'a party without a people',[17] while harsh on his former colleague, was accurate.

The Labour Party also campaigned on the lack of economic progress in the west and focused on the immediate local social and economic concerns of the people. As stated earlier, the party's new candidate in Galway was Gilbert Lynch, the self-styled 'Tenement TD'.[18] In his speeches Lynch criticised the different levels of prosperity in the county, repeated Fianna Fáil's call for more protection for the fisheries and local industries, and drew attention to the housing shortage in the county. In opening his campaign on 1 May, he declared that the government 'gave lip service to the Gaelic language and Gaelic culture' but 'made no provision in their budget for carrying into effect the recommendations of the Gaeltacht Commission'. Labour, he insisted, would provide an opposition in the Dáil that would focus attention on economic issues and protect the interests of the workers and the town tenants.[19]

Locally, the Labour Party's first preference vote dropped from 5.97 per cent in August 1923 to 4.60 per cent in June 1927. Yet despite the presence of so many contending parties it retained its seat in Galway, albeit on the last count. Nationally, Labour's first preference vote increased from 10.62 per cent to 12.55 per cent and the party won twenty-two seats compared to fourteen seats in August 1923. T. J. O'Connell, campaigning in Mayo, topped the poll in his native county and secured a new seat for the party in the Mayo South constituency.[20] With two Labour deputies from Connacht being returned to the Dáil, the June 1927 election marked the party's most successful performance in the region during the period 1923–32 (Table 7.1).

The local Cumann na nGaedheal candidates, on the other hand, campaigned on the president's 'good value' slogan and went to the county on the party's credible record of peace and security, law and order, the merit of its political experience, and the achievement of solvency, high financial credit and economic stability. The continued aim and purpose of the party, Cosgrave reminded the electorate, was

> an ordered society, hard work, constant endeavour, a definite settled policy of reconstruction and rehabilitation, recruitment to the public service on the basis of merit; efficient, upright, economic public service, greater national economy day by day, year by year; balanced budgets, a national revival of Irish culture; [and] the maintenance of peace.[21]

However, the government's recent legislative reforms had proved unpopular. In addition, Cumann na nGaedheal lacked a clear, concise economic policy to address the distress in the west and foster economic growth. Reacting to the criticisms of the government's hesitant response to the Gaeltacht Commission, Patrick Hogan insisted that 'they did not propose to spend money before an election to buy votes, and they would

Table 7.1 Labour seats in Connacht, 1923–32

	Galway	Mayo North	Mayo South	Leitrim-Sligo	Roscommon
Year	Seats	Seats	Seats	Seats	Seats
Aug. 1923	1	0	0	0	0
June 1927	1	0	1	0	0
Sept. 1927	0	No candidate	1	0	No candidate
Feb. 1932	0	No candidate	0	0	No candidate

not alter their programme merely because there was a general election in the offing'.[22] Defending the slow progress of the Land Commission, he reiterated that 'all the land could not be divided all over the country in one day' and once again insisted that 'it was more important to buy land cheaply than quickly'.[23] Speaking in Galway city, he told those gathered: 'The shower of rain that fell this morning is of much more importance to the farmers of County Galway than any discussion about the Oath or the Treaty.'[24] Significantly, the electorate's impatience with the land question did not translate into a substantial protest vote against the minister. Although his number of first preference votes decreased from August 1923, Hogan, for the third successive time, topped the poll in Galway (Figure 7.1). Throughout his campaign, he was accompanied by Michael Davitt, son of the great Land Leaguer, physician at the County Hospital, and president of the Galway branch of Cumann na nGaedheal in 1927. Davitt's appeal among the electorate, undoubtedly, did much to counter the National League's profession of allegiance to the old Land League.

Nevertheless, for all that the opposing local candidates tried to distance themselves from the language of the civil war and focus on socio-economic affairs, the treaty and the oath dominated the tone of the election campaign. The contest became a clash of rival legitimacies between those who created the Free State and those who had forcefully challenged it. While Hogan was received with enthusiastic ovations from Cumann na nGaedheal supporters, he was also bombarded by cries of 'Up the Republic'. At Derrybrien he retorted, 'God help the Republic if it has nothing to depend on but sound.'[25] The campaign was noted for its volatility and bitterness. Referring to de Valera during his opening remarks in south Galway, Hogan declared: 'He is finished – absolutely finished.' In Headford (north Galway) he stated that Brian Cusack did not have 'the ghost of a chance of getting in' (here, at least, he was right). At Ballinamore Bridge (north-east Galway) on 22 May he wagered his salary of £1,700 that Mark Killilea would not get elected (this would have been, if he had paid, a more costly error).[26] Hogan's loathing and distrust of de Valera and his party was well known. In 1922 he had described him as 'a criminal lunatic'.[27] At election time, much as the electorate may have desired otherwise, matters of state dominated the agenda.

Cumann na nGaedheal polled the highest number of first preferences in the county, gaining 35.02 per cent of the vote compared to Fianna Fáil's 33.55 per cent.[28] But the figure of 35.02 per cent represented a decrease of 8.65 per cent in Cumann na nGaedheal party support from August 1923. The result was a success for Fianna Fáil in Galway. In the party's first general election contest, it eclipsed the local Sinn Féin vote (which fell to 4.41 per cent), secured Padraig Ó Máille's seat at the expense of the government party and gained the majority of seats in the county. Despite the obvious uncertainty as to whether its candidates, if elected, would enter the Dáil, de Valera's progressive republican policy and the party's claim that peaceful change was possible attracted considerable republican support. Galway elected four Fianna Fáil, three Cumann na nGaedheal, one Labour and one National League candidate (Figure 7.2). Barney Mellows, the single Sinn Féin candidate, lost his seat.

Local political predictions were wholly inaccurate. The *Galway Observer* forecast that the National League candidates were certain to poll well and regarded it as a foregone conclusion that William Duffy, Thomas Sloyan, James Cosgrave and James Reddington would be elected. A cartoon sketch printed in the paper read: 'Who will you vote for? James Cosgrave, Padraic O'Maille, Gilbert Lynch, Jimmy Reddington, Tom Sloyan, and Willie Duffy. We can't let down the tried and tested.'[29] The 'tried and tested', it seemed, were judged to be neither members of Cumann na nGaedheal nor members of Fianna Fáil. Other correspondents had forecast a win for McDonogh (CNG), followed by Duffy (NL), Hogan (CNG) and Ó Máille (CÉ).[30] Despite the constitutional leanings of his new party, local commentators had anticipated that the election would greatly reduce de Valera's following.

In a concerted effort to bolster its electoral appeal, Cumann na nGaedheal's election committee had directed its candidates to focus their campaigns on areas where the party had not previously held strong levels of support.

> From the reports of the Parish Canvassers, and from the marked Registers, the Director should be able to form an idea of where our weakness in the constituency lies, and should concentrate on these places. Where apathy is apparent or where our support is weak should be the place of meeting selected for the ablest speaker.[31]

The local Cumann na nGaedheal candidates, however, failed to adhere to such directives. In fact, none of the other rival party candidates rose to the challenge of this new initiative. Instead, as had been the tendency in previous campaigns, they concentrated for the most part on their own local areas of support.[32] The size of the Galway constituency made it

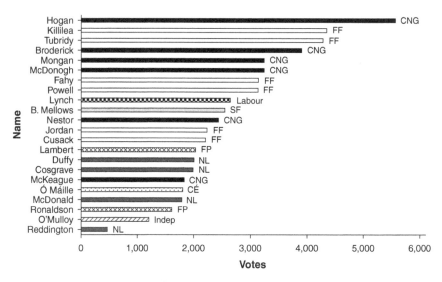

Figure 7.1 First preference vote in County Galway, June 1927

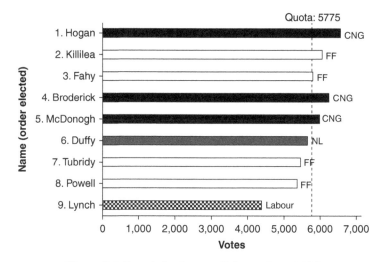

Figure 7.2 Result in County Galway, June 1927

almost entirely beyond the physical and financial reach of the candidates to canvass all the different regions.

Nonetheless, compared to the previous election, the June 1927 contest was noted for increased political activity and the local clergy played an active role in nominating candidates, presiding at party meetings and speaking at election rallies.[33] Yet Galway, for the third successive time,

registered the lowest percentage turnout in the country. It recorded a figure of 57.03 per cent compared to the national average of 66.26 per
cent.[34] Reacting to the poor turnout, Galway County Council ordered
that the attention of the Minister for Local Government be directed to
the fact that the arrangement of polling districts in such a large constituency caused significant inconvenience and hardship to rural voters and
resulted in a considerable amount of abstention from the polls.[35] Yet the
division of the county into smaller, more manageable electoral areas at
the local council elections did not produce a larger turnout at the polls.
Additionally, there were still problems with the electoral register. Although
reduced from an excess of 7,977 in 1923, Galway recorded a surplus of
3,696 relative to the population aged twenty-one and over in the county
in 1927.[36] A memorandum prepared by Cumann na nGaedheal after the
election stated that 'the public conception of the register is debased by the
fact that it is regarded as a legitimate battleground for political parties,
whereas it should be a coldly official document as accurate and automatic
as the conscription lists in countries where compulsory service prevails'.[37]
The register was still corrupt rather than correct. More significantly, the
dominance of the national question over local socio-economic issues was
generating a degree of apathy among the voting public.

In June 1927 the county returned another fragmented vote. The leading
candidates after the first count consisted of four Cumann na nGaedheal
and four Fianna Fáil candidates (Figure 7.1). No candidate was elected on
the first count and once more the large number of contestants resulted in
a long drawn-out count. Four counts were required before Patrick Hogan
(CNG), who topped the poll, reached the quota of 5,775 votes and was
declared elected. It took another five counts before Mark Killilea (FF),
who had received the second-largest first preference vote, reached the
quota. After nine rounds, only two candidates had been returned. By the
end of the twelfth count, two Fianna Fáil candidates, Killilea and Fahy,
and the two sitting Cumann na nGaedheal TDs, Hogan and Broderick,
had been elected. McDonogh (CNG) was elected on the fourteenth count
and the four remaining seats, Duffy (NL), Tubridy (FF), Powell (FF) and
Lynch (Labour), were eventually filled on the sixteenth and final count
(Figure 7.2). Of the nine candidates elected for Galway, only five deputies reached the quota. In June 1927, the local electorate's dissatisfaction
with the government's performance resulted in the loss of a number of
Cumann na nGaedheal first preference votes to the pro-treaty minority
parties, who between them polled 27.02 per cent of the local vote (Labour
4.60 per cent, National League 10.83 per cent, Farmers' 6.35 per cent,
Clann Éireann 3.13 per cent and Independents 2.11 per cent). Nationally,
the broad range of pro-treaty parties polled 42.81 per cent of the vote.[38]

Fianna Fáil was less exposed to a fragmentation of the anti-treaty vote. Party loyalty among its supporters was notably strong. For instance, after the seventh count, Stephen Jordan was the first Fianna Fáil candidate to be eliminated. The largest shares of his transfers divided 45 per cent for Killilea (FF), 23 per cent for Fahy (FF) and 5 per cent for Cusack (FF). At the next count Cusack's votes divided 65 per cent for Fahy and 16 per cent for Killilea. Killilea was then elected and 69 per cent of his surplus went to Fahy. In this manner the elimination of two Fianna Fáil candidates, as a minimum, ensured the election of two other party candidates. Fahy, who had received the seventh-highest number of first preference votes, was elected in third place.

One important correlation that emerged from the June election was the voting pattern of Cumann na nGaedheal and National League supporters. While a degree of party loyalty existed among Cumann na nGaedheal supporters, the party also lost a number of lower preference votes to the National League.[39] Within the National League, transfer loyalty was especially evident among supporters of the two former Irish Party MPs. For example, on the elimination of James Cosgrave after the thirteenth count, William Duffy received 59 per cent of his transfers, which helped secure the party's only seat.[40] However, many National League voters also showed considerable transfer loyalty to Cumann na nGaedheal candidates at the expense of their own party representatives. This was perhaps unsurprising in a group that resembled a cohort of personalities rather than a strongly organised political party. Ó Máille's Clann Éireann votes, on the other hand, were divided primarily between Cumann na nGaedheal (42 per cent) and Fianna Fáil (34 per cent). A degree of localism was also evident in the vote distribution, where the highest numbers of Ó Máille's preferences went to the three candidates most associated with Connemara – Martin McDonogh (CNG), Joseph Mongan (CNG) and Seán Tubridy (FF).

The June result signified the abandonment of the local electorate's popular support for *lámh láidir* (physical force) republicanism. It vindicated de Valera's split from the impolitic absolutes of Sinn Féin. Nevertheless, much as its TDs may have wanted to enter the Dáil, Fianna Fáil's abstentionist position ensured that the 'party's preliminary foray to Leinster House' on 23 June ended in rebuff when its deputies, having refused to take the oath, were denied admittance.[41] Hogan was delighted. Describing the events to his aunt, he wrote:

> We had a great day on the opening of Parliament. De Valera turned out with his following, all looking very nervous. We showed him into a room in the front hall, which is about fifty yards from the hall in which the Parliament sits. The Clerk of the Dáil inquired as to whether any of them were extremely

anxious to take the Oath. De Valera replied that he, the Clerk, had no right
to compel them to take the Oath. The door of the Parliament House was
then locked and they were left in the hall. They ambled about for about an
hour and then wandered away disgusted.[42]

Cumann na nGaedheal, as the single largest party in the Dáil, remained
in power. But it was frustrated by the result. Its national support had
dropped to 27.45 per cent – little more than a quarter of the vote.[43]
Locally, as already established, despite polling the highest number of
first preference votes, the party lost the majority of seats in Galway to
Fianna Fáil. 'All these wretched little parties', O'Higgins complained, had
weakened Cumann na nGaedheal's standing.[44] His analysis, although
petulant, was shrewd. The June election was a setback for the party. A
significant minority of the local electorate, while endorsing the political
institutions of the state, registered a protest vote against the government.
Cumann na nGaedheal's success in restoring law and order and securing
financial stability did not translate into marks on the ballot papers. In
Connacht, Cumann na nGaedheal's percentage vote decreased in each
of the five constituencies (Appendix A.3). The 'state of parties being
what they are', de Valera wrote, in a percipient letter to his supporters
in America, 'I think it unlikely that this parliament can live for anything
like its full term of five years, so another election may be rushed at any
time'.[45] O'Higgins's remark that the country had elected a Dáil but had
forgotten to elect a government was perhaps the most apt.[46] The indecisive result offered little hope of political stability.

September 1927

The political crisis that precipitated the September election has been
well documented. On 10 July Kevin O'Higgins, Minister for Justice,
was assassinated. Ten days later Cosgrave announced the introduction
of a drastic and far-reaching Public Safety Bill directed at the IRA; an
Electoral Amendment Bill requiring candidates to swear, at the time of
nomination, that they would take the oath of allegiance if elected; and a
third bill restricting the initiation of a referendum by petition to members
of the parliament who had taken the oath.[47] Facing permanent exclusion
from electoral politics, de Valera declared the oath to be an 'empty political formula' and Fianna Fáil entered the Dáil on 11 August. On 16
August the Labour Party proposed a motion of no confidence in the government. Believing he would be defeated, Cosgrave held a farewell party
for his staff on the evening before the vote.[48] The government, however, survived the motion on the casting vote of the Ceann Comhairle.
Nonetheless, Cosgrave dissolved the short fifth Dáil on 25 August.

Fianna Fáil's abandonment of abstention and the arrival of the party deputies into the chamber restored the natural balance of parliament. Cumann na nGaedheal now faced a real opposition rather than rows of empty seats in the Dáil. The September election would not be a battle of pro- or anti-state legitimacies, but a contest between two rival programmes for government. More importantly, Fianna Fáil now provided a viable constitutional alternative for the voters of an agriculturally depressed community.

At a first glance, the September 1927 election in Galway was another success for Fianna Fáil. The party swept up the Sinn Féin vote and retained the majority of seats it had won in the June election. A telegram from a delighted Seán Lemass to the local Fianna Fáil office read: 'Convey heartiest congratulations from H.Q. to all workers in Galway on magnificent victory.'[49] However, for the second successive election Cumann na nGaedheal gained more first preference votes than Fianna Fáil in County Galway, securing 45.48 per cent of the vote compared to Fianna Fáil's 42.71 per cent.[50] While Fianna Fáil increased its vote by 9.16 per cent, Cumann na nGaedheal increased its share by 10.46 per cent. The Cosgrave party recouped some ground in Galway. Yet it was recovering from a particularly low point (Appendix A.1 and A.2). At the June election the broad range of minority parties fractured the Cumann na nGaedheal vote. In September 1927, it was less susceptible to such a division. Neither the Farmers' Party, nor the National League, nor Clann Éireann contested the second election in Galway. In addition, Sinn Féin's continued policy of abstention debarred its candidates from contesting the election under the terms of the new Electoral Amendment Act 1927. Apart from the two main parties, only three alternative candidates contested the local election. Padraig Ó Máille (previously Clann Éireann), having failed to gain a nomination as a Fianna Fáil candidate, entered as an independent; James Cosgrave (previously National League), who lost his seat to his more popular running mate William Duffy in the June election, also contested as an independent; and Gilbert Lynch, having secured the final seat for the Labour Party in June, ran again as the Labour candidate (Figure 7.3). The reduced field simplified the September election and lessened the voters' choice. Evaluating the government's performance to date, the *Connacht Tribune* wrote:

> It may be argued that it was intolerant of criticism, autocratic, impatient; but all these arguments are the merest futilities when set against the higher interests of the country. They should not weigh with any sensible man to deflect a single vote from the Government.[51]

In a campaign dominated by national events, the minor parties were squeezed out. The contest became a straight fight between Cumann na nGaedheal and Fianna Fáil, and it is in this context that the government party's local performance was a disappointment.

Cumann na nGaedheal urged the electorate not to return another indecisive vote. Speaking in Gort (south Galway), Patrick Hogan declared 'I want you to return de Valera with a big majority or to return us with a big majority. Do one thing or the other. If you want a fight there is nothing like letting you have it. I want the country to call this bluff once [and] for all.'⁵² Hogan, in particular, had been deeply affected by the events of the summer and the murder of O'Higgins. Reacting to the death of his close friend, he wrote 'The Bishops here issued a pastoral recently: they are very concerned about short skirts; they don't seem nearly so concerned about perjury or murder, but there you are.'⁵³ During the election, he unleashed a barrage of criticism against the Fianna Fáil party. Fear – the fear of Fianna Fáil, the fear of instability, the fear of the gunman and the fear of war – dominated the tone of his powerful speeches. Addressing the crowd in Gort, he warned that

> if the country is bent on fighting England, there is no other way to settle it than to have a fight. Personally I would rather sell my cattle to England, and, so, too, I am sure, would the farmers. What would happen suppose there was a fight tomorrow … Your markets would be stopped and your roads blocked. There would be no fairs; no prices for stock, and the ordinary decent man and woman would have to pay the bill finally.⁵⁴

Hogan was unrelenting in his criticism. At Woodford (south Galway) he launched another broadside against his enemies: 'You need not mind either de Valera or Frank Fahy. They are beaten. I have been here, there, and everywhere, and I can tell you what the National Army gave them in 1922 is nothing to the beating they are going to get at this election.'⁵⁵ At a Cumann na nGaedheal rally in Tuam (north Galway), W. T. Cosgrave echoed the fiery speeches of his minister.

> We are going to throttle the gunman … on one party has fallen the responsibility of correcting evil tendencies throughout the country, of restoring some respect for civilisation and Christianity throughout the country, and then we are charged by those jelly-fish representatives of the people with being autocrats, despots, and so on.⁵⁶

Some of the other local Cumann na nGaedheal candidates were equally critical. At Moylough (north-east Galway), Seán Broderick stated that 'the Governor-General's signature was not dry on the Electoral Amendment Act until Fianna Fáil came creeping into the Dáil'. Speaking at Glynsk, in Connemara, he explained that the purpose of the Electoral Amendment Act 'was to prevent people being fooled any longer by Fianna Fáil, which secured votes from the people and then sat around the firesides and at the cross-roads and did nothing'.[57] Adding his support to the Cumann na nGaedheal campaign, Monsignor MacAlpine, parish priest of Clifden, declared that de Valera's policy 'was now the same as it was in the past – plunder, devastation, and ruin'.[58]

Responding to the near disaster of the June election, Cumann na nGaedheal, as mentioned in the previous chapter, employed the services of O'Kennedy-Brindley advertising agency to direct its national campaign in September 1927. In its post-election publication, *Making History: The Story of a Remarkable Campaign*, O'Kennedy described how almost 300 advertisements including seven full-page and 126 half-page posters had appeared in the press and not one had been repeated.[59] Referring to the amount of political propaganda packed into them, the *Irish Statesman* wryly commented that the election advertisements made much better reading than the election speeches.[60] Some of the more memorable slogans included 'Who are the War-makers?', 'Dev. in the Dumps and Dev. on the Warpath', 'Empty Formulas and Emptier Pledges', 'Economy – By Torch and Petrol Can' and 'Digging Freedom's Grave in 1922 – Poisoning the Wells of Freedom in 1927'. But its national advertising campaign did not penetrate the grassroots. Locally, only two election advertisements for Cumann na nGaedheal (and one for Fianna Fáil) appeared in the *Connacht Tribune* during the September campaign. Posters and painted slogans remained the features of the regional contests. The issues were clear – they screamed from the dead walls – but Cumann na nGaedheal's message did not speak to many key sectors of local society.

Nationally, the party improved its position from forty-seven seats and 27.45 per cent of the vote in June to sixty-two seats and 38.69 per cent of the vote in September and formed the new government with the support of the Farmers' Party and some independents.[61] At a local level, Hogan again topped the poll in Galway with 6,059 votes and was elected on the first count (Figure 7.3).[62] Cumann na nGaedheal recovered to its 1923 position, but it did not make significant new ground in the county. The first three candidates to be elected each represented the government party, but once more it lost the majority of seats to Fianna Fáil, on this occasion by five seats to four (Figure 7.4).

Tactically, the calling of a snap September election provided the government with an opportunity to test the national mood and take advantage of de Valera's reversal on the oath before Fianna Fáil had time to prove their constitutional capabilities in the Dáil. Fianna Fáil supporters, however, welcomed the strategic abandonment of protest politics. The party's entry into the Dáil did not impact negatively on its vote. It garnered the Sinn Féin vote and, as noted, retained the majority of seats in the county. In June 1927 there was an obvious pro-state loyalty among

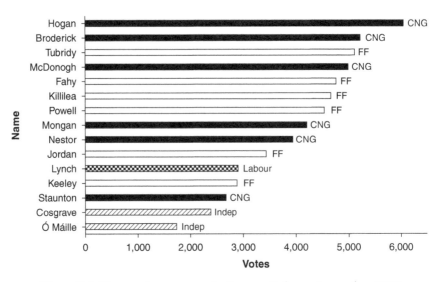

Figure 7.3 First preference vote in County Galway, September 1927

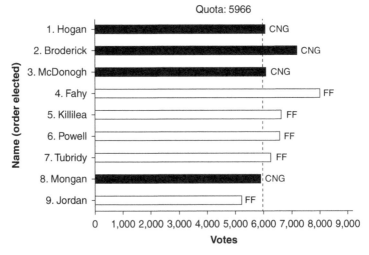

Figure 7.4 Result in County Galway, September 1927

transfer votes. In September Fianna Fáil's embrace of the political system, however grudging, secured for the party the benefit of some of these
vital transfers as the party began to attract support from middle ground,
disenfranchised, and non-aligned voters. 'If Fianna Fáil got into power',
Thomas Powell (FF) declared, 'they would restore the shilling to the old
age pensioners, cut down or revise useless departments, revise salaries

over £1,000 and look after the agricultural and fishing industry.'[63] Frank Fahy (FF), denouncing the draining effect of emigration on the country, claimed it was Fianna Fáil's duty to prevent the ostracism of the youth of the country. The farmer, he added,

> could not get as good a price now for his sheep as he would last May, and after the fair they saw him dodging down a back street to escape the eye of the shopkeeper who was trying to squeeze money out of him that he had not got.[64]

Between them Cumann na nGaedheal and Fianna Fáil won 88.19 per cent of the vote in Galway. Both parties were disciplined in their vote management. For instance, Patrick Hogan and Seán Broderick were the first Cumann na nGaedheal candidates to be elected. Of the available transfers, 82 per cent of Hogan's surplus and 94 per cent of Broderick's surplus went to the other Cumann na nGaedheal candidates. The elimination of Andrew Staunton (CNG) after the third count ensured the election of Broderick, who received 1,700 of the 2,828 available transfers and the distribution of Broderick's surplus secured the election of Martin McDonogh (CNG). Similarly, Frank Fahy and Mark Killilea were the first Fianna Fáil candidates to be elected. The distribution of their transfers also demonstrated a strong party allegiance: 91 per cent of Fahy's surplus and 94 per cent of Killilea's surplus went to the remaining Fianna Fáil candidates.

With the two main parties displaying such a loyalty of transfers, the voting patterns among the three other candidates are more revealing. Padraig Ó Máille and James Cosgrave, the two independent candidates, lacked party support and were the first to be eliminated. In a similar pattern to the June election, voters who had given their first preference to Ó Máille (Independent), once more tended to return a local ticket and distributed the highest number of preferences to the Connemara candidates McDonogh (CNG), Mongan (CNG) and Tubridy (FF). However unlike the June pattern, where McDonogh (CNG) received the largest share of the vote, in September the majority share went to the Fianna Fáil candidate, Tubridy. In June 1927 the majority of Ó Máille's transfers had gone to Cumann na nGaedheal. In September, this majority went to Fianna Fáil. The party won 49 per cent of the available transfers compared to Cumann na nGaedheal's 36 per cent (Figures 7.5 and 7.6). Similarly, while the majority of James Cosgrave's National League transfers went to his colleague William Duffy in the June election, Cumann na nGaedheal had gained a larger portion of Cosgrave's transfers than Fianna Fáil. In September this trend was again reversed. Cosgrave had voted against the government in the August no-confidence motion. In

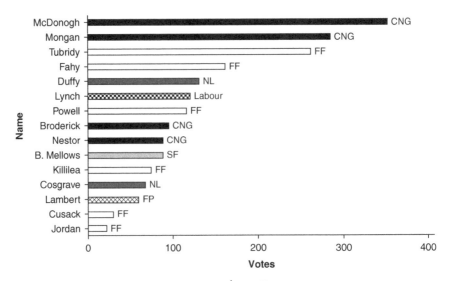

Figure 7.5 Distribution of Ó Máille's vote, June 1927

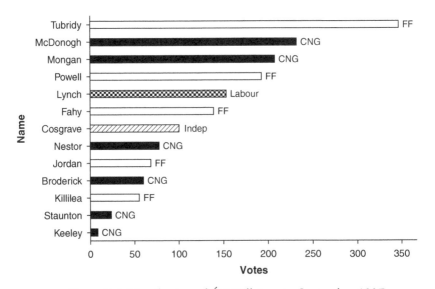

Figure 7.6 Distribution of Ó Máille's vote, September 1927

September, Fianna Fáil successfully gleaned some of this anti-government vote (Figures 7.7 and 7.8).

Labour's Gilbert Lynch was not eliminated until the tenth count. His transfers, therefore, do not mirror as strong a reflection of voting patterns as the earlier candidates, but the consistent feature of Fianna Fáil

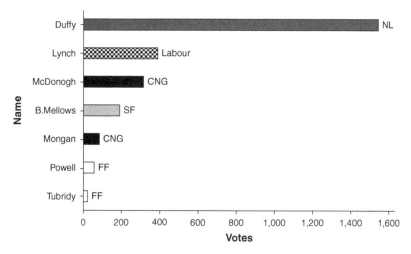

Figure 7.7 Distribution of Cosgrave's vote, June 1927

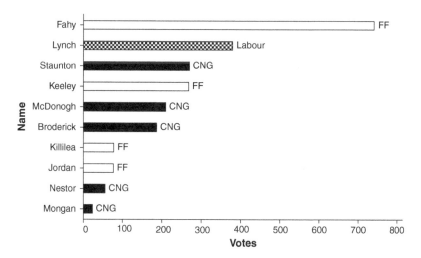

Figure 7.8 Distribution of Cosgrave's vote, September 1927

gains is again evident. The Fianna Fáil party's three remaining candidates won 74 per cent of the 2,937 available transfers compared to the two Cumann na nGaedheal candidates' 24 per cent. With the aid of these transfers, Fianna Fáil secured the final seat by a tight margin of 375 votes. Furthermore, the increase in Fianna Fáil support from June to September demonstrated that there were a substantial number of voters anxious to support the party but who were not prepared to waste their votes on an abstentionist candidate.[65] Constitutional republicanism not radical republicanism made the widest appeal to the mass of republican supporters in Galway.

Labour marginally increased its vote in Galway from 4.60 per cent in June to 4.88 per cent in September, but its funds were exhausted. Nationally, its support dropped from 12.55 per cent to 9.07 per cent. Its losses included its leader Thomas Johnson, William O'Brien, and almost half its parliamentary party. Locally, it lost its only seat in Galway (the party would not regain this seat until 1981 when Michael D. Higgins was returned for the Galway West constituency).[66] Padraig Ó Máille (Independent), polled the lowest first preference vote in the county and was the only candidate to lose his £100 deposit, having failed to secure a third of the quota (Figure 7.3). In his election programme he attempted, once more, to explain the basis for his decision to leave the Cumann na nGaedheal party.

> In 1921 I accepted, in your name, the Anglo-Irish Treaty … I did so as I believed that it was the best way to get, in Ireland, a foothold from which we could work for complete independence. When I saw that those in charge of the Executive Government were not utilising in that spirit the position gained, but were falling under pro-British and Imperialistic influences, and were, instead of advancing, becoming more and more reactionary, I felt I should not be true to Ireland nor to Galway, nor to my own principles, if I remained any longer in the Cumann na nGaedheal Party which they controlled.[67]

There is little gratitude in politics. Local loyalty was not enough to secure his election, especially when the voters closed ranks around the two principal parties.

Some lessons were learned from the June election and in September a more concerted effort was made to get the voters to the polling stations. It was reported that 'greater use than ever was made of motor cars for bringing people to the polls, and in this respect the Cumann na nGaedheal Party had greatly improved their organisation. They had also a larger number of workers than at the last election.'[68] Yet despite the intensity of the short campaign, the candidates once more concentrated primarily on their own districts. The fine weather and the fact that polling took place during the harvest season may have contributed to the disappointing turnout. Of the 101,256 persons eligible to vote, 59,655 valid votes were returned. While this represented a slight increase on the June 1927 figures, Galway, for the fourth successive general election, registered the lowest percentage turnout in the country, recording a figure of 58.92 per cent compared to the national average of 67.75 per cent.[69] Although the flawed and inflated nature of the electoral register, as referred to earlier, meant that the turnout figures for Galway between 1923 and 1927 were artificially low,[70] disaffection, indifference, and apathy at the polls had become a feature of Free State politics in Galway.

Frustrated by the county's poor participation, the editor of the *Connacht Tribune* offered his criticism of the Proportional Representation STV electoral system.

> We do not approve of the system of voting by proportional representation in the Saor Stát, but this is the fourth General Election at which it has been tried, and the people no longer have the excuse of unfamiliarity with it. The general prevailing political apathy, notwithstanding every device of the contestants, is in itself a damnatory evidence against proportional representation, and against the large area constituencies which its operation demands. The people will not eagerly vote for men whom they do not know, men whom they have in many cases never seen, and who may be the most undesirable mediocrities, simply because they belong to a political group. Moreover, proportional representation has taught the people that a candidate with political party funds and organisation behind him can manage to secure election in a wide constituency without the necessity for direct responsibility to the people whom he is supposed to represent. And direct responsibility to his constituents should be a first and guiding principle in all parliamentary representation.[71]

The editor of the *Connacht Sentinel* was equally critical. From 'every pulpit and platform and in every editorial page the people were urged to vote', yet this had little effect. Despondently, he asked 'should voting be made compulsory in the Saor Stát as it is in Belgium and other countries and as it has recently been made in Australia with quite remarkable results? The Irishman abhors compulsion, but if he will not fulfil the ordinary duties of a citizen without it, what else is there to be done?'[72] A Cumann na nGaedheal report on electoral reform contended that apart from apathy and ignorance the main reason for abstention was that the electoral system did not bring home any sense of personal liability or responsibility to the individual for his or her actions. The government was urged to consider whether non-voters should be penalised either by a fine or by a forfeiture of their civic rights for a specified period and disqualified from acting in a public capacity.[73]

In September 1927, the *Irish Independent* summed up the choice that faced the people: 'The electors have to choose whether they want the return to power of the present Government, with its established policy of peace, stability, and progress, or are prepared to take a leap in the dark.'[74] A divided local electorate once more straddled the partisan fence. Fianna Fáil's abandonment of abstention and entry into the Dáil should have been a moment of delight for Cumann na nGaedheal. Yet as Maryann Gialanella Valiulis has argued, they 'found themselves, in their implacable hostility to de Valera and their almost visceral distrust of their former chief, castigated as the pro-British party, foes of the Republic, thwarters of the goals of Irish nationalism. Consequently, they were unable to make political capital out of the fact they were indeed right in 1922.'[75] It was a fundamental flaw in the party's local electoral appeal. Cumann na nGaedheal had won widespread loyalty to the institutions of the new state.[76] It had fought an impressive and energetic campaign, but the dominance and salience of national affairs limited its creative thinking. It cast the September election as a choice between chaos, bankruptcy and the reimposition of the gunman or the security, strength and stability of the Free State. The prospect, let alone the promise, of material progress and increased social spending was not forthcoming.

February 1932

Fianna Fáil, as mentioned earlier, grasped the opportunity at the local elections of June 1928 to promote and advance the party organisation. However, its prediction of a landslide victory in the national election of February 1932 did not occur.[77] Although, County Galway's political ground certainly shifted in what the *Sunday Independent* astutely described as 'a land-annuity slide of quite considerable proportions'.[78] While the final result left the party representation unchanged in the county (five Fianna Fáil seats to four Cumann na nGaedheal seats), Fianna Fáil attracted almost 11,000 new votes in Galway. In 1923, the local republican vote had stood at 33.54 per cent. In June 1927, Sinn Féin, by that time barely functioning as a party, slumped to 4.41 per cent of the vote. Fianna Fáil, on the other hand, polled 33.55 per cent. In September 1927, the Fianna Fáil vote increased to 42.71 per cent. In 1932, it increased to 55.04 per cent (Appendix A.1 and A.2). Fianna Fáil's 'rare combination of a revolutionary objective with a conservative appeal'[79] was in step with Galway's progressive republican mentality. The party encapsulated all that the county's constitutional republicans desired – a link between the old republican ideology of Sinn Féin and the stability of the political structures of the Irish Free State. But, as Gallagher has pointed out, Fianna Fáil in many ways 'appeared radical only when compared with the very conservative Cumann na nGaedheal'.[80] More significantly, its alternative socio-economic programme for government evoked an instinctive response from the land-hungry farmers of the west. In 1932 more than half the Galway electorate was now prepared to endorse de Valera's version of the Free State.

    Yet in the mind of the Cumann na nGaedheal government, the opposition leader's appetite for the democratic process was far from certain.

In its eyes, Fianna Fáil still represented an anti-system opposition biding its time to bring down the institutions of the state. Owing to what Cumann na nGaedheal saw as de Valera's betrayal of democracy in 1922 and his party's continued sympathy for militant republicans, there was a legitimate mistrust and an anxiety over the Fianna Fáil party's commitment to constitutional politics. In June 1931 the IRA and Fianna Fáil had marched together in the annual pilgrimage to Wolfe Tone's grave at Bodenstown. The establishment of Saor Éire and the increase in IRA activity in that same year fuelled Cumann na nGaedheal's relentless insistence that Fianna Fáil – the Republican Party – was still under the control of the republican gunmen. Cosgrave had previously told the Dáil that he had 'no intention of accepting office in the mere capacity of a super-policeman to maintain law and order while allowing the country to drift along economically, nationally and internationally'.[81] But as Fanning has suggested, 'to deny the intention was but to acknowledge the reality that, for many, "super-policemen" was precisely what Cosgrave and his colleagues in government had become'.[82] Yet this sense of fear and resentment caused by the republicans cannot be underestimated.[83]

Against the backdrop of a grim recrudescence of IRA violence, Cumann na nGaedheal presented itself once more as the law and order party. As Dunphy wrote, 'the party's only political tactic seems to have been the sharpening up of its "tough-man" image'.[84] The government simply revamped its old 'Safety First' political philosophy into the party's new 'Danger Ahead!' slogan and 'the more danger the state appeared to be in, the better for Cumann na nGaedheal's electoral chances'.[85] Nevertheless, fighting the election on the communist red scare conspiracy and involving Fianna Fáil in the plot was a fundamental error.[86] As Keogh has argued, if the Cosgrave party was to capitalise on the red scare threat, 'the most appropriate moment for Cumann na nGaedheal to have gone to the country was in mid-November' when the conspiracy was deemed to be most dangerous and the bishops' pastoral fresh in the mind of the electorate. By February, the credibility of the red scare threat had waned.[87] Some of Cumann na nGaedheal's more extreme propaganda included a poster titled 'Don't let this happen', which depicted de Valera pulling open the door of a safe from which sinister-looking IRA and Saor Éire men carrying arms and explosives emerged from the shadows. A second poster, 'The shadow of the gunman', pictured a silhouette of a gunman towering over a county cottage, with the caption 'Keep it from your home: Vote Cumann na nGaedheal', and a newspaper advertisement printed on the eve of the election read: 'How will you vote tomorrow? The gunmen are voting for Fianna Fáil. The communists are voting for Fianna Fáil.'[88] Attempts to harness Catholicism exclusively to Cumann na nGaedheal were also misguided. The Catholic credentials of the Fianna Fáil leader were assured. When the Angelus bell tolled at Tulla, County Clare, de Valera transformed an election crowd into a reverent congregation. In Tuam (north Galway), on 12 February, he repeated the performance.[89]

In such deteriorating economic conditions it was difficult for the government to campaign on its own economic record. The achievements it presented – the restoration of law and order, the developments in agriculture, the judicious management of the country's finances, the positive part the state played in Commonwealth affairs, and the completion of the Shannon hydroelectric scheme[90] – stood in sharp contrast with the disappointing reality of the daily lives of many of the local electorate as the depression of the 1930s deepened. Cumann na nGaedheal claimed that its policy and its record were 'written clearly across the bright face of a reconstructed Ireland'.[91] The party's future policy was conspicuous by its absence. It had done little to soothe its detractors in Galway. Unemployment, the protection of the fisheries, land redistribution, schemes of afforestation, land reclamation and drainage, inadequate housing, poverty, the economic plight of the Gaeltacht, an emigrating population, the development of Galway port – the list of Galway grievances had differed little from year to year. Referring to the transatlantic port project at a Fianna Fáil rally, Seán Tubridy TD declared that 'Mr Cosgrave went to Furbo, threw a bag of cement on the waters and that was the last that was heard about the development'.[92] Popular applause had greeted some of the government's successes. The housing subsidy, temporary relief schemes, the Land Act, drainage schemes and road grants effected considerable local improvements. Galway's main roads, for instance, had been upgraded and the scheme provided much needed employment, but the county's secondary and trunk roads which linked the more isolated small villages to the bigger towns remained in a poor condition. The government 'gave good roads to motorists', Stephen Jordan (FF) asserted, but the farmers would need 'Russian boots going down the roads and boreens that branch off those steamrolled roads'.[93] Expectations in the west for practical socio-economic achievements were far greater. Cumann na nGaedheal's strict adherence to financial orthodoxy and the introduction of Blythe's recent supplementary budget had done little to galvanise its supporters. If anything, it added to the appeal of Fianna Fáil's nationalist economic rhetoric and its politics of promises. And such promises attracted new supporters. Fr Malachy Brennan, a committed Cumann na nGaedheal advocate, resigned from the party's National Executive in April 1927. A week before polling day in the 1932 general election, he publicly rebuked the policies of the government in a detailed statement to the press.

According to the latest census (1926), there were in County Galway alone 14,409 tenants with less than 15 acres of land, while at the same time there were 612,200 acres in the hands of 1,963 people, whose holdings ranged from 100 acres upwards ... I have always urged ... the Cumann na nGaedheal Organisation that those [uneconomic] tenants should be the first consideration of our Government, but, I must confess, without success ... I am going to vote for the Fianna Fáil candidates at the Election ... After ten years in office, it is plain to me that the present Government Party has failed to use the Treaty in accordance with the wishes of the vast majority of the people who accepted it for the best interests of the country and as a stepping-stone to complete independence ... They have taken away all powers of appointment to the more important positions from the popularly elected local councils ... They have adopted a policy of centralisation which brings all advantages of trade and industry to the City of Dublin and leaves the country districts and smaller towns poorer and more desolate than ever.[94]

Padraig Ó Máille (formerly of Cumann na nGaedheal and Clann Éireann) also joined Fianna Fáil and contested the Dublin County constituency on behalf of de Valera's party, although considerable opposition was manifested towards his nomination at the Dublin convention on the grounds that he was an outsider; that Labour was entitled to representation; and, rather ungenerously, that he was not a small farmer's representative but was really a rancher.[95] He failed to get elected. Nonetheless, Ó Máille, who was shot and wounded by the republicans on 7 December 1922, clearly identified the obvious distinction between Fianna Fáil's developing policy of constitutional republicanism and the fundamentalist republicanism of the civil war.

Owing to the electoral rebuff it had received in the county in 1927, Cumann na nGaedheal's complacency, naivety and, at times, arrogance was baffling. A statement issued by the party in 1931 read:

The Fianna Fáil Party fears, and it has good reason to fear, the verdict which the Country will pronounce upon its record of incompetency and play-acting in the Dáil when the General Election comes round ... Are the people going to throw over that Government and place the destinies of this country in the hands of the incompetent irresponsibles who for the greater part make up the Fianna Fáil party? I don't think there is the slightest fear of the majority of our people taking that mad leap in the dark.[96]

Despite its previous electoral defeat in Galway, the party simply did not believe it would be beaten on this occasion. Hogan was convinced that his party of law and order would hold firm. This was no time for revolutionary experiment. In his criticisms of de Valera's party, Hogan once more was vigorous and direct. He accused Fianna Fáil of defrauding the electors. 'Dangling the land annuities bait before the Irish people during the present bad times', he avowed, 'was damnable treason against the nation.'[97] If he had his way 'the Fianna Fáil party would be in jail long ago ... They were the real culprits for shielding the gunmen. But their party was incapable of governing as, after all, you must have breeding to govern.'[98] As Fianna Fáil's Gerald Bartley noted, this was 'a dirty election'.[99] Speaking in Galway city, Liam Ó Briain declared that the Fianna Fáil policy was 'full of colour, romance and imagination, but had no practical value'.[100] For much of the Galway electorate colour, romance and imagination were appealing qualities. They were not, however, a potential force for social revolution. At its core, Galway was too conservative to engage in a radical transformation of its society.[101] Cumann na nGaedheal's red scare tactics, however genuine, exposed how out of touch the party was with local grassroots politics. The people were familiar with the local Fianna Fáil TDs. While in opposition, they had toured the county organising the party, mobilising political support and educating the people on its party programme. Fanning described it as 'a time when Irish republicans no longer sulked in a self-imposed exile, but when they increasingly assumed the aspect of a government in waiting'.[102] Between 1927 and 1932 Fianna Fáil built up a strong organisation. The Cumann na nGaedheal government underestimated it. By 1932 the Galway electorate was well versed in the Fianna Fáil policy for government – so much so that one agitated local editor wrote:

> the pronouncements being made at the moment from one end of the country to the other have been heard so frequently for the last few years that their repetition has become wearisome to the last degree.[103]

The Galway electorate knew its politicians. Were these men suddenly in danger of subverting the state by gunman terror?

Fianna Fáil presented a vigorous programme of economic recovery to the electorate. Its manifesto was 'an ingenious amalgam which resolved many of the Sinn Féin positions of 1922, embracing within its remit Griffithite protectionism, de Valera's external association and Collins' stepping-stones'.[104] The party promised to abolish the oath, to retain the land annuities, establish new industries, introduce economic protection, increase rural employment, accelerate land division, maximise economic independence, preserve the home market for Irish farmers, reduce salaries in the public sector, stimulate local industries, promote additional welfare measures and revive the Irish language.[105] It also issued election leaflets targeting specific sections of the community – fishermen, the unemployed, farmers, labourers and the rural worker. The free trade philosophy of Cumann na nGaedheal was to be replaced by a policy of

protection and self-sufficiency. There was, of course, an air of the fantastic about a number of Fianna Fáil's policies; what William Redmond
denounced as the 'wholesale howling for tariffs'.[106] But the party's promises of subsidies and protection won strong support among those farmers whose interests had not rested in the export market. In a county
such as Galway, dominated by small farmers, de Valera's programme for
government appealed to the monetary necessities of a struggling community. The party presented itself as 'the champion of the dispossessed'
and won widespread popularity.[107] In 1932, the Galway electorate was
offered a choice between the stability of the status quo, or the wholesale
constitutional, economic and social changes proposed by Fianna Fáil.
De Valera's unique blend of constitutional republicanism and nationalist
economics, what Oliver MacDonagh described as 'a nice amalgam of
nationalism and democracy',[108] won the election and increased the party
support by 10,925 votes in County Galway. Writing to Michael Hayes
after the campaign, a downcast Ó Briain offered his appraisal of the new
Fianna Fáil voters.

> I met some hard-headed wealthy, middle-aged large familied Mayo shop-
> keepers that I knew in the train. Their enthusiasm and determination for
> the Fianna Fáil policy of high protection and development of the country's
> resources by strong measure was astonishing and the most curious thing
> was they had no delusion about Dev's [*sic*] own personality and were quite
> bitter about his responsibility and culpability in '22. 'But what matter now;
> he has the right policy and we'll see it through and make it succeed.' Voila!
> There is certainly a tide flowing somewhere in this country.[109]

Since the pact election of June 1922 a pragmatic Galway electorate
had supported the establishment of the Irish Free State and returned
Patrick Hogan (CNG) at the head of the poll at each successive general election. In February 1932, Fianna Fáil's Frank Fahy topped the
poll on the first count, followed by Thomas Powell (FF), relegating
Patrick Hogan to third place (Figure 7.9). Nevertheless despite the dra-
matic increase in the local Fianna Fáil vote, the complexities of the
Proportional Representation STV voting system ensured that Cumann
na nGaedheal, which polled 39.58 per cent of the vote, a loss of 5.90 per
cent from September 1927, retained its four seats. Fianna Fáil's strategic
cross-class electoral appeal won the party more votes, but no extra seats
in February 1932. It was not until the snap election of January 1933,
when the Fianna Fáil vote increased to 62.42 per cent in Galway that
the party's popular majority translated into more seats. At that election,
Frank Fahy, as outgoing Ceann Comhairle was returned automatically
and the seven other Fianna Fáil candidates polled the seven highest first

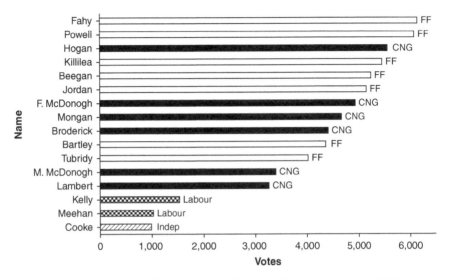

Figure 7.9 First preference vote in County Galway, February 1932

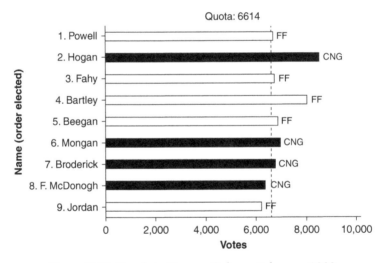

Figure 7.10 Result in County Galway, February 1932

preference votes.[110] In theory, had the contest been run on the old first past the post system, Fianna Fáil would have achieved its landslide victory in the county. Instead, under the Proportional Representation STV method, it increased its majority over Cumann na nGaedheal in Galway by six seats to three in 1933. The final result of the 1932 election, as noted, was five seats to four in favour of Fianna Fáil, but a tide *was* flowing in this western county (Figure 7.10).

Thus far, local issues had almost entirely failed to impinge on the political debate. Between 1923 and 1927 the treaty, stability and the legitimacy of the state had dominated Galway's electoral politics. In 1932, Fianna Fáil subtly relegated the national question to the sidelines as increasing emphasis was placed on the local economic and social conditions of the county. The issue, as the *Tuam Herald* noted,

> is plain to us all. It is not the Oath, for they have all taken it; it is not the Treaty, for they have all accepted it; it is not partnership in the British Empire, for that, too, is agreed to on all sides. It is simply a question with each of the contending parties as to what chance it has of obtaining the power and right to govern.[111]

Fianna Fáil's ability to sidestep the national question was due to the completion of de Valera's protracted 'crablike progress'[112] towards constitutionalism. The party deputies had been quick to neutralise all charges of its association with IRA violence, insisting on platform after platform that Fianna Fáil had no use for the gunmen. Addressing a meeting at Corofin (north Galway), Mark Killilea (FF) proclaimed that 'the gunman bogey had been exploded long ago. The suggestion of another round with England was merely an electioneering cry, intended to mislead the electors. Fianna Fáil stood for peace and stability.'[113] With its democratic credentials secure, the party concentrated on wining over the moderates, the uncommitted, the disaffected, and those disillusioned with the politics of Cumann na nGaedheal. A party directive advised its organisers that

> it must be remembered that the purpose of the whole campaign is to get people who voted against us before to vote for us on this occasion. This must never be lost sight of. Speeches, literature, etc., must be directed towards converting former opponents, not towards denouncing them.[114]

The twin elections of 1927 demonstrated that Fianna Fáil's republican vote was assured. It was the party's economic, social and welfare strategy, coupled with an evident dissatisfaction with the government's economic policies, which attracted its new supporters in 1932. If a vote for Fianna Fáil enhanced the possible attainment of the Republic, so much the better, but it was not the primary motivation governing the actions of these new voters. The party owed its electoral success in Galway to its ability to step past the national issue and identify with the immediate economic and social concerns of the people. It owed its success to its eventual realisation that the national question alone was not going to win votes for the party.

Fianna Fáil urged local party workers to keep the names of their candidates displayed on the walls and trees and roads and reminded them that valuable work had been done in previous by-elections elsewhere where candidates' names were white-washed in twenty-foot letters on prominent sloping fields.[115] The party also looked to break the trend of the previous campaigns where its candidates had tended to concentrate primarily on their own local areas of support.

> It should be clearly understood that the practice of dividing Constituencies into areas in which particular candidates are given instructions to seek No. 1 votes for themselves is not to be adopted. The Árd Fheis has decided that this practice must stop. All candidates should go before the whole electorate as a team and the people should be asked to vote for them in the order of their own choice.[116]

Fianna Fáil, however, did not follow its own advice. Locally, both Fianna Fáil and Cumann na nGaedheal openly encouraged such tactics and continued to urge the people in the different parts of the county to give their first preference vote to the candidate of that area.[117] That the latter strategy would become a recognised feature of future Irish election campaigns demonstrated the effectiveness of such tactics and the inability to ignore or eradicate the local grassroots character of Irish political life.

Despite being a winter campaign, noisy demonstrations were held across the county. In Clifden, for instance, there was some disturbance when supporters of the two main parties collided at intervals and several blows were struck.[118] In Loughrea the rival platforms on the main street were only twenty yards apart and supporters of the two main parties 'made the frosty air ring with their cheers'.[119] The concentrated effort that was made to get the voters to the polling stations in September 1927 was repeated in February 1932. Yet while polling across the county was reported to have been slow but steady, 'there was no great enthusiasm'.[120]

In February 1932, the scant coverage of the election in the local newspapers reflected the apathy and indifference shown by a large proportion of the Galway electorate in the previous elections. It was evident that not all of the people were interested in the machinations of party politics. The real issue was the worsening economic condition of the county. Even to the pressmen, the mudslinging and propaganda tactics of national politics in recent years had become a source of irritation. Referring to the infamous 1932 'Devvy's Circus' poster, the *Galway Observer* wrote

> What has become known as the 'Circus Poster' pasted on all the dead walls of Galway has been condemned on all sides. We are politicians first last and all the time, but the crude 'humour' of the artist with a big note of interrogation after the word artist stinks in our [opinion].[121]

Echoing such sentiments, Frank Kelly, one of the new Labour candidates for Galway, declared

> I suppose it is natural that being Irish we should enjoy what in vulgar parlance, is called a slinging match but when the mudslinging is continued for years and as a direct consequence we find thousands of our people destitute and starving and living in the vilest of conditions, then no longer is it a source of humour but tragic in the extreme.[122]

During the election campaign, few speeches were reported in the columns of the local press and scarcely any predictions were offered. In June 1927 the *Connacht Tribune* had run election forecast competitions for its readers. In February 1932, the paper in its editorial opted to discuss the fortunes of the Irish Hospital Sweepstakes rather than the results of the election.[123] There is more than a nibble of irony, then, in the fact that the county recorded its highest percentage turnout in the February election, recording a figure of 72.09 per cent. This compared to the national average of 75.30 per cent. Galway once more recorded the lowest turnout in Connacht, but was replaced at the foot of the national poll by the Dublin South, Dublin County, Dublin North and Kildare constituencies.[124] However, as Sinnott has suggested, the increase in the voting turnout in 1932, especially in the western counties, was, to some extent, more apparent that real, owing to the previously inflated nature of the election register. In September 1927, as stated earlier, the Galway electorate numbered 101,256 and 59,655 valid votes were returned (58.92 per cent turnout). In February 1932, the electorate was reduced to 91,746 but the number of valid votes returned increased to 66,136 (72.09 per cent turnout). In 1927 the Galway electoral register recorded a surplus of 3,696 voters relative to the population aged twenty-one and over. In 1932 it recorded a deficit of 7,720.[125] Fundamental problems still persisted, and the press reported that 'hundreds of people in the city and county were disappointed when they went to vote to find that they were not on the register'.[126]

In 1932, the strong party ticket voting that was prominent at the last election was again evident. Thomas Powell (FF) was the first candidate to be elected and 90 per cent of his surplus went to the other Fianna Fáil candidates. The elimination of Seán Tubridy (FF) after the eighth count ensured the election of Gerald Bartley (FF), who received 84 per cent of Tubridy's transfers, and the distribution of Bartley's surplus saw the election of Patrick Beegan (FF). In similar fashion, Patrick Lambert (formerly of the Farmers' Party) was the first Cumann na nGaedheal candidate to be eliminated. Of the 3,236 available transfers, 2,978 or 92 per cent was divided among the Cumann na nGaedheal candidates. Patrick Hogan was the first Cumann na nGaedheal candidate to be elected and 97 per cent of his surplus also stayed within the party. Overall, no candidate reached the quota on the first count in Galway and three sitting TDs, Martin McDonogh (CNG), who had been ill during the campaign, Mark Killilea (FF) and Seán Tubridy (FF), lost their seats. In an effort to regain its seat the Labour Party put forward two candidates, Edward Meehan and Frank Kelly, but neither candidate made a significant impression on the vote. Between them, they polled 3.88 per cent (a loss of 1 per cent from September 1927).[127] Meehan was eliminated after the second count. His transfers divided 62 per cent for his running mate Kelly, 23 per cent for Fianna Fáil and 15 per cent for Cumann na nGaedheal. After the third count Kelly was eliminated. Fianna Fáil received 66 per cent of his transfers and Cumann na nGaedheal 34 per cent. Lacking both organisation and finances, Labour, for the most part, had run a limp campaign. In Mayo, T. J. O'Connell, by then having succeeded to the leadership of the party, lost his seat and no Labour candidate was returned in any of the Connacht constituencies (see Table 7.1 above).[128] As one historian of the Labour Party has recently argued, 'it would be more accurate to say that they stood in the election rather than fought in it'.[129]

Although the first preference vote cast for the Fianna Fáil party had increased considerably in February 1932 to 55.04 per cent, some of the party's tactics were unsuccessful. For instance, in an effort to capitalise on the lack of economic progress in the west, Fianna Fáil chose to run a second Connemara candidate. However, Joseph Mongan, the Cumann na nGaedheal candidate most associated with the region, retained his seat. Rather than gaining an extra seat, the inclusion of a second Fianna Fáil candidate diverted a number of votes away from the party's sitting TD, Seán Tubridy. Tubridy, who had received some considerable support in Connemara at the last election, was replaced by his running mate Gerald Bartley from Clifden. The election of the Tuam solicitor Fred McDonogh was another accomplishment for Cumann na nGaedheal. McDonogh had concentrated his campaign almost entirely on his local region of North Galway and relied heavily on a strong personal vote. Mark Killilea, the Fianna Fáil candidate most associated with this area, lost his seat.

At a national level the Cumann na nGaedheal vote 'was buffered by the decline of the Farmers' Party, some of whose members actually joined Cumann na nGaedheal between 1927 and 1932, and by pre-election absorption of the remnants of the National League and some independents'[130] – adhesions which Fianna Fáil less charitably described as 'the alliance of a dog with its fleas'.[131] Yet in Galway, such alliances were more ambiguous. James Cosgrave, for example, did not follow William Redmond, his old National League leader, into Cumann na nGaedheal but (like Ó Máille) defected instead to Fianna Fáil. In the Dáil, Cosgrave had been a vocal critic of the government. In 1932, he failed to secure a nomination at the local Fianna Fáil convention, but was a regular speaker for the party on the election platforms.[132] Patrick Lambert, the former Farmers' Party candidate, as mentioned earlier, did join Cumann na nGaedheal. But he polled the lowest number of first preferences among the Cumann na nGaedheal candidates and failed to get elected (Figures 7.9 and 7.10). The reorientation of the Cumann na nGaedheal party, however, did consolidate the conservative element of its support base, united 'in their fear of the "wild men" of de Valera's party'.[133] For some Galway voters, the anti-republican prejudice of the party was its very attraction. Others feared the grave repercussions that Fianna Fáil's commitment to economic protection and land redistribution would have on the large export-orientated farming interests that Cumann na nGaedheal supported.[134] In February 1932, Cumann na nGaedheal retained its core conservative vote in the county, losing only 954 first preference votes compared to the previous election. The party's downfall lay in its inability to attract new voters. Fianna Fáil had gained almost 11,000 new supporters. In Connacht, Fianna Fáil returned the highest percentage vote in each of the five constituencies (Appendix A.4).[135] From this perspective Hogan's claim that Cumann na nGaedheal 'are winning all over the Free State, and will win'[136] was bordering on the fantastic. They were not and did not. With 44.47 per cent of the national vote and seventy-two seats, Fianna Fáil was still short of an overall Dáil majority, but de Valera succeeded to power on 9 March 1932 with the support of the Labour Party. The storms were threatening, sinister even, but the heavens did not fall. Nevertheless it did mark the end of Cumann na nGaedheal's ascendancy, although few would have realised it at the time.

Political instability and adverse economic conditions took their toll on the Cosgrave party, and the absence of a specific programme to effect socio-economic change militated against its ability to retain local popular appeal. Galway society required economic investment that the government felt, particularly in inopportune post-war circumstances, the country could not afford. Cumann na nGaedheal was unable to temper economic harshness with assurances of sufficient tangible advantages for the west of Ireland.

Notes

1 *Connacht Tribune*, 14 May 1927.
2 Martin McDonogh (1860–1934) was a native of Lettermullen, Connemara. Proprietor of the Galway firm Thomas McDonogh & Co. in Galway city,

he was also a director of the Midland Great Western Railway and a member of the Governing Body of University College Galway, the Galway Race Committee, and the Board of Guardians. In addition, he served as chairman of the Urban District Council, the Galway Harbour Commissioners and Galway Steamship Company. Stephen Gwynn in *Memories of Enjoyment* (Tralee, 1946), offers a sympathetic portrait of McDonogh's personality. However, as John Cunningham has pointed out, McDonogh's hostility towards trade unionism and his abrasive nature also gained him an 'exalted position in the demonology of working class tradition in Galway'. Cunningham, *Labour in the West of Ireland*, pp. 152–4.

3 'Individual Elections 1927–57', UCDA, de Valera papers, P150/2094.
4 Moss, *Political Parties in the Irish Free State*, p. 125.
5 *Connacht Tribune*, 11 June 1927.
6 Dunphy, *The Making of Fianna Fáil Power in Ireland 1923–1948*, p. 75. In October 1926 the IRA issued a general order forbidding its members to run as parliamentary candidates. Nevertheless, twenty-two officers (including the three Galway officers) contested the election in June 1927 and fifteen were elected. See Hanley, *The IRA*, pp. 208–9.
7 *Connacht Tribune*, 4 June 1927; Moss, *Political Parties in the Irish Free State*, p. 161. The same advertisement was printed in the *Irish Independent* on 3 June 1927.
8 Election pamphlet, June 1927, UCDA, MacEntee papers, P67/344/2.
9 *Irish Independent*, 7 June 1927.
10 Moss, *Political Parties in the Irish Free State*, p. 154.
11 *Connacht Tribune*, 7 May 1927.
12 *Ibid.*
13 *Galway Observer*, 7 May 1927.
14 *Ibid.*, 21 May 1927.
15 *Connacht Tribune*, 7 May 1927.
16 *Ibid.*, 18 June 1927.
17 Broderick speech at Kilconoly (north Galway), *ibid.*, 30 Apr. 1927.
18 *Ibid.*, 21 May 1927. The local press often referred to Lynch as 'the Lancashire Galwegian'. He fought alongside James Connolly in the GPO in Easter 1916 and was secretary of the Galway branch of the Irish Transport and General Workers' Union and treasurer of the Galway Trades' Council.
19 *Ibid.*, 7 May 1927.
20 Gallagher (ed.), *Irish Elections 1922–44*, pp. 45–6, 64, 70, 84–5.
21 Cosgrave, 'Policy of the Cumann na nGaedheal Party', 1927, NAI, DT, S7440/B.
22 NAI, DT, S7439; *Connacht Tribune*, 29 Jan. 1927.
23 *Connacht Tribune*, 30 Apr. 1927.
24 *Ibid.*, 11 June 1927.
25 *Ibid.*, 4 June 1927.
26 *Ibid.*, 30 Apr., 28 May 1927. Killilea polled the highest first preference vote among the Fianna Fáil candidates and was the second candidate to be declared elected after Hogan.

27 Letter from Hogan to his aunt Mere Wilfreda, London, 28 Dec. 1922. Cited in Cullen, 'Patrick J. Hogan, T.D., Minister for Agriculture, 1922–1932', p. 52.

28 Gallagher (ed.), *Irish Elections 1922–44*, p. 64.

29 *Galway Observer*, 7 May 1927. Thomas Sloyan later withdrew from the contest. He was replaced by James McDonnell, former chairman of Galway County Council.

30 *Ibid.*, 11 June 1927.

31 Cumann na nGaedheal Election Committee, 'Election Handbook', 1927, UCDA, Mulcahy papers, P7b/61/1.

32 For detailed colour maps showing the distribution of party meetings and candidate meetings in the different regions of County Galway for the June 1927 election, see, Úna Newell, 'The West must wait? People, poverty and politics in Free State Galway 1922–1932', PhD thesis, University College Dublin, 2010, p. 171.

33 Murray, *Oracles of God*, p. 122.

34 Gallagher (ed.), *Irish Elections 1922–44*, p. 84.

35 Minutes of Galway County Council, 13 Aug. 1927, GCCA, Galway County Council minute books, GC1/4.

36 Sinnott, *Irish Voters Decide*, pp. 85–6.

37 'Preparation of Election Registers and the use of the Vote', 9 July 1927, NAI, DJ, H49/24.

38 Gallagher (ed.), *Irish Elections 1922–44*, pp. 64, 84.

39 For a detailed colour breakdown of the distribution of preference votes by candidate and by party in June 1927, see Newell, 'The West must wait?', pp. 177–80.

40 The National League's only other success in Connacht was the election of John Jinks in the Leitrim-Sligo constituency. Jinks, the former Mayor of Sligo, would become better known for his absence from the Dáil during the vote of confidence in the government on 16 August 1927 'having unwisely accepted the lunchtime hospitality of a pro-government T.D. and the editor of the *Irish Times*'. O'Halpin, 'Politics and the state, 1922–32', p. 122. Commenting on the event, a contributor to the journal of Commonwealth affairs, the *Round Table*, wrote of 'high jinks in the Dáil'. Dermot Keogh, *Twentieth-Century Ireland: Nation and State* (Dublin, 1994), p. 48.

41 O'Halpin, 'Politics and the state, 1922–32', pp. 109, 120.

42 Hogan to Mere Wilfreda, 11 July 1927. Cited in Cullen, 'Patrick J. Hogan, T.D., Minister for Agriculture, 1922–1932', p. 202.

43 Gallagher (ed.), *Irish Elections 1922–44*, p. 84.

44 Cited in Meehan, *The Cosgrave Party*, p. 83.

45 Letter from de Valera to republicans in America following the election results, 16 June 1927, UCDA, de Valera papers, P150/2094.

46 Reprinted in *Irish Independent*, 20 Feb. 1932.

47 The third bill was designed to block Fianna Fáil's attempt to petition for a referendum for the removal of the oath from the Constitution. In 1927, the bill did not proceed beyond its second reading. However in 1928, as de

Valera began to mount his petition, the government forced through 'a constitutional amendment abolishing the initiative altogether'. O'Halpin, 'Politics and the state, 1922–32', pp. 121, 123; Regan, *The Irish Counter-Revolution 1921–1936*, p. 274.

48 Arthur Mitchell, *Labour in Irish Politics 1890–1930* (Dublin, 1974), p. 261. For more on de Valera's interpretation of the oath, see Lord Longford and T. P. O'Neill, *Eamon de Valera* (London, 1970), pp. 246–58; Lee, *Ireland 1912–1985*, pp. 154–5. In the Dáil six of the nine Galway deputies, Gilbert Lynch (Labour), the four Fianna Fáil TDs and William Duffy (NL), supported Johnson's motion of no confidence. The three Cumann na nGaedheal TDs, as was to be expected, voted with the government.

49 *Connacht Sentinel*, 20 Sept. 1927.

50 Gallagher (ed.), *Irish Elections 1922–44*, p. 102.

51 *Connacht Tribune*, 3 Sept. 1927.

52 *Ibid.*, 10 Sept. 1927.

53 Hogan to Mere Wilfreda, 19 Oct. 1927. Cited in Regan, *The Irish Counter-Revolution 1921–1936*, p. 286. O'Higgins was gunned down by three IRA men while on his way to mass in Booterstown, County Dublin. He was thirty-five years of age. Hogan had been waiting in O'Higgins's house for a friend to take him to play golf when he heard the burst of revolver fire. Cited in Terence de Vere White, *Kevin O'Higgins* (London, 1948), p. 240. For further details on the assassination see Regan, *The Irish Counter-Revolution 1921–1936*, pp. 272–3; John P. McCarthy, *Kevin O'Higgins: Builder of the Irish State* (Dublin, 2006), pp. 287–92.

54 *Connacht Tribune*, 10 Sept. 1927.

55 *Irish Independent*, 5 Sept. 1927.

56 *Tuam Herald*, 10 Sept. 1927.

57 *Irish Independent*, 5 Sept. 1927; *Connacht Tribune*, 10 Sept. 1927.

58 *Irish Independent*, 10 Sept. 1927. Cited in Murray, *Oracles of God*, p. 127.

59 Brian O'Kennedy, *Making History: The Story of a Remarkable Campaign* (Dublin, 1927).

60 Cited in McCracken, *Representative Government in Ireland*, p. 83.

61 Gallagher (ed.), *Irish Elections 1922–44*, pp. 84–5, 115–16.

62 *Ibid.*, p. 102.

63 *Galway Observer*, 3 Sept. 1927.

64 *Connacht Sentinel*, 30 Aug. 1927.

65 Manning, *Irish Political Parties*, p. 42.

66 Gallagher (ed.), *Irish Elections 1922–44*, pp. 84, 115; Brian Walker (ed.), *Parliamentary Election Results in Ireland 1918–1992* (Dublin, 1992), p. 241.

67 *Tuam Herald*, 10 Sept. 1927.

68 *Connacht Tribune*, 17 Sept. 1927.

69 Gallagher (ed.), *Irish Elections 1922–44*, pp. 114–15.

70 See Sinnott, *Irish Voters Decide*, pp. 82–7; Gallagher (ed.), *Irish Elections 1922–44*, p. 125.

71 *Connacht Tribune*, 17 Sept. 1927.

72 *Connacht Sentinel*, 20 Sept. 1927.
73 'Preparation of Election Registers and the use of the Vote', 9 July 1927, NAI, DJ, H49/24.
74 *Irish Independent*, 8 Sept. 1927.
75 Maryann Gialanella Valiulis, '"The man they could never forgive": The view of the opposition: Eamon de Valera and the civil war', in John. A. Murphy and John P. O'Carroll (eds), *De Valera and His Times* (Cork, 1983), p. 99.
76 Jackson, *Ireland 1798–1998*, p. 282.
77 For a cartoon sketch of the Cumann na nGaedheal house being swept away, see 'The landslide', *Irish Press*, 13 Feb. 1932.
78 *Sunday Independent*, 21 Feb. 1932, UCDA, FitzGerald papers, P80/1136.
79 Nicholas Mansergh, *The Irish Free State: Its Government and Politics* (London, 1934), pp. 289–90.
80 Gallagher, 'Electoral support for Irish political parties, 1927–1973', p. 19.
81 Cited in Ronan Fanning, '"The four-leaved shamrock": electoral politics and the national imagination in independent Ireland', O'Donnell Lecture (Dublin, 1983), p. 6.
82 Fanning, 'The four-leaved shamrock', p. 6.
83 Ferriter, *The Transformation of Ireland, 1900–2000*, p. 312.
84 Dunphy, *The Making of Fianna Fáil Power in Ireland 1923–1948*, p. 117.
85 Regan, *The Irish Counter-Revolution 1921–1936*, p. 287.
86 Keogh, 'De Valera, the Catholic Church and the "Red Scare", 1931–1932', in Murphy and O'Carroll (eds), *De Valera and His Times*, p. 155.
87 *Ibid.*, p. 144.
88 UCDA, Blythe papers, P24/662 (b) 8; NLI, Ephemera collection, EPH F53; *Irish Independent*, 15 Feb. 1932.
89 Lee, *Ireland 1912–1985*, p. 170; *Irish Press*, 13 Feb. 1932.
90 Manning, *Irish Political Parties*, p. 14.
91 Cited in Meehan, *The Cosgrave Party*, p. 174.
92 *Galway Observer*, 23 Jan. 1932.
93 Speech by Jordan in Williamstown (north Galway), *Connacht Tribune*, 19 Dec. 1931.
94 *Irish Press*, 10 Feb. 1932. For a similar rebuke of Cumann na nGaedheal by UCC's Alfred O'Rahilly, see *ibid.*, 1 Feb. 1932.
95 Report from the convention for the selection of candidates in County Dublin, 21 Jan. 1932, UCDA, Fianna Fáil archives, P176/830 (4).
96 Cumann na nGaedheal election statement, 1931, UCDA, FitzGerald papers, P80/1126.
97 *Irish Independent*, 15 Feb. 1932.
98 *Irish Press*, 15 Feb. 1932.
99 *Connacht Tribune*, 27 Feb. 1932.
100 *Connacht Sentinel*, 16 Feb. 1932.
101 For a wider discussion on the conservative nature of the Free State see, for instance, Michael Laffan, '"Two Irish states" in Ireland: dependence and independence', *The Crane Bag*, vol. 8, no. 4 (1984), pp. 26–40.
102 Fanning, *Independent Ireland*, p. 93.

103 *Tuam Herald*, 23 Jan. 1932.
104 Regan, *The Irish Counter-Revolution 1921–1936*, p. 306.
105 For a detailed outline of the party's mandate see UCDA, de Valera papers, P150/2096; Daly, *Industrial Development and Irish National Identity, 1922–1939*, pp. 69–70.
106 *Connacht Tribune*, 6 Feb. 1932.
107 Ferriter, *The Transformation of Ireland, 1900–2000*, p. 358.
108 Oliver MacDonagh, *Ireland: The Union and its Aftermath* (2nd edn, Dublin, 2003), p. 123.
109 Liam Ó Briain to Michael Hayes, 8 Mar. 1932, UCDA, Hayes papers, P53/74.
110 Gallagher (ed.), *Irish Elections 1922–44*, pp. 134, 165.
111 *Tuam Herald*, 16 Jan. 1932.
112 Fanning coined this phrase in reference to de Valera's pragmatic approach to his constitutional objectives between 1932 and 1937. See Fanning, *Independent Ireland*, p. 112.
113 *Galway Observer*, 23 Jan. 1932.
114 'Fianna Fáil scheme of election organisation', UCDA, Aiken papers, P104/1598.
115 *Ibid*.
116 *Ibid*.
117 See *Connacht Tribune*, 13 Feb. 1932.
118 *Connacht Sentinel*, 16 Feb. 1932.
119 *Irish Independent*, 12 Feb. 1932.
120 *Ibid.*, 17 Feb. 1932.
121 *Galway Observer*, 13 Feb. 1932. The Devvy Circus poster announced the arrival of 'the greatest road show in Ireland today' featuring, among others, 'Señor de Valera – World-famous Illusionist, Oath swallower and Escapologist. See his renowned Act: "Escaping from the Straight [*sic*] Jacket of the Republic"', and 'Monsignor Lemass – Famous tight-rope performer. See him cross from the Treaty to the Republic on the tight-rope every night.' NLI, Ephemera collection, EPH F50.
122 *Galway Observer*, 13 Feb. 1932.
123 See *Connacht Tribune*, 27 Feb. 1932. Coverage of the election was relegated to a short report on page 12.
124 Gallagher (ed.), *Irish Elections 1922–44*, p. 147.
125 Sinnott, *Irish Voters Decide*, pp. 85–7.
126 *Irish Press*, 18 Feb. 1932.
127 Gallagher (ed.), *Irish Elections 1922–44*, p. 134.
128 O'Connell took over the leadership of the party after the defeat of Thomas Johnson in the September 1927 general election.
129 Niamh Puirséil, *The Irish Labour Party 1922–73* (Dublin, 2007), p. 36.
130 Sinnott, *Irish Voters Decide*, pp. 101–2.
131 Cited in Moss, *Political Parties in the Irish Free State*, p. 180.

132 In such a large constituency the attraction of greater party support may also have been a factor in his decision, particularly as the electorate closed ranks around the two main parties after June 1927.

133 Tom Garvin, *The Evolution of Irish Nationalist Politics* (2nd edn, Dublin, 2005), pp. 161–2.

134 McGarry, *Eoin O'Duffy*, p. 202.

135 In February 1932, Fianna Fáil won the majority of seats in four of the five Connacht constituencies – Galway, Roscommon, Mayo South and Leitrim-Sligo. In Mayo North, Fianna Fáil and Cumann na nGaedheal won two seats each.

136 *Connacht Sentinel*, 16 Feb. 1932.

Epilogue

In Galway, the language of Free State politics – the treaty, the state and the fear of the gunman – differed significantly from the language of local Free State society – land, distress and disappointment. The advent of political independence did not and could not, in itself, produce solutions to the pressing social and economic problems confronting the county. The civil war shattered the confidence of the people. A new government, coming to power after a revolution and looking to consolidate a new state, adopted an economically and socially conservative attitude. A government, whose first priority was to secure the survival of the state, was not going to introduce radical reform. This is not to advocate the proposition that Cumann na nGaedheal directed a deliberate counter revolution against the republicanism of 1919–21, but rather to suggest that its actions were shaped by the circumstances it found itself in.

Cumann na nGaedheal faced a formidable task. Vehemence, civil war and republican violence stripped the party of its strongest leaders – Griffith, Collins and then O'Higgins. The IRA was ruthlessly repressed in 1922–23; the infrastructure of the country was ruined; but the republicans, although conceding defeat, only dumped their arms. They did not surrender them.

With single-mindedness, collective ability, a strong civil service and sureness in decision-making, the Cosgrave government established efficient, stable government and enhanced its authority. It secured the loyalty of the people to the institutions of the state and marginalised the radical republican elements of local society. It demobilised most of the army, released the civil war prisoners, prevented a widespread eruption of anarchy in the rural countryside and restored a respect for law and order. In external affairs it successfully asserted the Irish Free State's status as a member of the Commonwealth. While the formal political divisions of the civil war survived, Cumann na nGaedheal's commitment to the democratic foundations of the treaty, its defence of majority rule and its consolidation of the authoritative political institutions lured, or indeed forced, constitutional republicans back to the political fold. Its successes in state-building enabled a peaceful transition of power, at the behest of the voting public, to an increasingly assertive Fianna Fáil party in 1932.

Cumann na nGaedheal's steely approach to national and international affairs was laudable. Its ability to confront and tackle the agricultural poverty of the west of Ireland was not. The incessant problems of land congestion and economic degradation remained unresolved. Given the difficult political conditions of the time, this was perhaps understandable. The persistent pattern of poverty in the west was one inherited, not created, by Cumann na nGaedheal. Economic policy would inevitably be curbed. The government could only afford what it decided it could afford. High levels of socio-economic development were not assured. Constrained by a stringent fiscal policy, the west would have to wait.

Nonetheless, the political elite failed to develop an effective long-term response to the instance of distress in the west. The cure for Connemara was work, not charity. In addition, the Irish language was still woven into a life of poverty and hardship, not the possibility of obtaining preferential treatment in the acquisition of a teaching, policing or civil service position. A fundamental weakness in Cumann na nGaedheal's policy of constructive gaelicisation was that it did not sufficiently promote the Irish language as being a demonstrable financial asset or a language of modernisation. During the first decade of independence Galway did not go down a republican road. But neither did it go down a road to economic recovery (although the local bishops did make every effort to set the people on a road towards moral recovery).

Bargaining, not bloodshed, would govern the process of land division. Yet notwithstanding the allocation of large sums of money towards the implementation of the 1923 Land Act, the progress of the Land Commission was slow and dilatory. Patrick Hogan's task was an impossible one. In the language of the Irish Free State, the old cry of the 'land for the people' would necessarily translate as some of the land for some of the people.

Despite winning the civil war, Cumann na nGaedheal remained extremely vulnerable.[1] As Hogan reminded the Dáil in February 1928, 'the smell of petrol had hardly left the country'.[2] But, as J. J. Lee has commented, the Irish Free State also began with many advantages compared to other new states – 'No new nation had to be created in 1922, only a new state.'[3] And it was this ability (or indeed inability) to reconcile stability with progress that was the government's weakness. By 1932, Cumann na nGaedheal signified peace if not prosperity, continuity if not change, stability if not creativity. Stability and continuity were not words to inspire a depressed west.

186   *Epilogue*

Notes

1 Daly, *The First Department*, p. 156.
2 DE, vol. 22, 28 Feb. 1928. Cited *ibid.*, p. 144.
3 Lee, *Ireland 1912–1985*, p. 93. For a discussion on a number of British influ-
ences and legacies (both positive and negative) – including education, bank-
ing, policing, partition, and the civil service – which impacted on the Free
State, see *ibid.*, pp. 88–93.

Appendix

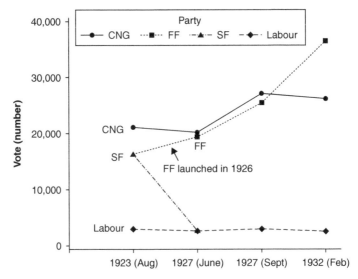

Figure A.1 County Galway first preference voting pattern, 1923–32

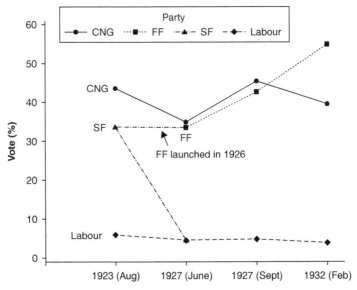

Figure A.2 County Galway percentage voting pattern, 1923–32

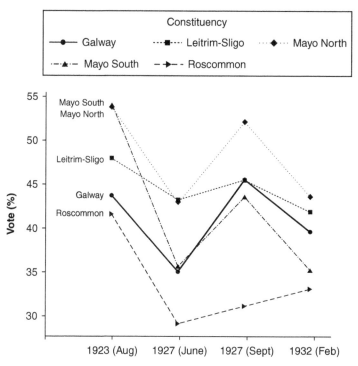

Figure A.3 Cumann na nGaedheal percentage vote in Connacht, 1923–32

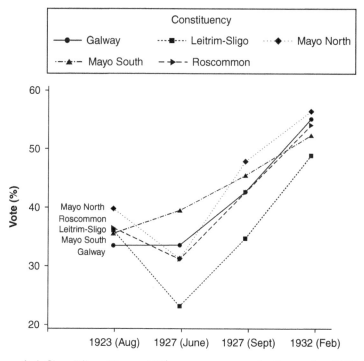

Figure A.4 Sinn Féin – Fianna Fáil percentage vote in Connacht, 1923–32

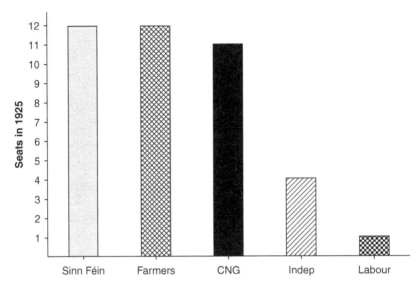

Figure A.5 Composition of Galway County Council by party, 1925

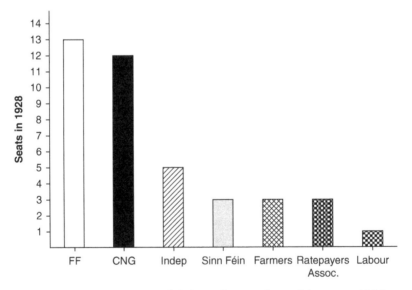

Figure A.6 Composition of Galway County Council by party, 1928

Sources and bibliography

1. Primary sources

A. Manuscripts

Galway Diocesan Archives
Thomas O'Dea papers
Thomas O'Doherty papers

Tuam Archdiocesan Archives
Thomas Gilmartin papers

Galway County Council Archives
Tomás Bairéad papers

NUI, Galway, Special Collections Department
Brian Cusack papers
Joseph Finlay papers
Patrick and Harry Loughnane files

University College Dublin, Archives Department
Frank Aiken papers
Ernest Blythe papers
Cumann na nGaedheal party minute books
Eamon de Valera papers
Fianna Fáil archives
Desmond FitzGerald papers
Michael Hayes papers
Seán MacEntee papers
Eoin MacNeill papers
Mary MacSwiney papers
Richard Mulcahy papers
Ernie O'Malley notebooks
Ernie O'Malley papers
Maurice Twomey papers

National Archives of Ireland
Bureau of Military History 1913–21: Witness statements
Clann na Poblachta and Sinn Féin collection

B. Government records

National Archives of Ireland
Department of Agriculture
Department of Finance
Department of Justice
Department of Local Government
Department of the Taoiseach

National Library of Ireland
RIC County Inspectors' Reports, CO 904/100–107

Galway County Council Archives
Galway County Council minute books 1921–32
Galway Rural District Council minute books 1922–25
Ballinasloe Rural District Council minute books 1922–25
Clifden Rural District Council minute books 1922–25
Loughrea Rural District Council minute books 1922–25
Tuam Rural District Council minute books 1922–25

Galway City Council Archives
Galway Urban District Council minute books 1921–32

C. Official publications

Census of Ireland, 1911. General Report, with Tables and Appendix (London, 1913)
Census of Ireland, 1926 (Dublin, 1927 and subsequent dates)
Census of Ireland, 1966 (Dublin, 1967 and subsequent dates)
Report of the Commission on the Gaeltacht, 1926 (Dublin, 1926)
Commission on the Gaeltacht: Statement of Government Policy on the Recommendations of the Commission (Dublin, 1928)
Report of the Commission on the Relief of the Sick and Destitute Poor, including the Insane Poor, 1927 (Dublin, 1927)
Dáil Éireann Debates

D. Newspapers and periodicals

Church of Ireland Gazette
Connacht Sentinel
Connacht Tribune
Daily Bulletin
Daily Sheet
East Galway Democrat
Éire – The Irish Nation
Freeman's Journal
Gaelic American
Galway Observer
Irish Independent
Irish Press

Irish Statesman
Irish Times
Leader
Nation
An tÓglach
An Phoblacht
Tuam Herald
Western News
Westmeath Independent

E. Other primary sources

National Library of Ireland
Ephemera collection
Pamphlet collection

National Photographic Archive
Congested Districts Board photographic collection
Independent Newspapers (Ireland) collection
Keogh collection
Lawrence collection
Levingston collection
Valentine collection

National Folklore Collection, University College Dublin
Manuscripts – MS 1634, MS 1637, MS 1707, MS 1738, MS 1766, MS 1768, MS 1769, MS 1770
Tape Recordings – MD0042, MD0043
Domhaill Ó Cearbhaill photographic collection

Radió Telifís Éireann Libraries and Archives
Looking West by John Raftery (2 Mar. 1984), produced by Jim Fahy

2. Secondary sources

A. Guides and works of reference

Edwards, Ruth Dudley, *An Atlas of Irish History* (3rd edn, London, 2005)
Gallagher, Michael (ed.), *Irish Elections 1922–44: Results and Analysis* (Limerick, 2003)
Helferty, Seamus and Refaussé, Raymond (eds), *Directory of Irish Archives* (4th edn, Dublin, 2003)
Irish Catholic Directory (Dublin, 1923 and subsequent dates)
Irish Times, The Sinn Féin Rebellion Handbook (Dublin, 1917)
McGuire, James and Quinn, James (eds), *Dictionary of Irish Biography: From the Earliest Times to the Year 2002* (Cambridge, 2009)
O'Farrell, Padraic, *Who's Who in the Irish War of Independence and Civil War 1916–1923* (Dublin, 1997)

Thom's Directory (Dublin, 1922 and subsequent dates)

Vaughan, W. E. and Fitzpatrick, A. J. (eds), *Irish Historical Statistics: Population, 1821–1971* (Dublin, 1978)

Walker, Brian. M. (ed.), *Parliamentary Election Results in Ireland 1801–1922* (Dublin, 1978)

Walker, Brian. M. (ed.), *Parliamentary Election Results in Ireland 1918–1992* (Dublin, 1992)

B. Books and articles

Akenson, D. H. and Fallin, J. F., 'The Irish civil war and the drafting of the Free State constitution: the drafting committee and the boundaries of action', *Éire – Ireland*, vol. 5, no. 1 (Spring, 1970), pp. 10–26

Akenson, D. H. and Fallin, J. F., 'The Irish civil war and the drafting of the Free State constitution: the drafting process', *Éire – Ireland*, vol. 5, no. 2 (Summer, 1970), pp. 42–93

Akenson, D. H. and Fallin, J. F., 'The Irish civil war and the drafting of the Free State constitution: Collins, de Valera and the pact – a new interpretation', *Éire – Ireland*, vol. 5, no. 4 (Winter, 1970), pp. 28–70

Allen, Gregory, *The Garda Síochána: Policing Independent Ireland 1922–82* (Dublin, 1999)

Arensberg, Conrad, *The Irish Countryman: An Anthropological Study* (London, 1937)

Augusteijn, Joost, *From Public Defiance to Guerrilla Warfare: The Experience of Ordinary Volunteers in the Irish War of Independence 1916–1921* (Dublin, 1996)

Augusteijn, Joost, *Patrick Pearse: The Making of a Revolutionary* (Basingstoke, 2010)

Augusteijn, Joost (ed.), *Ireland in the 1930s: New Perspectives* (Dublin, 1999)

Augusteijn, Joost (ed.), *The Irish Revolution 1913–23* (Basingstoke, 2002)

Bartlett, Thomas, *Ireland: A History* (Cambridge, 2010)

Bartlett, Thomas, Curtin, Chris, O'Dwyer, Riana and Ó Tuathaigh, Gearóid (eds), *Irish Studies: A General Introduction* (Dublin, 1988)

Blanshard, Paul, *The Irish and Catholic Power* (London, 1954)

Boyce, D. G. (ed.), *The Revolution in Ireland, 1879–1923* (London, 1988)

Brady, Ciaran (ed.), *Interpreting Irish History: The Debate on Historical Revisionism 1938–1994* (Dublin, 1994)

Brady, Conor, *Guardians of the Peace* (2nd edn, London, 2000)

Breathnach, Ciara, *The Congested Districts Board of Ireland, 1891–1923: Poverty and Development in the West of Ireland* (Dublin, 2005)

Breathnach, Ciara (ed.), *Framing the West: Images of Rural Ireland 1891–1920* (Dublin, 2007)

Brown, Terence, *Ireland: A Social and Cultural History 1922–2002* (London, 2004)

Bulfin, William, *Rambles in Eirinn* (Dublin, 1907)

Bull, Philip, *Land, Politics and Nationalism: A Study of the Irish Land Question* (Dublin, 1996)

Butterfield, Herbert, *The Whig Interpretation of History* (London, 1931)

Campbell, Fergus, *Land and Revolution: Nationalist Politics in the West of Ireland 1892–1921* (Oxford, 2005)

Carr, Edward Hallett, *What is History?* (London, 1961)

Chubb, Basil, *The Government and Politics of Ireland* (3rd edn, London, 1992)

Claffey, John (ed.), *Glimpses of Tuam since the Famine* (Tuam, 1997)

Clear, Caitriona, *Women of the House: Women's Household Work in Ireland 1926–1961* (Dublin, 2000)

Clear, Caitriona, *Social Change and Everyday Life in Ireland, 1850–1922* (Manchester, 2007)

Coakley, John and Gallagher, Michael (eds), *Politics in the Republic of Ireland* (3rd edn, London, 1999)

Coleman, Marie, *County Longford and the Irish Revolution 1910–1923* (Dublin, 2003)

Comerford, R. V., *Ireland* (London, 2003)

Coogan, T. P., *The I.R.A.* (5th edn, London, 2000)

Coogan, T. P. and Morrison, George, *The Irish Civil War* (London, 1990)

Cronin, Mike and Regan, John M. (eds), *Ireland: The Politics of Independence, 1922–49* (Basingstoke, 2000)

Cumann na mBan, *The Story of Liam Mellows* (Dublin, 1929)

Cumann na mBan, *Liam Mellows: His Life and Aims* (Dublin, 1933)

Cunningham, John, *Labour in the West of Ireland: Working Life and Struggle 1890–1914* (Belfast, 1995)

Cunningham, John, *'A Town Tormented by the Sea': Galway, 1790–1914* (Dublin, 2004)

Curran, Joseph M., *The Birth of the Irish Free State, 1921–1923* (Alabama, 1980)

Daily Express, 'Mr Balfour's tours in Connemara and Donegal' (Dublin, 1890)

Daly, Mary E., *Industrial Development and Irish National Identity, 1922–1939* (Dublin, 1992)

Daly, Mary E., *The Buffer State: The Historical Roots of the Department of the Environment* (Dublin, 1997)

Daly, Mary E., *The First Department: A History of the Department of Agriculture* (Dublin, 2002)

Daly, Mary E., 'Late nineteenth and early twentieth century Dublin', in Harkness, David and O'Dowd, Mary (eds), *The Town in Ireland, Historical Studies XIII* (Belfast, 1981), pp. 221–52

Daly, Mary E., 'Irish nationality and citizenship since 1922', *Irish Historical Studies*, vol. 32, no. 127 (May, 2001), pp. 377–407

Daly, Mary E. and O'Callaghan, Margaret (eds), *1916 in 1966: Commemorating the Easter Rising* (Dublin, 2007)

Delaney, Enda, *Irish Emigration since 1921* (Dundalk, 2002)

Dillon, Eilís, *The Bitter Glass* (London, 1958)

Dolan, Anne, *Commemorating the Irish Civil War: History and Memory, 1923–2000* (Cambridge, 2003)

Dolan, Martin, 'Galway 1920–21', *Capuchin Annual* (1970), pp. 384–95

Donnelly, Brian, *For the Betterment of the People: A History of Wicklow County Council* (Wicklow, 1999)

Donnelly, James S., 'The land question in nationalist politics', in Hachey, Thomas E. and McCaffrey, Lawrence J. (eds), *Perspectives on Irish Nationalism* (Kentucky, 1989), pp. 79–98

Donnelly, James S., Jr, 'Bishop Michael Browne of Galway (1937–76) and the regulation of public morality', *New Hibernia Review*, vol. 17, no. 1 (Spring, 2013), pp. 16–39

Dooley, Terence, *The Decline of the Big House in Ireland: A Study of Irish Landed Families 1860–1960* (Dublin, 2001)

Dooley, Terence, *'The Land for the People': The Land Question in Independent Ireland* (Dublin, 2004)

Dooley, Terence, *The Big Houses and Landed Estates of Ireland: A Research Guide* (Dublin, 2007)

Dooley, Terence, 'Land and politics in independent Ireland, 1923–48: the case for reappraisal', *Irish Historical Studies*, vol. 34, no. 134 (Nov., 2004), pp. 175–97

Drudy, P. J. (ed.), *Ireland: Land, Politics and People* (Cambridge, 1982)

Dunphy, Richard, *The Making of Fianna Fáil Power in Ireland 1923–1948* (Oxford, 1995)

Earner-Byrne, Lindsey, *Mother and Child: Maternity and Child Welfare in Dublin 1922–1960* (Manchester, 2007)

English, Richard, *Radicals and the Republic: Socialist Republicanism in the Irish Free State, 1925–1937* (Oxford, 1994)

Fanning, Ronan, *Independent Ireland* (Dublin, 1983)

Fanning, Ronan, '"The Four-Leaved Shamrock": electoral politics and the national imagination in independent Ireland', O'Donnell Lecture (Dublin, 1983)

Farrell, Brian (ed.), *The Irish Parliamentary Tradition* (Dublin, 1973)

Farry, Michael, *Sligo 1914–1921: A Chronicle of Conflict* (Trim, 1992)

Farry, Michael, *The Aftermath of Revolution: Sligo 1921–23* (Dublin, 2000)

Ferriter, Diarmaid, *Cuimhnigh ar Luimneach: A History of Limerick County Council 1898–1998* (Limerick, 1999)

Ferriter, Diarmaid, *Lovers of liberty? Local Government in Twentieth-Century Ireland* (Dublin, 2001)

Ferriter, Diarmaid, *The Transformation of Ireland, 1900–2000* (London, 2004)

Ferriter, Diarmaid, *What if? Alternative Views of Twentieth-Century Ireland* (Dublin, 2006)

Ferriter, Diarmaid, *Judging Dev: A Reassessment of the Life and Legacy of Eamon de Valera* (Dublin, 2007)

Ferriter, Diarmaid, *Occasions of Sin: Sex and Society in Modern Ireland* (London, 2009)

Fitzpatrick, David, *Irish Emigration 1801–1921* (Dublin, 1984)

Fitzpatrick, David, *Politics and Irish Life 1913–1921: Provincial Experience of War and Revolution* (2nd edn, Cork, 1998)

Fitzpatrick, David, *The Two Irelands 1912–1939* (Oxford, 1998)

Fitzpatrick, David, 'The geography of Irish nationalism 1910–1921', *Past and Present*, no. 78 (Feb., 1978), pp. 113–44

Fitzpatrick, David, 'Strikes in Ireland, 1914–21', *Saothar*, 6 (1980), pp. 26–40

Fitzpatrick, David, 'Ethnic cleansing, ethical smearing and Irish historians', *History*, vol. 98, no. 329 (2013), pp. 135–44

Fitzpatrick, David, 'Protestant depopulation and the Irish Revolution', *Irish Historical Studies*, vol. 38, no. 152 (Nov., 2013), pp. 643–70

Fitzpatrick, David (ed.), *Revolution? Ireland, 1917–1923* (Dublin, 1990)

Foster, R. F., *Modern Ireland 1600–1972* (London, 1988)

Foster, R. F., *Paddy and Mr Punch: Connections in Irish and English history* (London, 1993)

Foster, R. F., *The Irish Story: Telling Tales and Making it up in Ireland* (London, 2001)

Freeman, T. W., *Ireland: A General and Regional Geography* (4th edn, London, 1969)

Gallagher, Michael, 'Electoral support for Irish political parties 1927–1973', *Contemporary Political Sociology Series*, vol. 2 (London, 1976), pp. 1–75

Gallagher, Michael, 'The pact general election of 1922', *Irish Historical Studies*, vol. 21, no. 84 (Sept., 1979), pp. 405–21

Gallagher, Michael and Marsh, Michael, *Days of Blue Liberty: The Politics of Membership of the Fine Gael party* (Dublin, 2002)

Garvin, Tom, *Nationalist Revolutionaries in Ireland, 1858–1928* (Oxford, 1987)

Garvin, Tom, *The Evolution of Irish Nationalist Politics* (2nd edn, Dublin, 2005)

Garvin, Tom, *1922: The Birth of Irish Democracy* (2nd edn, Dublin, 2005)

Garvin, Tom, Manning, Maurice and Sinnott, Richard (eds), *Dissecting Irish Politics: Essays in Honour of Brian Farrell* (Dublin, 2004)

Gaughan, J. Anthony (ed.), *Memoirs of Senator Joseph Connolly (1885–1961): A Founder of Modern Ireland* (Dublin, 1996)

Gogarty, Oliver St John, *Rolling down the Lea* (London, 1950)

Greaves, Charles Desmond, *Liam Mellows and the Irish Revolution* (London 1971)

Greaves, Charles Desmond, *The Irish Transport and General Workers' Union: The Formative Years 1909–1923* (Dublin, 1982)

Gwynn, Denis, *The Irish Free State 1922–1927* (London, 1928)

Gwynn, Stephen, *A Holiday in Connemara* (London, 1909)

Gwynn, Stephen, *The Famous Cities of Ireland* (Dublin, 1915)

Gwynn, Stephen, *Experiences of a Literary Man* (London, 1926)

Gwynn, Stephen, *Memories of Enjoyment* (Tralee, 1946)

Hanley, Brian, *The IRA, 1926–1936* (Dublin, 2002)

Hanley, Brian, 'The IRA and trade unionism, 1922–72', in Devine, Francis, Lane, Fintan and Puirséil, Niamh (eds), *Essays in Irish Labour History: A Festschrift for Elizabeth and John W. Boyle* (Dublin, 2008), pp. 157–77

Hardiman, James, *The History of the Town and County of the Town of Galway: From the Earliest Period to the Present Time* (Dublin, 1820, reprint, Galway, 1975)

Hart, Peter, *The I.R.A. and its Enemies: Violence and Community in Cork 1916–1923* (Oxford, 1998)

Hart, Peter, *The I.R.A. at War 1916–1923* (Oxford, 2003)

Hart, Peter, *Mick: The Real Michael Collins* (London, 2005)

Hart, Peter, 'The Protestant experience of revolution in Southern Ireland', in English, Richard and Walker, Graham (eds), *Unionism in Modern Ireland: New Perspectives on Politics and Culture* (London, 1996), pp. 81–98

Hart, Peter, 'The geography of revolution in Ireland 1917–1923', *Past and Present*, no. 155 (May, 1997), pp. 142–73

Hayes, Michael, 'Dáil Éireann and the Irish Civil War', *Studies*, vol. 58 (Spring, 1969), pp. 1–23

Higgins, Roisín, *Transforming 1916: Meaning, Memory and the Fiftieth Anniversary of the Easter Rising* (Cork, 2012)

Higgins, Roisín and Uí Chollatáin, Regina (eds), *The Life and After-Life of P. H. Pearse. Pádraic Mac Piarais: Saol agus Oidhreacht* (Dublin, 2009)

Hill, J. R. (ed.), *A New History of Ireland, vol. VII. Ireland 1921–84* (Oxford, 2003)

Honohan, Iseult (ed.), *Republicanism in Ireland: Confronting Theories and Traditions* (Manchester, 2008)

Hopkinson, Michael, *The Irish War of Independence* (Dublin, 2002)

Hopkinson, Michael, *Green against Green: The Irish Civil War* (2nd edn, Dublin, 2004)

Howe, Stephen, *Ireland and Empire: Colonial Legacies in Irish History and Culture* (Oxford, 2000)

Jackson, Alvin, *Ireland 1798–1998: Politics and War* (Oxford, 1999)

Kalyvas, Stathis N., *The Logic of Violence in Civil War* (Cambridge, 2006)

Keogh, Dermot, *The Vatican, the Bishops and Irish Politics, 1919–1939* (Cambridge, 1986)

Keogh, Dermot, *Twentieth Century Ireland: Nation and State* (Dublin, 1994)

Keogh, Dermot, 'The Catholic Church and politics in Ireland', in O'Connell, Maurice R. (ed.), *People Power: Proceedings of the Third Annual Daniel O'Connell Workshop* (Dublin, 1993), pp. 57–79

Keogh, Dermot, 'The Catholic Church and the Irish Free State 1923–1932', *History Ireland*, vol. 2, no. 1 (Spring, 1994), pp. 47–51

Kiberd, Declan, *Inventing Ireland: The Literature of the Modern Nation* (London, 1995)

King, Clara, *Michael Davitt* (Dublin, 2009)

Kinsella, Anthony, 'The Special Infantry Corps', *Irish Sword*, vol. 20, no. 82 (Winter, 1997), pp. 331–454

Kissane, Bill, *Explaining Irish Democracy* (Dublin, 2002)

Kissane, Bill, *The Politics of the Irish Civil War* (Oxford, 2005)

Kissane, Bill, 'Defending democracy? The legislative response to political extremism in the Irish Free State, 1922–39', *Irish Historical Studies*, vol. 34, no. 134 (Nov., 2004), pp. 156–74

Kotsonouris, Mary, *Retreat from Revolution: The Dáil Courts, 1920–24* (Dublin, 1994)

Laffan, Michael, *The Partition of Ireland 1911–1925* (Dundalk, 1983)

Laffan, Michael, *The Resurrection of Ireland: The Sinn Féin Party, 1916–1923* (Cambridge, 1999)

Laffan, Michael, 'The unification of Sinn Féin in 1917', *Irish Historical Studies*, vol. 17, no. 67 (Mar., 1971), pp. 353–79

Laffan, Michael, 'Violence and terror in twentieth century Ireland: IRB and IRA', in Mommsen, Wolfgang J. and Hirschfeld, Gerhard (eds), *Social Protest, Violence and Terror in Nineteenth and Twentieth Century Europe* (London, 1982), pp. 155–74

Laffan, Michael, '"Two Irish States" in Ireland: dependence and independence', *The Crane Bag*, vol. 8, no. 4 (1984), pp. 26–40

Laffan, Michael, '"Labour must wait": Ireland's conservative revolution', in Corish, Patrick (ed.), *Radicals, Rebels and Establishments, Historical Studies XV* (Belfast, 1985), pp. 203–22

Laffan, Michael, 'Insular attitudes: the revisionists and their critics', in Ní Dhonnchadha, Máirín and Dorgan, Theo (eds), *Revising the Rising* (Derry, 1991), pp. 106–21

Laffan, Michael, 'The sacred memory: religion, revisionism and the Easter Rising', in Devlin, Judith and Fanning, Ronan (eds), *Religion and Rebellion, Historical Studies XX* (Dublin, 1997), pp. 174–91

Lane, Fintan and Ó Drisceoil, Donal (eds), *Politics and the Irish Working Class, 1830–1945* (Basingstoke, 2005)

Lee, J. J., *Ireland 1912–1985: Politics and Society* (Cambridge, 1989)

Lee, J. J., 'Some aspects of modern Irish historiography', in Schulin, E. (ed.), *Gedenkschrift Martin Göhring: Studien zur Europäischen Geschichte* (Wiesbaden, 1968), pp. 431–43

Lee, J. J., 'Irish Nationalism and Socialism: Rumpf reconsidered', *Saothar*, 6 (1980), pp. 59–64

Longford, Lord and O'Neill, Thomas P., *Eamon de Valera* (London, 1970)

Luddy, Maria, 'Sex and the single girl in 1920s and 1930s Ireland', *Irish Review*, no. 35 (Spring, 2007), pp. 79–91

Lynd, Robert, 'Galway of the Races', in McMahon, Seán (ed.), *Robert Lynd, Galway of the Races: Selected Essays* (Dublin, 1990), pp. 58–87

Lyons, F. S. L., *Ireland since the Famine* (2nd edn, London, 1973)

Lyons, F. S. L., *Culture and Anarchy in Ireland 1890–1939* (Oxford, 1979)

Lyons, F. S. L., 'From war to civil war in Ireland: three essays on the treaty debate', in Farrell, Brian (ed.), *The Irish Parliamentary Tradition* (Dublin, 1973)

Macardle, Dorothy, *The Irish Republic* (2nd edn, London, 1968)

McCarthy, John P., *Kevin O'Higgins: Builder of the Irish State* (Dublin, 2006)

McCracken, J. L., *Representative Government in Ireland: A Study of Dáil Éireann 1919–48* (London, 1958)

MacDonagh, Oliver, *States of Mind: A Study of Anglo-Irish Conflict 1780–1980* (London, 1983)

MacDonagh, Oliver, *Ireland: The Union and its Aftermath* (2nd edn, Dublin, 2003)

Mac Eoin, Uinseann (ed.), *Survivors* (Dublin, 1980)

McGarry, Fearghal, *Eoin O'Duffy: A Self-Made Hero* (Oxford, 2005)

McGarry, Fearghal (ed.), *Republicanism in Modern Ireland* (Dublin, 2003)

McKay, Enda, 'Changing with the tide: the Irish Labour Party, 1927–1933', *Saothar*, 11 (1986), pp. 27–38

MacMahon, Bryan, *Here's Ireland* (London, 1971)

McMahon, Deirdre, *Republicans and Imperialists: Anglo-Irish Relations in the 1930s* (Yale, 1984)

McMahon, Timothy G., *Pádraig Ó Fathaigh's War of Independence: Recollections of a Galway Gaelic Leaguer* (Cork, 2000)

McNiffe, Liam, *A History of the Garda Síochána* (Dublin, 1997)

Macken, Walter, *The Scorching Wind* (London, 1964)

Madden, Jim, *Fr John Fahy: Radical Republican and Agrarian Activist* (Dublin, 2012)

Manning, Maurice, *Irish Political Parties: An Introduction* (Dublin, 1972)

Manning, Maurice, 'Women in Irish national and local politics 1922–77', in MacCurtain, Margaret and Ó Corráin, Donncha (eds), *Women in Irish Society: The Historical Dimension* (Dublin, 1978), pp. 92–102

Mansergh, Nicholas, *The Irish Free State: Its Government and Politics* (London, 1934)

Martin, F. X., '1916 – myth, fact, and mystery', *Studia Hibernica*, no. 7 (1967), pp. 7–126

Martin, F. X., 'The 1916 Rising – a coup d'etat or a "bloody protest"?', *Studia Hibernica*, no. 8 (1968), pp. 106–37

Martin, Micheál, *Freedom to Choose: Cork and Party Politics in Ireland 1918–1932* (Cork, 2009)

Maye, Brian, *Fine Gael 1923–1987: A General History with Biographical Sketches of Leading Members* (Dublin, 1993)

Micks, William L., *An Account of the Constitution, Administration and Dissolution of the Congested Districts Board for Ireland from 1891 to 1923* (Dublin, 1925)

Middlemas, Keith (ed.), *Thomas Jones Whitehall Diary, vol. III. Ireland 1918–1925* (Oxford, 1971)

Mitchell, Arthur, *Labour in Irish Politics 1890–1930* (Dublin, 1974)

Meehan, Ciara, *The Cosgrave Party: A History of Cumann na nGaedheal, 1923–33* (Dublin, 2010)

Meenan, James, *The Irish Economy since 1922* (Liverpool, 1970)

Moran, Gerard and Gillespie, Raymond (eds), *Galway: History and Society* (Dublin, 1996)

Morrison, George, *The Irish Civil War* (Dublin, 1981)

Moss, Warner, *Political Parties in the Irish Free State* (New York, 1933)

Murphy, Brian, 'The Stone of Destiny: Father John Fahy (1894–1969), Lia Fail and smallholder radicalism in modern Irish society', in Moran, Gerard (ed.), *Radical Irish Priests 1660–1970* (Dublin, 1998)

Murphy, Daniel J. (ed.), *Lady Gregory's Journals*, vol. 1, Books 1–29, 10 Oct. 1916–24 Feb. 1925 (Gerrards Cross, 1978)

Murphy, John A., *Ireland in the Twentieth Century* (Dublin, 1975)

Murphy, John A., 'Priests and people in modern Irish history', *Christus Rex*, vol. 23, no. 4 (October, 1969), pp. 235–59

Murphy, John A. and O'Carroll, John P. (eds), *De Valera and His Times* (Cork, 1983)

Murray, James P., *Galway: A Medico-Social History* (Galway, 1994)

Murray, Patrick, *Oracles of God: The Roman Catholic Church and Irish Politics 1922–37* (Dublin, 2000)

Newell, Úna, 'The rising of the moon: Galway 1916', *Journal of the Galway Archaeological and Historical Society*, vol. 58 (2006), pp. 114–35

Ní Chinnéide, Síle, 'Coquebert de Montbret's impressions of Galway city and county in the year 1791', *Journal of the Galway Archaeological and Historical Society*, vol. 25 (1952), pp. 1–14

Ní Chinnéide, Síle, 'A Frenchman's tour of Connacht in 1791: Part I', *Journal of the Galway Archaeological and Historical Society*, vol. 35 (1976), pp. 52–66

Ní Chinnéide, Síle, 'A Frenchman's tour of Connacht in 1791: Part II', *Journal of the Galway Archaeological and Historical Society*, vol. 36 (1977), pp. 30–42

Nolan, William, 'New farms and fields: migration policies of state land agencies 1891–1980', in Smyth, William J. and Whelan, Kevin (eds), *Common Ground: Essays on the Historical Geography of Ireland* (Cork, 1988), pp. 296–319

O'Brien, Flann, *Stories and Plays* (London, 1941)

O'Brien, Flann, *The Third Policeman* (London, 1967)

O'Brien, George, 'Patrick Hogan: Minister for Agriculture 1922–1932', *Studies*, vol. 25 (Sept., 1936), pp. 353–68

O'Brien, Máire Cruise, *The Same Age as the State: The Autobiography of Máire Cruise O'Brien* (Dublin, 2003)

Ó Cadhain, Máirtín, *The Road to Brightcity and Other Stories*, translated by Eoghan Ó Tuairisc (Dublin, 1981)

O'Callaghan, Margaret, 'Religion and identity: the Church and Irish independence', *The Crane Bag*, vol. 7, no. 2 (1983), pp. 65–76

O'Callaghan, Margaret, 'Language, nationality and cultural identity in the Irish Free State, 1922–7: the *Irish Statesman* and the *Catholic Bulletin* reappraised', *Irish Historical Studies*, vol. 24, no. 94 (Nov., 1984), pp. 226–45

Ó Cearbhaill, Diarmuid (ed.), *Galway: Town and Gown 1484–1984* (Dublin, 1984)

Ó Cléirigh, Nellie, *Hardship and High Living: Irish Women's Lives 1808–1923* (Dublin, 2003)

Ó Comhraí, Cormac, *Revolution in Connacht: A Photographic History 1913–23* (Cork, 2013)

O'Connor, Emmet, *A Labour History of Ireland 1824–1960* (Dublin, 1992)

O'Connor, Gabriel, *A History of Galway County Council: Stair Chomhairle Chontae na Gaillimhe* (Galway, 1999)

O'Dowd, Peadar, *In from the West: The McDonogh Dynasty* (Galway, 2002)

Ó Drisceoil, Donal, *Peadar O'Donnell* (Cork, 2001)

Ó hÉochaidh, Éamonn, *Liam Mellows* (Dublin, 1975)

Ó Fathartaigh, Micheál, 'Cumann na nGaedheal, the land issue and west Galway 1923–1932', *Journal of the Galway Archaeological and Historical Society*, vol. 60 (2008), pp. 154–77

Ó Fathartaigh, Micheál, 'Cumann na nGaedheal, sea fishing and west Galway, 1923–32', *Irish Historical Studies*, vol. 36, no. 141 (May, 2008), pp. 72–90

O'Flaherty, Liam, *The House of Gold* (London, 1929)

Ó Gadhra, Nollaig, *Civil War in Connacht 1922–1923* (Dublin, 1999)

Ó Gaora, Colm, *Mise*, translated by Michael Ó hAodha and Ruán O'Donnell, *On the Run: The Story of an Irish Freedom Fighter* (Cork, 2011)

Ó Gráda, Cormac, *Ireland: A New Economic History 1780–1939* (Oxford, 1994)

O'Halpin, Eunan, *Defending Ireland: The Irish State and its Enemies since 1922* (Oxford, 1999)

O'Halpin, Eunan, 'Army, politics and society in independent Ireland, 1923–1945', in Fraser, T. G. and Jeffery, Keith (eds), *Men, Women and War, Historical Studies XVIII* (Dublin, 1993), pp. 158–74

O'Halpin, Eunan, 'Parliamentary party discipline and tactics: the Fianna Fáil archives, 1926–1932', *Irish Historical Studies*, vol. 30, no. 120 (Nov., 1997), pp. 581–90

O'Halpin, Eunan, 'The geopolitics of republican diplomacy in the twentieth century', in Bric, Maurice J. and Coakley, John (eds), *From Political Violence to Negotiated Settlement: The Winding Path to Peace in Twentieth-Century Ireland* (Dublin, 2004), pp. 81–98

O'Kennedy, Brian W., *Making History: The Story of a Remarkable Campaign* (Dublin, 1927)

Ó Laoi, Padraic, *History of Castlegar Parish* (Galway, 1998)

O'Leary, Cornelius, *Irish Elections 1918–77: Parties, Voters and Proportional Representation* (Dublin, 1979)

O'Malley, Cormac K. H., and Ó Comhraí, Cormac (eds), *The Men Will Talk to Me: Galway Interviews by Ernie O'Malley* (Cork, 2013)

O'Malley, William, *Glancing Back: 70 Years' Experiences and Reminiscences of Pressman, Sportsman and Member of Parliament* (London, 1933)

O'Neill, Thomas P., 'In search of a political path: Irish republicanism, 1922 to 1927', in Hayes-McCoy, G. A. (ed.), *Historical Studies X* (Dublin, 1976), pp. 147–71

Oram, Hugh, *The Newspaper Book: A History of Newspapers in Ireland, 1649–1983* (Dublin, 1983)

O'Shiel, Kevin, 'Memories of my lifetime', *Irish Times*, 11–23 Nov. 1966

O'Sullivan, M. D., *Old Galway: The History of a Norman Colony in Ireland* (2nd edn, Galway, 1983)

Ó Tuathaigh, M. A. G., 'Language, literature and culture in Ireland since the War', in Lee, J. J. (ed.), *Ireland 1945–70* (Dublin, 1979), pp. 111–23

Ó Tuathaigh, M. A. G., 'The historical pattern of Irish emigration: some labour aspects', in Galway Labour History Group, *The Emigrant Experience* (Galway, 1991), pp. 9–28

Ó Tuathaigh, M. A. G., 'Galway in the modern period: survival and revival', in Clarke, Howard B. (ed.), *Irish Cities* (Dublin, 1995), pp. 136–49

Ó Tuathaigh, M. A. G., 'The state and the language since 1922', *Irish Times*, 19 Apr. 1977

Pakenham, Frank (Lord Longford), *Peace by Ordeal* (London, 1935)

Prager, Jeffrey, *Building Democracy in Ireland: Political Order and Cultural Integration in a Newly Independent Nation* (Cambridge, 1986)

Price, Alan (ed.), *J. M. Synge: Collected works. Volume II, Prose* (Gerrards Cross, 1982)

Price, Dominic, *The Flame and the Candle: War in Mayo 1919–1924* (Cork, 2012)

Puirséil, Niamh, *The Irish Labour Party 1922–73* (Dublin, 2007)

Pyne, Peter, 'The third Sinn Féin party: 1923–1926', *Economic and Social Review*, vol. 1, no. 1 (1969–70), pp. 29–50

Pyne, Peter, 'The third Sinn Féin party: 1923–1926', *Economic and Social Review*, vol. 1, no. 2 (1969–70), pp. 229–57

Regan, John M., *The Irish Counter-Revolution 1921–1936: Treatyite Politics and Settlement in Independent Ireland* (Dublin, 1999)

Regan, John M., *Myth and the Irish State: Historical Problems and Other Essays* (Kildare, 2013)

Regan, John M., 'The politics of reaction: the dynamics of treatyite government and policy 1922–33', *Irish Historical Studies*, vol. 30, no. 120 (Nov., 1997), pp. 542–63

Riordan, Susannah, 'Venereal disease in the Irish Free State: the politics of public health', *Irish Historical Studies*, vol. 35, no. 139 (May, 2007), pp. 345–64

Robinson, Lennox (ed.), *Lady Gregory's Journals 1916–1930* (New York, 1947)

Rouse, Paul, *Ireland's Own Soil: Government and Agriculture in Ireland, 1945 to 1965* (Dublin, 2000)

Rumpf, E. and Hepburn, A. C., *Nationalism and Socialism in Twentieth Century Ireland* (Liverpool, 1977)

Sammon, Patrick J., *In the Land Commission: A Memoir 1933–1978* (Dublin, 1997)

Sanderlin, Walter S., 'Galway as a transatlantic port in the nineteenth century', *Éire – Ireland*, vol. 5, no. 3 (Autumn, 1970), pp. 15–31

Shaw, George Bernard, *The Plays of Bernard Shaw: John Bull's Other Island* (London, 1927)

Sinnott, Richard, *Irish Voters Decide: Voting Behaviour in Elections and Referendums since 1918* (Manchester, 1995)

Speakman, Harold, *Here's Ireland* (New York, 1926)

Stafford, Séan, 'Taibhdhearc na Gaillimhe: Galway's Gaelic Theatre', *Journal of the Galway Archaeological and Historical Society*, vol. 54 (2002), pp. 183–214

Thompson, D'Arcy Wentworth, 'Galway; or, the city of the tribes' (reprint, with intro. by Tadhg Foley, of orig. edn, first published in *Macmillan's Magazine*, vol. 12, May, 1865), *Journal of the Galway Archaeological and Historical Society*, vol. 54 (2002), pp. 88–102

Tóibín, Colm, *Lady Gregory's Toothbrush* (Dublin, 2002)

Towey, Thomas, 'The reaction of the British government to the 1922 Collins–de Valera Pact', *Irish Historical Studies*, vol. 22, no. 85 (Mar., 1980), pp. 65–76

Townshend, Charles, *Political Violence in Ireland: Government and Resistance since 1848* (Oxford, 1983)

Townshend, Charles, *Easter 1916: The Irish Rebellion* (London, 2005)

Townshend, Charles, *The Republic: The Fight for Irish Independence, 1918–1923* (London, 2013)

Valiulis, Maryann Gialanella, 'After the revolution: the formative years of Cumann na nGaedheal', in Eyler, A. and Garratt, R. F. (eds), *The Uses of the Past: Essays in Irish Culture* (Delaware, 1988), pp. 131–42

Varley, Tony, 'Agrarian crime and social control: Sinn Féin and the land question in the west of Ireland in 1920', in McCullagh, Ciaran, Tomlinson, Mike and Varley, Tony (eds), *Whose Law and Order? Aspects of Crime and Social Control in Irish Society* (Belfast, 1988), pp. 54–75

Varley, Tony, 'Irish land reform and the west between the wars', *Journal of the Galway Archaeological and Historical Society*, vol. 56 (2004), pp. 213–32

Vaughan, W. E. (ed.), *A New History of Ireland, vol. VI. Ireland under the Union, II, 1870–1921* (Oxford, 1996)

Waldron, Kieran, *The Archbishops of Tuam 1700–2000* (Galway, 2008)

Weber, Eugen, *Peasants into Frenchmen: The Modernization of Rural France 1870–1914* (Stanford, 1976)

White, Terence de Vere, *Kevin O'Higgins* (London, 1948)

Whitmarsh, Victor, *Shadows on Glass: Galway 1895–1960 – A Pictorial Record* (Galway, 2003)

Williams, T. D. (ed.), *The Irish Struggle, 1916–1926* (London, 1966)

Whyte, J. H., *Church and State in Modern Ireland 1923–70* (Dublin, 1971)

C. Academic theses

Boran, Marie, 'Manifestations of Irish nationalism' (University College Galway, MA, 1989)

Cullen, Joan M., 'Patrick J. Hogan, T.D., Minister for Agriculture, 1922–1932: a study of a leading member of the first government of independent Ireland' (Dublin City University, PhD, 1993)

Moran, Mary Denise, 'A force beleaguered: the Royal Irish Constabulary 1900–1922' (University College Galway, MA, 1989)

Newell, Úna, 'Awakening the West? Galway 1916–18' (University College Dublin, MA, 2004)

Newell, Úna, 'The West must wait? People, poverty and politics in Free State Galway 1922–1932' (University College Dublin, PhD, 2010)

O'Connor, Sanchia Katherine, 'Public opinion and the Irish civil war in Connaught, 1921–1923' (NUI, Galway, MA, 2000)

Index

Index